# Commendations for *Why Believe*

"Tawa Anderson has the heart of a pastor and mind of a scholar, writing an enjoyable, readable, and philosophically, biblically, scientifically, and historically informed apologetic for theism and Christianity. His patient and accessible, lucid and inviting prose deftly canvasses a wide swath of evidential terrain, each step successively building toward a powerful cumulative case. In the process his impressive approach models what a laudably expansive, philosophically rigorous, existentially satisfying, and large-hearted apologetic ought to look like. Warmly recommend!"

—*David Baggett, professor of philosophy and director of the center for moral apologetics, Houston Baptist University*

"If you've never looked into the bases for Christianity's truth claims including the existence of a creating and law-giving God, the reality of Jesus, and his resurrection from the dead, you may be surprised at the sheer number of lines of reasoning Tawa Anderson brings forward for these remarkable claims. His real-life examples will keep you turning the pages.

Christians are called to provide reasons for their hope and, with the plethora of faith and worldview options today, good reasons are needed more than ever. This book provides them in a highly readable and engaging form. But this book does more than satisfy one's intellect. It also brings out the appeal of the Christian message. Anderson shows that whether you believe it or not, once you really grasp it, you may just wish it were true."

—*Paul Chamberlain, associate professor of apologetics and director of the Institute for Christian Apologetics, ACTS Seminaries*

"Apologetics is as important today as it has ever been. Yet, in an age when most apologetic texts are either overly technical or too watered down to be of great use, Tawa Anderson's *Why Believe* is a breath of fresh air. As a trusted intellect and gifted writer, Anderson provides an outstanding resource for those interested (no matter their motivations) in the great questions about Christian faith. This book will have a long life and use in the courses I teach!"

—*James K. Dew Jr., president, New Orleans Baptist Theological Seminary*

"Tawa Anderson skillfully shows, in plain language, that there are good reasons to want and believe Christianity is true. Fully conversant with the contemporary landscape regarding the questions of God, faith, and the Bible, Anderson's *Why Believe* is essential reading for anyone seeking truth. Believers will be nourished and strengthened. Unbelievers will be challenged and set on a path, that if faithfully followed, leads to Jesus."

—*Paul Gould, associate professor of philosophy of religion and director, M.A. Philosophy of Religion program, Palm Beach Atlantic University*

"Tawa Anderson provides an incredibly clear and easy-to-follow overview from pertinent preliminaries, to God's existence and the truth of Christianity. It includes excellent discussions, penetrating questions, and helpful summaries of very complex arguments in a conversational and easily read manner. The result is a robust, yet concise and easily followed summary of the major issues across the spectrum, including scientific, rational, anthropological, and historical considerations that make Christianity unique. Highly recommended."

—*Gary Habermas, distinguished research professor of apologetics and philosophy, Liberty University*

"*Why Believe* is a straightforward, easy-to-read, but surprisingly detailed guide to why Christianity is believable. Tawa Anderson has provided a useful resource to place in the hands of skeptics as well as Christians who are struggling with evidence for their faith."

—*Timothy Paul Jones, chair, department of apologetics, ethics, and philosophy, The Southern Baptist Theological Seminary*

"In a world where Christians are often portrayed as anti-science and anti-intellectual, this is a refreshing book that challenges both of those convictions. Tawa Anderson articulates a fourfold case for the rationality of the Christian faith. He argues that it matters whether Christianity is true, that it is true, that Jesus really was the incarnate son of God, and that the major objections to Christianity fall by the wayside. The final result is an articulate and winsome defense of the historic Christian faith, a faith very much able to withstand careful scrutiny and the challenges of science. Highly recommended."

—*Stewart Kelly, professor of philosophy, Minot State University*

"Does God exist? Are science and religion in conflict? Why does God allow evil, pain, and suffering? What can we *really* know about Jesus? Professor Tawa Anderson answers these questions and others in this important book. Highly recommended for students, young and old alike!"

—*Michael R. Licona, associate professor of theology, Houston Baptist University, and president, Risen Jesus, Inc.*

"I really enjoyed reading *Why Believe*. Professor Anderson has a firm grasp of the issues and relevant literature, and he clearly knows his way around an argument. The selection of content is excellent. But what really drew me in was the way the book reads like a personal conversation between Anderson and the reader. The tone is warm, conversational, and engaging. And even though no relevant stone is left unturned, *Why Believe* is written at a very accessible level without being simplistic.

This would serve as an excellent text for a course on worldview or apologetics. It also equips the reader to share his or her faith. I highly recommend it."

*—J. P. Moreland, distinguished professor of philosophy, Talbot School of Theology, Biola University*

"*Why Believe* offers an accessible introduction to key issues in Christian apologetics. Tawa Anderson's charitable tone, willingness to engage fairly with objections, and clear, thoughtful explanations make this a volume that will be of value both to the inquiring skeptic and to the budding apologist."

*—Holly Ordway, fellow of faith and culture, Word on Fire Institute*

"Culture is becoming more and more non-religious. People are weary of agendas and propaganda. And yet, people are still incredibly hungry for truth, hope, and peace. Everyone desires to believe in something that will bring meaning to their life. That is why I am so excited to enthusiastically recommend *Why Believe,* by my friend Dr. Tawa Anderson. This book is timely and applicable. Grab multiple copies. One for you, and others to gift to those who are searching. This is a must read!"

*—Shane Pruitt, national next gen evangelism director, North American Mission Board*

"*Why Believe* is an elegantly balanced work: rigorous and yet accessible, rooted in the traditions of the church while being fully engaged in contemporary debates, solidly academic and also warmly pastoral, confident, and yet not triumphalistic. This is apologetics as it should be written, seasoned with intellect, wisdom, and passion to grow disciples in the grace and knowledge of Jesus Christ."

*—Randal Rauser, professor of historical theology, Taylor Seminary*

"This is a remarkable book! Some books today on Christian apologetics are over the head of the average reader (or too long). Others understate the seriousness of the challenges that contemporary believers face, or misrepresent those challenges, and then give answers that really aren't sufficient for the task. The result is that readers are left with a false sense of confidence that is easily overcome by a moderately well-informed skeptic. This book finds the literary Goldilocks zone (i.e., it is just right for what it is). Tawa Anderson identifies the issues that matter most, states them succinctly, and then communicates complex ideas in simple and useful ways, making them understandable yet without dumbing them down. Better still, like the proverbial chicken on the highway, he lays it on the line and does it in a hurry. But what really sets this book apart is Anderson's modesty and hopefulness. This is an honest treatment of the issues that recognizes that there is more to be said but leaves the reader wanting Christianity to be true because Anderson has presented it for what it truly is: reasonable and desirable."

"*Why Believe* is an outstanding resource for contemporary apologetics and evangelism. In the true spirit of Pascal's famous dictum, Anderson builds a compelling case for why one should *want* Christianity to be true prior to laying out, in an attractive conversational tone, the best reasons to believe that it actually *is* true. This book is a wonderfully versatile tool for training Christians, encouraging doubters, and overcoming the common apathy of nonbelievers. I will be recommending it frequently."

# Commendations for Hobbs College Library

"This series honors a wonderful servant of Christ with a stellar lineup of contributors. What a gift to the body of Christ! My hope and prayer is that it will be widely read and used for the glory of God and the good of his Church."

—*Daniel L. Akin, president, Southeastern Baptist Theological Seminary*

"This series is a must-have, go-to resource for everyone who is serious about Bible study, teaching, and preaching. The authors are committed to the authority of the Bible and the vitality of the local church. I am excited about the kingdom impact of this much-needed resource."

—*Hance Dilbeck, executive director, Baptist General Convention of Oklahoma*

"This series offers an outstanding opportunity for leaders of all kinds to strengthen their knowledge of God, his word, and the manner in which we should engage the culture around us. Do not miss this opportunity to grow as a disciple of Jesus and as a leader of his church."

—*Micah Fries, senior pastor, Brainerd Baptist Church, Chattanooga, TN*

"The best resources are those that develop the church theologically while instructing her practically in the work of the Great Commission. Dr. Thomas has assembled an impressive host of contributors for a new set of resources that will equip leaders at all levels who want to leave a lasting impact for the gospel. Dr. Hobbs exemplified the pastor-leader-theologian, and it's inspiring to see a series put out in his name that so aptly embodies his ministry and calling."

—*J.D. Greear, pastor, The Summit Church, Raleigh-Durham, NC, and president, the Southern Baptist Convention*

# WHY BELIEVE

HOBBS COLLEGE LIBRARY

# WHY BELIEVE

*Christian Apologetics
for a Skeptical Age*

TAWA J. ANDERSON

HEATH A. THOMAS, *Editor*

OBU

NASHVILLE, TENNESSEE

# Contents

# Acknowledgments

This book has been a joy to write! It has consumed numerous evenings and weekends and has cost me considerable blood, sweat, and tears, but it has been worth it, at least from my perspective. I can only hope that you feel the same way!

Many people have contributed in one way or another to the process. Forgive any oversights, but some thanks must be delivered.

My former dean, and now president, at Oklahoma Baptist University is Dr. Heath Thomas. Heath, who serves as the general editor for B&H's Hobbs College Library series, challenged (commissioned? ordered?) me to write this book in the first place. If it's terrible—blame him. If it's great—well, he deserves at least some of the thanks.

My 2019 Contemporary Christian Apologetics class (Brandon Alley, Emileigh Goad, Deborah Fidler, Chad Jordan, Pablo Villa, Paige Lehrmann, Joshua Knox, and Chapman Pennington) at OBU read this book as it was being written between August and December. An additional set of colleagues and friends performed in-depth reviews of the manuscript in January and February of 2020: Eleanor Bayne, Susan Booth, Gunner Briscoe, Nolan Cannon, Mark Coppenger, Aaron Hembree, Noah Jones, Stewart Kelly, and Chandler Warren. Together they provided invaluable feedback, helping to eliminate numerous typos, potential heresies, and howling logical fallacies; they even precipitated a major structural reorganization. These dear friends made several helpful suggestions for improvement of primary content, and the book is far better for the time and effort they poured into it. If the book remains terrible, just think how much worse it would have been if not for their input! If it's great—well, they deserve at least some of the credit.

Finally, my family puts up with the time commitments involved in writing projects. I am grateful for their love, support, and encouragement—particularly that of my long-suffering wife, Vanessa. If you wonder whether miracles happen, consider that she has remained married to me for more than twenty-five years now!

Our older daughter is named after the Greek word for *truth*, αλεθεια. Alethea has always had character, spunk, and an eagerness to hear (and challenge) ideas and stories. As our miracle baby graduates from high school and continues to blossom into a beautiful, talented, intelligent young woman, she is a constant reminder of the need to pursue truth in all things. This book is a humble attempt to identify reasons to believe that Christianity is true. I lovingly dedicate this book to our incredible no-longer-little girl, Alethea Janae.

# *About the Library*

The Hobbs College Library equips Christians with tools for growing in the faith and for effective ministry. The library trains its readers in three major areas: Bible, theology, and ministry. The series originates from the Herschel H. Hobbs College of Theology and Ministry at Oklahoma Baptist University, where biblical, orthodox, and practical education lies at its core. Training the next generation was important for the great Baptist statesman Dr. Herschel H. Hobbs, and the Hobbs College that bears his name fosters that same vision.

The Hobbs College Library: Biblical. Orthodox. Practical.

# Introduction: What Is This Book All About, Anyway?

I don't know whether you bought this book, received it as a gift, inherited it as assigned reading, or stumbled across it in a book store. Whichever way, thank you for reading (at least this far). I hope you will continue. To encourage you to do so, I thought it might help to introduce my purpose in writing and who I envision you (my reader) to be.

I hope this book will foster a fruitful conversation about reasons that exist to support religious (specifically Christian) faith. There is a widespread, usually unstated, understanding in Europe and North America that Christian faith is held without supporting reasons, evidence, or argumentation. Strangely, it is not just everyday people who think faith has no reasons. Christians often share that understanding. For everyday people, the apparent dissociation of faith and reason provides motivation to (continue to) avoid or reject religious beliefs. For Christians, that same dissociation can be a source of honor, shame, or mere confusion.

My goal is to draw the spheres of (Christian) faith and (everyday) reason back together. I suggest that Christianity is a reasonable faith—that there is a tremendous confluence of scientific, logical, and historical evidence that points toward the truth of the Christian worldview.

1

I envision six distinct people reading this book. You may not belong neatly to any of these "categories," but knowing the types of people I have in mind should help you understand why I write what I do and how I do.

First, I see a *hardened skeptic*. You have never been a religious believer, certainly not a Christian. In your experience, Christians tend to be somewhat weak-minded. You have never encountered a good, let alone persuasive, argument for the existence of God. If this is you, then you probably think my purpose is futile—a chasing after the wind. Read on! I do not presume that you will be persuaded to adopt my beliefs, but I do hope to challenge your perception that Christianity is unreasonable. You are cordially invited to adjudicate my success (and please share your evaluation with me, at tawa.anderson@gmail.com).

Second, I see a *former believer*. You grew up within the church, perhaps were baptized as a Christian, and certainly considered yourself a follower of Jesus. Later, however, possibly as an older teen or young adult, you began to question aspects of the Christian faith. In the midst of your questions and doubts, you found no answers that supported Christianity but much that prompted a move away from the church. Slowly or swiftly, you discarded your Christian beliefs and adopted a skeptical or naturalistic worldview. If this is you, then you probably think there cannot possibly be reasons for supporting Christianity that you would not have encountered before rejecting your faith. I hope that I will surprise you—that you will see that people who deal with questions and doubts like yours *can* find reasons to remain within their faith rather than making the move away. I do not expect to convince or (re-)convert you, but I do hope to present reasons for you to reconsider your deconversion!

Third, I see a *questioning seeker*. You are not a Christian, but you are curious about matters of faith. If good reasons exist to believe that Christianity is true, you would give them serious consideration. If this is you, then you are probably highly motivated to read onward. Whether or not you come to share my beliefs, I hope my contribution is helpful in your search for truth.

Fourth, I see a *disinterested secularist*. You are not a Christian and do not consider yourself a particularly religious person. You have not really given much thought to questions about the existence of God, the basis of morality, or life after death. If this is you, then you are probably not very motivated to keep reading. Let me gently encourage you to at least consider Chapter 1, where I suggest that we should all care to seek out answers to the big questions of life and propose reasons for desiring Christianity to be true. If, after reading Chapter 1, you are still uninterested, then so be it.

Fifth, I see a *struggling follower*. You are a Christian and quite possibly have been for a very long time, but you sense increasing doubts about your faith. You believe that we should have reasons and evidence for significant beliefs, and you have not encountered any such reasons and evidence that support Christianity. You are not necessarily looking to ditch your faith. But if you cannot see good reasons for continuing to believe, you sense you might be on your way out of the church. If this is you, then I earnestly plead that you carefully read not only *this* book, but also many of the resources I will reference. I pray that you will find much encouragement and support for your faith in these pages.

Sixth, I see a *tentative apologist*. You are a Christian and thoroughly enjoy sharing your faith with friends and neighbors. In your conversations, however, you are often asked to provide evidence and arguments supporting your beliefs. Too frequently, you find yourself unable to articulate reasons, unable to answer specific questions, and unable to respond to particular objections. You are looking for tips and tools that can help you spread a winsome, reasonable Christian faith. If this is you, then I hope you find (at least some of) what you are looking for in this book. If you do not, then I have failed spectacularly. (Again, please share your evaluation with me—I need to know!)

Whoever you are—you may resemble one of these six imaginary readers, or you may think yourself quite distinct from all of them—I will write, generally, as if you are a tentative apologist. I will seek to set forth reasons that support the faith that you hold dear and to provide resources to help you share those reasons with others.

I contend that the Christian faith is, in Doug Groothuis's words, "objectively true, rationally compelling and existentially or subjectively engaging."[1] In the coming pages, I will defend that contention, providing reasons, evidence, and arguments to that end. There are four stages to the cumulative argument that I build, corresponding to the four parts of this book.

First, in part 1 ("Why Bother?"), I argue that we should all be committed to the pursuit of finding true answers to the big questions of life. In particular, we should be motivated to discover whether or not Christianity is true. Chapter 1 ("Who Cares?") addresses professed disinterest in the truthfulness of Christianity. Here I argue that, regardless of what we currently believe, we should all care deeply about the "big questions of life" and should be particularly motivated to discover whether Christianity provides true answers. Chapter 2 ("Why Apologeticize?") outlines the nature of apologetics, provides the biblical mandate for giving reasons for Christian faith, and considers the desperate need for a reasoning and reasonable faith in contemporary Western society. In Chapter 3 ("Why Truth?"), I argue that truth exists and provide tools for testing various truth claims. There *are* answers to the big questions of life, even if they may be difficult to *find* and even more difficult to *agree* upon!

---

[1] Douglas Groothuis, *Christian Apologetics: A Comprehensive Case for Biblical Faith* (Downers Grove, IL: IVP Academic, 2011), 24.

Then, in part 2 ("Why God?"), I argue that there are strong reasons to believe that God exists. Everyday people, even Christians, frequently assert that belief in God is at best based on personal experience; at worst it flies in the face of overwhelming evidence to the contrary. I show that this popular perception is woefully ill-informed and that the preponderance of reason and evidence strongly supports the existence of a transcendent, powerful, creative, personal God. In Chapter 4 ("Science"), I articulate a wealth of contemporary scientific evidence that points to a creator who brought the universe into being (the cosmological argument) and fine-tuned it to support the existence and flourishing of living creatures, including humanity, on earth (the teleological or fine-tuning argument). In Chapter 5 ("Reason"), I outline two rational arguments that point to the existence of God. First, I discuss the ontological (ontology = the study of being/existence) argument, which suggests that, given the universally understood conception of God, such a God logically must exist in reality. Second, I identify what I consider to be the most persuasive contemporary clue for God—the moral argument, which shows that human understandings of morality demonstrate the necessity of God. In Chapter 6 ("Humanity"), I suggest that several universal aspects of the human experience (religious experience, transcendent desire, appreciation of beauty, consciousness and free will, and rationality) point strongly toward a divine creator.

Given the existence of objective truth, and the strong reasons to believe that there is a God, we can then move on to ask whether there is good reason to believe that Christianity specifically is true—for that, we need primarily to examine the question of Jesus of Nazareth.

Then in part 3 ("Why Jesus?"), I argue that there is good evidence supporting the Christian belief that Jesus of Nazareth was a divine being—a unique God-man—who died to provide humanity a means to return to right relationship with God and rose from the dead both to demonstrate his identity as the divine Son of God *and* to confer the gift of eternal life to those who trust in and follow him. Chapter 7 ("The Story") examines the nature of the New Testament Gospels. Most of what we know or think about Jesus is based on these four books; thus, it is essential to see that we have good reason to trust these accounts. Chapter 8 ("The Man") shows that Jesus of Nazareth was a unique figure who believed himself to be divine and confirmed his identity through both words and deeds. Chapter 9 ("The Fulcrum") outlines the crucial events of Easter Sunday. Here I outline the historical evidence (biblical and nonbiblical) that supports the central miracle claim of Christianity: Jesus's resurrection from the dead. I will argue that the traditional belief that God raised Jesus from the dead is the only satisfactory explanation for the data; it is more reasonable to embrace the risen Jesus than to reject him.

Finally, in part 4 ("What About?"), I respond briefly to some of the most frequently stated objections to Christian faith. Even if one grants the relative strength of the arguments I have made in the first nine chapters, many will insist that there are compelling objections and counterarguments. Chapter 10 ("Cross-Examined") looks at five reasons often given for *not* believing that Christianity is true: (1) the problem of evil and suffering, (2) the hypocrisy of many Christians (3) injustices perpetrated by the church, (4) the conflict between contemporary science and Christian faith, and (5) the exclusive (narrow) nature of Christian salvation. I will argue that although these objections may involve important insights, they ultimately do not provide a reason to reject Christianity.

In the conclusion ("Why Believe?"), I briefly retrace our steps and suggest that there are good reasons for our *hearts* to *desire* Christianity to be true and for our *heads* to *believe* Christianity to be true.

That, in a nutshell, is what I seek to show in these pages. I hope you will take this journey with me, and I trust it will be rewarding and worthwhile. I do not expect to present anything revolutionary; I do not presume to alter your entire worldview; I do not assume you will be persuaded that my arguments are accurate. I do, however, hope that as you engage this little book, whatever your starting point, you will find food for thought and be stimulated to think about reasons for Christian faith that you had not previously acknowledged. Thank you for coming this far with me. I invite you to hop aboard and take the next stage of our journey together.

# PART 1

# WHY BOTHER

As noted in the introduction, my goal in this book is to suggest that there are good reasons for accepting Christianity as the way, the truth, and the life. But why bother with this kind of a project at all? After all, some people do not care whether Christianity is true; others think it is either impossible and/or unnecessary to present reasons for Christian belief; still others think there is no such thing as "truth" in religion or worldview. So why bother with the task of trying to show that Christianity is true and worth believing?

First, in Chapter 1, I propose that we should *all* care to learn whether Christianity is true. Furthermore, I argue that we should *want Christianity to be true*—that is, the nature of Christianity is such that we should deeply desire its truth. What's more, I think Christians have a responsibility to provide others with *reasons to think that Christianity is true*. Christian apologetics involves "the rational defense of the Christian worldview as objectively true, rationally compelling and existentially or subjectively engaging."[1] Chapter 2 is addressed to fellow Christians: feel free to skip this chapter altogether if you are not in that camp! For my Jesus-following friends, I will unpack our apologetic mandate from biblical commands and examples along with insights from our contemporary context.

---

[1]  Groothuis, *Christian Apologetics*, 24. (see intro., n. 1).

A precondition for defending Christianity as "objectively true" is establishing the existence of objective truth. Once upon a time, you could take for granted that virtually everyone you met would acknowledge that truth exists and that we have at least a strong fighting chance of obtaining truth through vigorous effort. In our contemporary culture, that is no longer true (pardon me, that is no longer the case). The concept of truth has fallen on hard times.

So, in Chapter 3, I outline the postmodern flight from truth and provide illustrations of the relativism that increasingly marks Western society. After highlighting some of the implications of relativism, I show why relativism is necessarily false and not worth holding. I close with a discussion of the nature of truth.

**Chapter 1. Who Cares?** Why We Should *Want* and *Believe* Christianity to Be True

**Chapter 2. Why Apologeticize?** Why Christians Must Provide Reasons for Faith

**Chapter 3. Why Truth?** The Existence and Nature of Truth

CHAPTER 1

## *Who Cares?*

### Why We Should *Want* and *Believe* Christianity to Be True

I think *all* of us should care to know whether Christianity is true. By *all*, I mean those who live in the contemporary Western world—roughly encompassing Western Europe, North America, and Australasia. Yes, I think people in other parts of the world should care, too, but we in the West have a particularly vested interest in knowing whether Christianity is true. Why? Because much of our legal, political, economic, scientific, and social structure is built upon the foundation of a Christian worldview. Have we built our society upon secure philosophical foundations? Or have we built social castles in the clouds—appealing structures that do not rest on a solid foundation and therefore are susceptible to sudden collapse or disintegration? Have we built our house upon solid rock or shifting sand? We should care to know.

But many, perhaps most, contemporary Westerners are singularly uninterested in knowing whether Christianity is true—indeed, you may be disinterested yourself! The attitude of general disinterest in such religious questions is known as *apatheism*.

## The Challenge: Apatheism

Why are we here? What is the meaning of life? Does God exist? If not, what does his nonexistence mean for us? If yes, can we know God, and what does his existence entail? What is right? What is wrong? How can we live a good (moral) life? How can we live a good (fulfilled, contented) life? What are human beings? Where did we come from? Are we responsible for how we live? Do we have free will? What happens after we die? Why are we so smitten with beauty? Can we know the answers to such questions? Can we know anything at all?

Philosophy, I often argue, is seeking consistent, reasonable answers to the "big questions of life, the universe, and everything." Central among those big questions of life are existence questions—questions related to the existence (or nonexistence) of God and the implications of religious beliefs for human existence.

Apatheism is a disinclination to care much about religious matters. For an apatheist, the big questions of life are relatively unimportant. It is not necessarily that apatheists actively disbelieve in God; they simply do not care about the questions related to God's existence or lack thereof.

Apatheism burst into the public intellectual sphere through Jonathan Rauch's iconic 2003 essay in *The Atlantic* titled "Let It Be." In his article, Rauch self-identifies as an apatheist, acknowledging, "I used to call myself an atheist . . . but the larger truth is that it has been years since I really cared one way or another. I'm . . . an apatheist."[1] Rauch, it seems to me, speaks for a large segment of the North American population that does not care to think about, discuss, or come to conclusions regarding existence questions.

---

[1]  Jonathan Rauch, "Let It Be," *The Atlantic*, May 2003. Rauch's article can be read in full at https://www.theatlantic.com/magazine/archive/2003/05/let-it-be/302726/.

The obstacle for Christian faith should be obvious. If people do not care about the question to begin with, it is pretty difficult to convince them that *this particular answer* is true and compelling. Consider an analogy. I do not much care about the identity of the greatest baseball player of all time. Imagine that I am at a dinner party with a few people who are passionately debating the relative merits of Babe Ruth, Roger Clemens, Ted Williams, Lou Gehrig, and Cy Young. Someone asks me what I think: which of them is the GOAT (greatest of all time)? I would be hard pressed to answer. Why? Because I simply do not care. My friends can debate and discuss until they're blue in the face; I will probably sit and drink my lemonade with a bemused smirk, wondering at the misplaced passion of these baseball fanatics.

At times, I think this is how Christians are perceived when asking someone in contemporary culture to embrace the truthfulness of Christianity. It's as if you are being asked, Which is the greatest religion in the world? Don't you agree that it's Christianity? Shouldn't you embrace Christian beliefs and practice as your own? Those questions are heard like I hear the baseball questions, Who is the greatest baseball player of all time? Don't you agree that it's Cy Young? Shouldn't you embrace Young as your favorite too? The short answer is, I simply do not care.

So if I present to an apatheist chapters 4–6 of this book (arguments for the existence of God) and/or chapters 7–9 (arguments for the deity and resurrection of Jesus), the apatheist may sit with a bemused smirk, wondering at the misplaced passion of this religious fanatic. The short answer is, they simply do not care.

And if individuals do not care about the subject or issue being discussed, it will be exceedingly difficult for them to seriously consider the truth claims that others raise.

The apatheistic disinterest in religious questions could be the result of mere laziness, or a conviction that religious beliefs are irrelevant and just cause conflict, or some other cause(s) altogether. Although I am interested in understanding and addressing the causes of apatheism, for my purposes here, it is more necessary to respond to the apatheistic position.

### Contra Apatheism: Why We Should Care to Know Whether Christianity Is True

Chances are, if you opened this book in the first place, you already care about the big questions of life. If you do not, you will not likely hang in there for long! But, at the risk of "preaching to the choir," let me suggest that we should all—Christians and everyday people alike—*care to know whether* Christianity is true. That is, we should give attention to learning what the claims of Christianity are, understanding why people argue that it is true, and discerning whether its claims are actually true. Why should we care about the truthfulness (or lack thereof) of the Christian faith? I see two broad reasons.

### The Essential Nature of Existence Questions

The first broad reason has less to do with Christianity specifically and more to do with the importance of a philosophical/religious quest for answers to the big questions of life. The questions introduced above—the meaning of life, the existence of God, life after death, moral questions, the possibility of knowledge, the nature of human beings, among others—are the most central and significant questions we can ask. Insofar as apatheism represents an avoidance of these significant questions, apatheism is avoiding a critically important aspect of our human nature and existence! We can and should encourage one another to think deeply about the big questions of life—in other words, *not* to be apatheists.

The seventeenth-century French mathematician and philosopher Blaise Pascal had powerful thoughts in this respect. Pascal, born in 1623, was religiously apathetic in his teens and early twenties. He self-identified throughout as a Catholic Christian, but his faith had little to no impact on his life, and he was unconcerned with matters of religious truth. In November 1654, however, Pascal experienced a radical conversion to Christ, which he recorded in "The Memorial," a piece of parchment sewn into his overcoat and carried with him until his death in 1662.[2] After his conversion, Pascal embarked on a twofold mission: (1) to compose a great treatise explaining and defending the reasonability and winsomeness of the Christian faith; and (2) to demonstrate to his upper-class French peers that their apatheism was not a virtue but a vice of the gravest order.

One of the oldest religious questions, and certainly one of the central existence questions (EQs), is, What happens when we die?[3] Apatheism, remember, is an indifference and lack of concern for such EQs. So apatheists, as a general rule, will not care much about how they (or anyone else) answer the question of humanity's postmortem faith. Pascal has incisive and insightful words for someone who is apathetic about what will happen to him when he dies. It is worth quoting Pascal at some length:

---

[2]  Blaise Pascal, "The Memorial," in *The Mind on Fire: An Anthology of the Writings of Blaise Pascal*, ed. James M. Houston (Portland, OR: Multnomah, 1989), 41–42.

[3]  The question of life after death is the first philosophical question I remember asking in my childhood. After my great-grandma Ross's death in 1983, I asked my mother on the way home from violin lessons, "Where is Great-Grandma now?" After a short pause, my mother answered, "Nowhere. When we die, that's it." (Or something to that general effect.) I recall thinking, as an eight-year-old twerp, "Well, that sucks, doesn't it?" Thus was born a promising career in philosophy.

The immortality of the soul is something of such vital importance to us, affecting us so deeply, that one must have lost all feeling not to care about knowing the facts of the matter. All our actions and thoughts must follow such different paths, according to whether there is hope of eternal blessings or not, that the only possible way of acting with sense and judgment is to decide our course in the light of this point, which ought to be our ultimate objective.

. . . And that is why, amongst those who are not convinced [that there is life after death], I make an absolute distinction between those who strive with all their might to learn and those who live without troubling themselves or thinking about it.

I can feel nothing but compassion for those who sincerely lament their doubt . . . and who . . . make their search their principal and most serious business.

But as for those who spend their lives without a thought for this final end of life . . . I view them very differently.

This negligence in a matter where they themselves, their eternity, their all are at stake, fills me more with irritation than pity; it astounds and appalls me; it seems quite monstrous to me. . . . We ought to have this [passion to know the answer] from principles of human interest and self-esteem. . . .

Nothing is so important to man as his state: nothing more fearful than eternity. Thus the fact that there exist men who are indifferent to the loss of their being and the peril of an eternity of wretchedness is against nature. With everything else they are quite different; they fear the most trifling things, foresee and feel them; and the same man who spends so many days and nights in fury and despair at losing some office or at some imaginary affront to his honour is the very one who knows that he is going to lose everything through death but feels neither anxiety nor emotion. It is a monstrous thing to see one and the same heart at once so sensitive to minor things and so strangely insensitive to the greatest. It is an incomprehensible spell, a supernatural torpor.[4]

The question of life after death is among the most significant of all EQs and is a central question in all worldviews (religious and nonreligious alike). The apatheist does not care to consider the content or the manner of afterlife belief—and that, I propose, is a grave (pardon the pun) mistake.

We should *care* whether or not Christianity is true, because Christianity offers a unique and powerful answer to the age-old question of life after death. If Christianity is true, then this life is the gateway to eternity, and how we relate to God in this life determines how and where we will spend eternal life. If Christianity is not true, then what happens after we die (heaven, hell, or something else) is irrelevant. But what Christianity is not and cannot be is irrelevant in this regard! Either there is heaven and hell, or there is not! Either eternity is predicated upon our relationship to Jesus Christ, or

---

[4]   Blaise Pascal, *Pensées*, ed. A. J. Krailsheimer, rev. ed. (New York: Penguin, 1995), Pensée 427.

it is not! The answer to the questions matters. Indeed it is (as Pascal argued) of the utmost importance!

So one ought to care to know if Christianity is true, because the answers to the fundamental questions of "life, the universe, and everything" matter supremely. But there is a second broad reason we ought to care to know if Christianity is true: the foundations of our society are built upon a Christian view of reality.

### Western Civilization Is Built upon the Foundations of a Christian Worldview

There are seven elements of typical Western societies (known collectively as Western civilization) that are built upon the philosophical and theological foundations of a biblical Christian worldview. That fact does not make Christianity true, not by any stretch! But it should provide motivation to care about the truth value of those foundations. If the foundations are found to be false, then perhaps we need to question the elements of society built upon those foundations—if not, at the very least, we need to find an alternative means of grounding or justifying these elements of society. So here are seven elements of modern Western civilization that are dependent (historically and/or ideologically) upon the theological and philosophical foundations provided by Christianity.[5]

---

[5] I hasten to add, in the seven elements of society that follow, that I am not pretending that everyone agrees with me! I am presenting these elements of Western society in fairly short order and not interacting with scholars who might dispute their basis in a Christian worldview. Please understand, first, that there is a lot of debate about these matters and, second, that I am aware of that debate but remain convinced that these elements of our society did grow out of a Christian worldview.

Some of the philosophical foundations of Western civilization (e.g., democracy, capitalism) could potentially be supported or justified by other worldviews; in those cases, Christianity serves only as the historical source of our civilizational structure. Other elements of our society (e.g., recognition of universal human rights, modern science), it seems to me, can be adequately grounded only by a Christian worldview;

First, Christianity teaches that the natural order is created by a rational God and is both regular (ordered, lawlike) and knowable. These theological foundations are necessary for the development of modern science.[6]

Second, Christianity teaches that the physical world (the natural order) is created by God and is created with intrinsic goodness and objective reality. As such, the natural world is seen by Christians as both beautiful and morally good and therefore worthy of being protected and nurtured.[7]

Third, Christianity teaches that all human beings are created in the image of God, a doctrine that has several significant implications.

a. Because God is a rational being, human beings are also created with trustworthy reason. As such, we can use our reasoning capacities (and sensory perception) to learn about the world around us, and we can trust the deliverances of our reason.

b. Accordingly, we can come to know things truly about the world (and the world's Creator, incidentally), *and* we can teach those things accurately to others. That is, education is both possible and worthwhile.

c. More significantly, if all human beings are created in the image of God, then all human persons are, as the United

in those cases, Christianity is both the historical source of and the necessary philosophical foundation for modern social structures.

[6] See, e.g., Nancy R. Pearcey and Charles B. Thaxton, *The Soul of Science: Christian Faith and Natural Philosophy* (Wheaton, IL: Crossway, 1994), esp. chaps. 1–5; Rodney Stark, *For the Glory of God: How Monotheism Led to Reformations, Science, Witch-Hunts, and the End of Slavery* (Princeton, NJ: Princeton University Press, 2003), chap. 2: "God's Handiwork: The Religious Origins of Science."

[7] See, e.g., Mitch Hescox and Paul Douglas, *Caring for Creation: The Evangelical's Guide to Climate Change and a Healthy Environment* (Minneapolis: Bethany House, 2016).

States' Declaration of Independence puts it, "created equal, [and] endowed by their Creator with certain unalienable Rights." Christianity therefore provides the necessary philosophical and theological foundation for the development of universal human rights.[8] Although Christians have certainly not always lived as if this were true, it is worth noting that the Christian worldview alone provides a sufficient ground upon which universal human rights can be articulated.

d. Along these lines, it is Christianity's doctrine of the *imago Dei* (image of God) that provided the required philosophical and theological basis for the antislavery movement, both in the ancient world (the first–fifth centuries, Roman Empire) and in the modern European and American contexts.[9]

e. Similarly, the brotherhood of humanity—the understanding that we are all created in the image of God—provides the foundation for social welfare and charity, cornerstones of modern liberal democratic states.

f. Finally, more broadly, our creation in the image of God establishes a responsibility within Christian theology to have a special concern and care for the most vulnerable members of society, including prisoners, the poor, widows, orphans, the mentally and physically disabled, the unborn, and the aged.

Fourth, Christendom gives birth to modern democracy. If God is the supreme sovereign, then human rulers have only derivative legitimacy and authority. Given the correlative doctrine of creation in the

---

[8]  See, e.g., Jacques Maritain, *Christianity and Democracy & The Rights of Man and the Natural Law* (1944; repr., San Francisco: Ignatius, 2011), 65–138.

[9]  See, e.g., Stark, *For the Glory of God*, chap. 4: "God's Justice: The Sin of Slavery."

image of God, rulers then have limited power and are required biblically to exercise that power in the best interests of their subjects.[10]

Fifth, Christianity provides a foundation for private property, with the balance of God's ultimate ownership of all things. As such, Western society recognizes the rights of private citizens to own property and accumulate wealth, while rejecting our absolute or final ownership of anything.[11]

Sixth, Christianity historically gives birth to modern capitalism, which, despite its abuses, provides the engine for economic growth and prosperity that has raised billions of humans out of poverty.[12]

Seventh, Christianity teaches that there is a transcendent moral lawgiver—a personal, divine moral being—who alone can serve as a sufficient foundation for both objective morality and the legitimate rule of law. On the one hand, objective moral values and duties require a transcendent moral standard, something beyond human beings, that serves as the "rule" or example by which our moral beliefs and actions can and should be judged. On the other hand, the legitimate rule of law requires the existence of a divine being who rightly serves as the transcendent moral authority *and* judge, such that the rule of law is right not just because of the governmental might behind it but because it adheres to the transcendent moral law.

Western civilization as we know it is based on all seven of these foundational pillars. Perhaps you think one or more of these pillars counts against Western civilization; that is, perhaps you think private property is a bad idea. So be it. Nonetheless, Western society is (historically and/or philosophically) built upon these pillars; if you

---

[10]   See, e.g., Maritain, *Christianity and Democracy*, 3–64.

[11]   See, e.g., Ronald J. Sider, *Rich Christians in an Age of Hunger: Moving from Affluence to Generosity*, rev. and updated ed. (Nashville: Thomas Nelson, 2015), 97–101.

[12]   See, e.g., Michael Novak, *The Spirit of Democratic Capitalism* (New York: Touchstone, 1982), esp. 13–186; 333–60.

live in Western society, I suggest you at least care whether or not the philosophical foundations for these pillars are true. As such, we all ought to care to know if Christianity is true.

### *Heart: Why We Should* Want *Christianity to Be True*

Apatheists contend that it is appropriate not to care about the answers to the big questions of life. I have suggested that we have two broadly compelling reasons to care deeply about such questions. First, these questions lie at the very core of human existence. To fail to care about fundamental philosophical questions is to fail to be fully human. Second, our Western civilization is built upon Christian answers to many of these significant questions of life: as such, we should care whether the philosophical foundations of our society are true.

But we can and should go further. I also suggest that we should *want* Christianity to *be true*. That is, regardless of what we actually believe right now, we should personally desire that Christianity be found to provide true answers to the big questions of life. Why? Simply put, Christianity provides a thoroughly satisfying and desirable worldview.

In seven areas we can see the winsomeness of a Christian worldview that prompts us to desire its truth. I am not arguing that Christianity is the only worldview that can support *each* of these seven areas. But I think Christianity alone can support *all seven*.

First, Christianity provides objective and knowable moral values and duties. As we will see in Chapter 5, we all tend to live as if there are objective moral values and duties, even if our worldview explicitly or implicitly rules out the existence of objective morality. There is, then, a deep-seated intuition that objective moral values exist; Christianity provides us with a foundation for such objective morality. Furthermore, Christianity provides the foundation for those moral values and duties to be *known*. On one hand, we can discover significant moral truths through our investigation of God's natural created order—a discipline known as natural law ethics. On the other hand, we can discover significant moral truths by studying God's divine self-revelation in Scripture. From these combined sources, we can develop a holistic and robust moral system of objective moral values and duties.

Second, Christianity provides the platform for an objective and knowable physical reality. We all, I submit, desire to know reality; if Christianity is true, then there is an objective reality that exists, and God has created us with trustworthy sensory and cognitive faculties that can come to know truths about that objective physical reality. Some worldviews deny either the objectivity (extreme postmodernism) or knowability (much of Hinduism and Buddhism) of objective reality; other worldviews are incapable of grounding the trustworthiness of our senses and reason in rightly knowing reality (atheism).

Third, Christianity provides for an objective and transcendent value to human life (and other aspects of creation). If Christianity is true, then each and every human person has innate value, dignity, and worth. No person is insignificant, regardless of how young or old, powerful or powerless, rich or poor, famous or unknown, healthy or sick. Some worldviews elevate some human persons over others (textbook Hinduism) or implicitly label all persons as equally insignificant (atheism).

Fourth, Christianity provides for an objective and transcendent purpose and meaning in human life. Other worldviews might enable us to construct proximate meaning in our lives and chart our own paths that create purpose for ourselves. Christianity, however, declares that there is a meaning and purpose for all human life and invites us to discover that purpose in Christ.

Fifth, Christianity provides a basis for the possibility of temporal and eternal forgiveness for wrongdoing. On the one hand, given the grace and forgiveness of God, most radically expressed through the death of Jesus Christ on the cross, Christianity provides the offer of eternal forgiveness for one's own wrongdoing. On the other hand, the reality and depth of divine forgiveness supplies both motivation and mandate for temporal forgiveness. We can forgive others as God has forgiven us, and we can ask others to forgive us as we seek to make things right with them. Christianity, then, provides a way out of the human drive for vengeance as well as an escape from self-loathing for wrongdoing.

Sixth, Christianity guarantees the reality of life after death, with three significant implications.

a. We are invited to enjoy eternal life in heaven, an unending existence of paradise, exploration, joy, and worship. Even archskeptic Michael Shermer, in a 2012 dialogue with Gary Habermas about life after death, acknowledged (and I paraphrase), "Well of course I want the Christian vision of life after death to be true! Eternal bliss, peace, and unending life! Who wouldn't want that?!"[13]

b. The Christian afterlife offers a lastingness to earthly relationships. It is not that our relationships will continue in heaven precisely as they are on earth, but we are promised a familiarity and continuity in the afterlife that makes earthly relationships even more meaningful.

---

[13]   Michael Shermer, "There Is No Life after Death." *Is There Life after Death? The 2012 Greer-Heard Point-Counterpoint Forum.* April 13–14, 2012 at New Orleans Baptist Theological Seminary. See Shermer's "Opening Speech," 0:55–1:10. Shermer goes on to insist (correctly) that his desire for something to be true does not make that something true.

c. Christianity also offers the means for postmortem justice, the righting of earthly wrongs after this life is over. Accordingly, those who suffer wrongs in this life can have those wrongs righted by God; those who have callously perpetrated wrongs upon others in this life will pay for their wrongdoing. A naturalistic worldview spectacularly fails to establish any semblance of eternal or transcendent justice: those who suffer in this life have no hope for anything better or further. As such, we should desire for the Christian picture of life after death to be true.

Seventh, Christianity offers the fulfillment of a core human desire: to know and to be known by God in an ultimate divine/human relationship.

Christianity offers a vision of life that satisfies the deepest yearnings of the human heart.[14] We can embrace and know objective morality and physical reality; we can embrace and find objective and transcendent value, meaning, and purpose in human life; we can experience divine and temporal forgiveness for wrongdoing; we can receive eternal life; and we can know and be known by the majestic creator and Lord of all that is. Indeed, it seems to me that we should all deeply desire for Christianity to be true.

### *Head: Why We Should* **Believe** *Christianity to Be True*
But facts do not care about our feelings. Perhaps you agree that you should (and perhaps do) *want* Christianity to be true, but a desire for Christianity to be true does not *make* Christianity *be* true. I might

---

[14] For more on this front, see Clifford Williams, *Existential Reasons for Belief in God: A Defense of Desires & Emotions for Faith* (Downers Grove, IL: IVP Academic, 2011), esp. chaps. 1–3, 8–9; and Gregory E. Ganssle, *Our Deepest Desires:*

desperately want it to be true that I am a world-famous hockey player; but no matter how zealously I desire that to be true, it simply is not going to be true! Passion and fanaticism do not create truth.

Perhaps our hearts should *want* Christianity to be true. But is there reason for the head to follow the heart and *believe* Christianity to be true? In a nutshell, yes: logic, evidence, and rational arguments point to the truth of the Christian worldview. I will endeavor to provide some of those reasons in chapters 4–9. Read on!

## Recommended Resources for Further Exploration

Ganssle, Gregory E. *Our Deepest Desires: How the Christian Story Fulfills Human Aspirations.* Downers Grove, IL: IVP Academic, 2017.

Maritain, Jacques. *Christianity and Democracy & The Rights of Man and the Natural Law.* San Francisco: Ignatius, 2011.

Pascal, Blaise. *Pensées.* Translated by A. J. Krailsheimer. New York: Penguin, 1995.

Stark, Rodney. *For the Glory of God: How Monotheism Led to Reformations, Science, Witch-Hunts, and the End of Slavery.* Princeton, NJ: Princeton University Press, 2003.

---

*How the Christian Story Fulfills Human Aspirations* (Downers Grove, IL: IVP Academic, 2017).

# CHAPTER 2

## *Why Apologeticize?*

### Why Christians Must Provide Reasons for Faith

In my teaching role at Oklahoma Baptist University, I have helped to design apologetics undergraduate and graduate curricula. In the context of my academic ministry, I am frequently confronted by questions such as, Why do we need apologetics? Aren't evangelism and discipleship all that matter? Why waste time on rational arguments and evidences for the Christian faith?

Many people feel that apologetics is an exercise in futility: there are no good reasons to believe Christianity is true, so why bother pretending? Many well-meaning Christians, similarly, are unsure of the value of apologetics; they feel it is unnecessary, perhaps even counterproductive. I trust later chapters will respond to the first group of skeptics by showing excellent reasons supporting Christian faith. In this chapter, I will respond to the latter and suggest that far from being unnecessary or counterproductive, apologetics is actually an indispensable aspect of Christian faith, discipleship, and ministry. We will walk through four areas together. First, I will briefly identify and define apologetics. Second, I will outline the biblical mandate for apologetics, showing how Scripture commands followers of Jesus to be engaged in apologetic encounters. Third,

I will provide biblical examples of apologetics in action. Fourth, I will discuss the desperate need for apologetics in our contemporary post-Christian cultural context.

## What Is Apologetics?

A contemporary follower of Jesus Christ needs to be a competent apologist. Our own spiritual growth, our mentoring of peers, our ministry on campus and in our churches, and our evangelistic outreach all require us to engage in robust and informed apologetic discussions. To become a competent apologist, we must know something about the nature of apologetics.

The term *apologetics* comes from the Greek απολογια (*apologia*). The Greek term denotes a courtroom scene and suggests presenting one's defense in the face of prosecution—providing the reasoning for one's legal position. The term rises to prominence in the life of Socrates, the ancient Greek philosopher, after he is arrested on charges of atheism and corrupting the youth of Athens. Socrates presents a defense for his ministry and his philosophy to the Athenian court—that defense comes down to us as a classic work in Western philosophy known as *The Apology*. Apologetics, then, is a giving of reasons for what one believes or practices.

As Douglas Groothuis notes, an apologist is simply "a defender and an advocate for a particular position."[1] You can be an apologist for Christianity, but you can also be an apologist for Islam or capitalism or even the sport of hockey. *Christian* apologetics, then, is *the explanation and defense of the Christian faith*. More fully, Christian apologetics is "the rational defense of the Christian worldview as objectively true, rationally compelling and existentially or

---

[1]   Groothuis, *Christian Apologetics*, 23 (see intro., n. 1).

subjectively engaging."[2] So Christian apologetics is about providing reasons and evidence for believing that the Christian faith is reasonable, true, and worth embracing.

## The Biblical Mandate for Apologetics

In some circles, *apologetics* is a dirty word. Popular blogs question whether Jesus or the apostle Paul would be bothered to engage in modernistic reasoning, trying to persuade people to embrace the reasonability of Christian discipleship. The great Danish philosopher Søren Kierkegaard argued in *Works and Love* that belief and disbelief are alike moral responses to God and that trying to present reasons to believe in Jesus is akin to beating the air. German theologian Karl Barth, in his *Church Dogmatics*, declared that attempting to rationally demonstrate God's existence is an anti-Christian endeavor. So the question here is not, *can* apologetics be done; that is, can we provide good reasons to believe that Christianity is true? Rather, it is the foundational question, *should* apologetics be done? Is it consistent with Christian faith and/or honoring to God to articulate a reasonable faith? Everyday non-Christians may be curious: are there good reasons to believe Christianity is true? For Christians, the previous question is more important. For them, the Word of God (written and incarnate) is authoritative. What the Bible says and shows about apologetics, then, ought to determine how we approach providing reasons for our faith.

So what *does* the Bible say about apologetics? In short, the Bible commands all believers everywhere to always be ready to be

---

[2]   Groothuis, 24.

engaged in apologetics. The key apologetic mandate comes from 1 Pet 3:13–17:

> Who is going to harm you if you are eager to do good? But even if you should suffer for what is right, you are blessed. "Do not fear what they fear; do not be frightened." But in your hearts set apart Christ as Lord. Always be prepared to give an answer to everyone who asks you to give the reason for the hope that you have. But do this with gentleness and respect, keeping a clear conscience, so that those who speak maliciously against your good behavior in Christ may be ashamed of their slander. It is better, if it is God's will, to suffer for doing good than for doing evil.

In verse 15, Peter commands his listeners to *be prepared*. Be prepared for *what*? To give *an answer*. What *kind* of answer? An answer for the reason for the hope that you have. In other words, God, through the apostle Peter, is commanding all Christians to be ready to answer questions that people have concerning our faith. It is not the great apologetic *suggestion*, where God gives us the option, if we are so inclined and if we have the right abilities and character, to try to answer people's questions. Instead, God delivers the apologetic *mandate*, commanding all believers everywhere to always be prepared to give an answer to everyone who asks you to give the reason for the hope that you have. In the same way that the Ten Commandments are *not* the Ten Considerations, so, too, here in 1 Peter 3, we do not have the apologetic exhortation, but rather the apologetic mandate. All believers are commanded to participate in apologetics.

In Mark 12, a teacher of the law asked Jesus which is the most important of all God's laws. Read Jesus's response, in verse 30: "Love the Lord your God with all your heart and with all your soul and with all your mind and with all your strength." J. P. Moreland has a wonderful little book called *Love Your God with All Your Mind*.[3] Moreland notes that the Christian church in the twentieth century has been pretty good at loving God with heart, soul, and strength but has fallen short at loving God with all their *mind*, in terms of intellectual discipleship. By and large, the North American church has not encouraged young Christians to develop a robust rational faith in Jesus Christ. Rather, the trend has been toward a faith that is embraced either in the absence of evidence or in the face of contrary evidence. But that tendency is not the scriptural imperative. Jesus tells us to love God with all of our being—heart, soul, mind, and strength. We are not to "check our brains at the door."[4] Apologetics is an endeavor to say yes, we can use our minds to develop our faith, to give answers to the questions people have, and to provide reasons for the hope and the faith that we have.

So the Bible clearly commands all believers to be engaged in apologetics.

## Biblical Examples of Apologetics

The Bible also provides many examples of apologetic ministry. We do not have time or space to consider every such example, but I will present a select few from both the Old and New Testaments.

---

[3]   J. P. Moreland, *Love Your God with All Your Mind: The Role of Reason in the Life of the Soul* (Colorado Springs: NavPress, 1997).

[4]   Josh McDowell and Bob Hostetler, *Don't Check Your Brains at the Door: Know What You Believe and Why* (Nashville: Thomas Nelson, 2011).

Some Christian critics of apologetics claim it is untoward to use human reason in our Christian faith; some everyday people assume that Christians are incapable of combining faith and reason. Through the prophet Isaiah, however, God invites us to do just that: "Stop doing wrong, learn to do right! Seek justice, encourage the oppressed. Defend the cause of the fatherless, plead the case of the widow. 'Come now, let us reason together,' says the LORD. 'Though your sins are like scarlet, they shall be as white as snow; though they are red as crimson, they shall be like wool'" (Isa 1:16–18).

Elsewhere, the Hebrew poet King David invites his hearers to behold the works of nature and consider what they imply about nature's Creator: "The heavens declare the glory of God; the skies proclaim the work of his hands. Day after day they pour forth speech; night after night they display knowledge. There is no speech or language where their voice is not heard. Their voice goes out into all the earth, their words to the ends of the world" (Ps 19:1–4).

From creation, Jeremiah builds a strong argument for the existence of Yahweh, the God of Israel, to the exclusion of the gods of other nations.

> Hear what the Lord says to you, O house of Israel. . . .
> "Do not learn the ways of the nations. . . . For the customs of the peoples are worthless; they cut a tree out of the forest, and a craftsman shapes it with his chisel. They adorn it with silver and gold; they fasten it with hammer and nails so it will not totter. Like a scarecrow in a melon patch, their idols cannot speak; they must be carried because they cannot walk. Do not fear them; they can do no harm nor can they do any good." (Jer 10:1–5)

Jeremiah reminded the people of how idols (statues of gods) are fashioned and how those idols are incapable of moving or acting, let alone creating all that exists. Jeremiah then points to the creative work evident throughout the earth and to Yahweh as the source of all that is.

> Tell them this: "These gods, who did not make the heavens and the earth, will perish from the earth and from under the heavens." But God made the earth by his power; he founded the world by his wisdom and stretched out the heavens by his understanding. When he thunders, the waters in the heavens roar; he makes clouds rise from the ends of the earth. He sends lightning with the rain and brings out the wind from his storehouses. (Jer 10:11–13)

Here Jeremiah provides a rational argument for abandoning idol worship and returning to Yahweh worship—an apologetic against the ways of the nations and for the God of Israel.[5]

Turning from the Old Testament (the Hebrew Scriptures) to the New Testament (the Greek Scriptures), we find that the author of the Gospel of Luke articulates a clearly apologetic purpose.

> Many have undertaken to draw up an account of the things that have been fulfilled among us, just as they were handed down to us by those who from the first were eyewitnesses and servants of the word. Therefore, since I myself have carefully investigated everything from the beginning, it seemed good also to me to write an orderly account for you, most excellent Theophilus, so that you

---

[5] A very similar argument against idolatry can be found in Isaiah 44.

may know the certainty of the things you have been
taught. (Luke 1:1–4)

Luke begins his Gospel by insisting that, although he is not an
eyewitness to Jesus's life, he has nonetheless thoroughly researched
the events of Jesus's life and ministry. Luke has applied careful
research skills, thought the matter over carefully, and decided (reasoned out) that it would be beneficial for him to present an orderly
account of Jesus of Nazareth. Why? Luke's purpose is to provide
his readers with reasons for his belief—certainty in the things he
had been taught. Luke's Gospel is a sustained, reasoned, apologetic
treatise.

John begins his first letter (epistle) by explaining why his readers ought to take his words concerning Jesus seriously:

That which was from the beginning, which we have heard,
which we have seen with our eyes, which we have looked
at and our hands have touched—this we proclaim concerning the Word of life. The life appeared; we have seen
it and testify to it, and we proclaim to you the eternal life,
which was with the Father and has appeared to us. We
proclaim to you what we have seen and heard, so that you
also may have fellowship with us. (1 John 1:1–3)

John's words matter because he is relating what he has personally
witnessed and experienced. John gives his readers reasons for their
heeding the encouragements, instructions, and commands that follow.

The book of Acts is full of apologetic reasoning. For example,
Peter's sermon on the day of Pentecost, recorded in Acts 2:14–36,
argues for the divinity of Jesus based on Old Testament prophecy
and his own eyewitness testimony of the resurrection.

Men of Israel, listen to this: Jesus of Nazareth was a man accredited by God to you by miracles, wonders and signs, which God did among you through him, as you yourselves know. . . .

God has raised this Jesus to life, and we are all witnesses of the fact. (Acts 2:22, 32)

Peter further explains that the psalmist David had declared (Ps 16:8–11) that God would not abandon the body of God's "Holy One" to decay in the grave. Given that all good Jews knew not only that David had died, but also where his tomb could be found (Acts 2:29), Peter argues that David, under the inspiration of the Holy Spirit, was speaking of the future resurrection of God's Christ (Acts 2:30–31). In other words, Peter gives the reasons for the hope that he has.

In my estimation, the preeminent apologist in the New Testament is the apostle Paul. In 2 Cor 10:5, Paul emphasizes the need to "demolish arguments and every pretension that sets itself up against the knowledge of God" and to "take captive every thought to make it obedient to Christ." Some critics take this to mean that Paul is going to aim a shotgun blast at his pagan opponents, plugging his ears with his fingers and raining blows upon nonbelievers until they cease and desist. But such an understanding badly misses the point. How does one demolish arguments? One cannot demolish an argument with a sledgehammer or a shotgun, nor can one demolish an argument by ignoring the argument and speaking over it. Rather, Paul both insists and models that arguments are demolished through the use of reason and evidence—by bringing *better arguments* to the table!

In the second half of the book of Acts, we see the apologist Paul in action. Let's look at Acts 17 to see how Paul operates in two different settings.

> When [Paul and his companions] had passed through
> Amphipolis and Apollonia, they came to Thessalon-
> ica, where there was a Jewish synagogue. As his custom
> was, Paul went into the synagogue, and on three Sab-
> bath days he reasoned with them from the Scriptures,
> explaining and proving that the Messiah had to suffer and
> rise from the dead. "This Jesus I am proclaiming to you
> is the Messiah," he said. Some of the Jews were per-
> suaded and joined Paul and Silas, as did a large number
> of God-fearing Greeks and quite a few prominent women.
> (Acts 17:1–4)

Note how Paul acts here. He *reasons* with Jews in Thessalon-ica, *explaining and proving* the death and resurrection of Jesus. The result? Many were *persuaded*. Paul does not appeal only to their hearts; he appeals to their reasoning capacities, showing how belief in Jesus as the risen Messiah made sense. The very terminology of the passage emphasizes that Paul is presenting rational arguments in support of his Christian faith. To those, then, who wonder whether Paul would "waste his time" constructing logical arguments or try-ing to rationally persuade others of the truth of Christianity, Acts 17 provides a clear and resounding answer.

Later Paul in Athens speaks to Greek philosophers:

> Paul then stood up in the meeting of the Areopagus and
> said: "Men of Athens! I see that in every way you are very
> religious. For as I walked around and looked carefully at

your objects of worship, I even found an altar with this inscription: to an unknown god. Now what you worship as something unknown I am going to proclaim to you.

"The God who made the world and everything in it is the Lord of heaven and earth and does not live in temples built by hands. . . . God did this so that men would seek him and perhaps reach out for him and find him, though he is not far from any one of us. 'For in him we live and move and have our being.' As some of your own poets have said, 'We are his offspring.'

"Therefore since we are God's offspring, we should not think that the divine being is like gold or silver or stone—an image made by man's design and skill. . . . For he has set a day when he will judge the world with justice by the man he has appointed. He has given proof of this to all men by raising him from the dead."

When they heard about the resurrection of the dead, some of them sneered, but others said, "We want to hear you again on this subject." At that, Paul left the Council. A few men became followers of Paul and believed. Among them was Dionysius, a member of the Areopagus, also a woman named Damaris, and a number of others. (Acts 17:22–34)

Earlier, when speaking to Jews in Thessalonica, Paul begins with Old Testament Scripture. Why? His Jewish audience accepts Scripture as authoritative, and so citing the Old Testament provides common ground upon which both parties can stand and reason. Paul uses Scripture as a springboard to the reasons for the hope that he has.

In Athens, Paul's apologetic approach is different. He notes points of commonality with the people of the city, and even *commends* their religiosity despite their pagan idolatry (Acts 17:22–23). The people of Athens are religious and even have an altar inscribed TO AN UNKNOWN GOD. Paul proposes to show them who that God is. Paul continues with natural revelation—evidence for God's existence that can be discerned from the world around us—noting that the divine being who created heaven and earth cannot be contained by human-built temples. Paul then quotes from two Greek poets to drive his point home (Acts 17:28). Why? Paul desires to reach the Athenian people where they are, using whatever common ground he can, in order to share with them the reason for the hope that he has. After establishing common ground and providing a basic argument for God from creation, Paul closes with a uniquely Christian apologetic surrounding the resurrection of Jesus. The result? "A few men became followers of Paul and believed" (Acts 17:34).

I could multiply examples, but I trust the point is clear: throughout Scripture, God encourages his people to think, to reason to their faith, to reason for their faith, and to give reasons that others ought to believe. We see examples in the Old Testament and New Testament of the people of God engaged in robust apologetics. There are, therefore, powerful scriptural reasons to engage in apologetic ministry, to share the gospel with those who do not believe. Put simply, God commands it, the Bible demonstrates it, and Christians ought to be doing it.

## The Contemporary Need for Apologetics

God commands his followers to be involved in apologetics and provides examples of believers giving reasons for their faith throughout the Bible. In light of these examples, one can acknowledge the deficiency in apologetic ministry both inside and outside the Christian church. I want to get at this side of things by sharing the stories of three different people.[6]

Gary grew up in a strong Christian family. His parents had been members of their Baptist church since their wedding. Gary accepted Jesus as his Savior and Lord when he was nine years old and was active in Sunday school and youth group throughout school. However, in college Gary began to have doubts about the truth of Christianity. Some things in the Gospels did not seem to add up. Matthew and Luke had different genealogies for Jesus. The details surrounding Jesus's empty tomb varied: how many women were there? Were there angels or men at the tomb? How many of them? He questioned the character of God in parts of the Old Testament. Why did God hate Esau? How could a loving God order the annihilation and extermination of entire people groups in the Promised Land? And how can God be both three and one?

Joy became a Christian in junior high school after her single mother started going to church and got involved in fellowships and Sunday school classes. Joy was baptized during high school and emerged as a vibrant, budding believer. A popular and outgoing young woman, Joy was surrounded by numerous friends who were involved with other religions. Many of her friends launched specific objections against Christianity and challenged Joy to see the truth of *their* beliefs. Joy wanted to see her friends come to know Christ but felt pressured and attacked. She often didn't know how to respond to the objections her friends presented to Christianity. How could she show her friends that Christianity is the only way to salvation? What were the differences between Christianity and other religions? How could she demonstrate lovingly but truthfully the problems, falsehoods, or inconsistencies in her friends' religious beliefs?

---

[6] The names and some minor details have been changed, but these reflect real people I know and love dearly.

Peter led a college-age Bible study group in his Baptist church. He became increasingly concerned that many students were dropping out of church. When he asked them why they had stopped attending, some cited growing doubts about the truth of their faith. Their college professors taught them that God was a figment of one's imagination and that humanity is a product of undirected, random, atheistic evolution. They could not reconcile the faith of their parents' church with what they were being taught at college. They were not about to drop out of college. Rather, they dropped out of church.

Gary, Joy, and Peter have something in common: each is in desperate need of apologetic investigation and training. An active apologetic ministry—in their personal lives and ministries or in the ministries of their local church and/or parachurch organization—would be an immense blessing to them.

In our contemporary world, people have questions and doubts about the truthfulness of the Christian faith. For many, Christianity is incredible and unbelievable; they cannot see any possible reason to think it might be true. Christians need to take questions and doubts (their own and those of others) seriously and apply the apologetic mandate by seeking to provide reasonable answers and responses.

Surveys and studies show that a large proportion of children raised in Christian homes walk away from Christianity as students or young adults. Although statistics differ based on the survey and the location, it is reasonable to infer that 70 to 85 percent of Christian teenagers drop out of church before age twenty-five. Why is this exodus happening? Sometimes, according to the research, it is due to church fatigue or a change in life situation (e.g., moving and not finding a new home church). But sometimes other reasons—moral and intellectual—are cited for youth dropping out of church. Two most commonly cited reasons are moral rebellion (usually sexual sin) and unresolved questions and doubts—especially concerning the problem of evil and the relationship between science and Christianity. Honest, genuine questions need honest, genuine responses, and often youth are not getting such answers.

Carol Anway did an extensive study of American women who converted to Islam, motivated in part by her own daughter's conversion. Anway was curious what prompted women to embrace Islam, especially those who moved away from Christianity. She writes,

> Three of the women, prior to converting to Islam, were hoping to convert their [Muslim] husband to Christianity by agreeing to study Islam if the husband would consider Christianity. One woman started asking questions of ministers and theologians to help her prove the superiority of Christianity to her husband. She said, "I wanted it so badly; I cried to several of them to help me and most of them said, 'I'm sorry—I don't know' or 'I'll write to you,' but I never heard from them.' . . . Nine of the women expressed problems with the belief in Jesus as God, Jesus as the Son of God, or the concept of the Trinity. Five others said they had major questions about Christianity that no one had satisfactorily answered.[7]

A friend of mine pastors a little country church in Alabama. One summer he polled his congregation, asking them to submit ideas and questions they would like him to address in Bible studies and sermons. The questionnaire results shocked his deacons (though not him). Here are some of them:

---

[7] Carol Anway, "American Women Choosing Islam," in *Muslims on the Americanization Path?*, ed. Yvonne Haddad and John Esposito (New York: Oxford University Press, 2000), 150.

What is the difference between the God Christians worship and the gods of other religions?

Is God real?

Is the story of creation a myth?

Pastor, my friends and I are not bad people. So, isn't it true that people are basically good?

Is the Bible really true?

At school, many say the Bible has errors in it. Is this true?

I've heard you say that Jesus is the God-man. Is Jesus a man? Or is he God?

My friends tell me that all religions lead to heaven. Is Jesus the only way to heaven?

If there is a God that is good, then why is there evil?

When I served as English pastor at Edmonton Chinese Baptist Church, I also had the privilege of serving part time as the BCM chaplain at the University of Alberta, a public university with 30,000 undergraduate students. Numerous young men and women would come by my office to ask questions or express doubts about the Christian faith. Frequently students would talk with me for an hour or more. At the end of our conversation, they would say something like, "Thank you for talking with me about this. I tried to ask my pastor these questions, and he said good Christians don't ask questions like this." Or, "I told my parents I had these doubts, and they treated me as if I were a drug-abusing demon-possessed rebel."

When students, children, friends, neighbors, or coworkers are asking honest, searching, deep questions about the truthfulness of Christianity, it is not enough for Christian leaders to say, "Don't ask these questions. Just believe!" If you are a Christian, you should expect that people will regularly ask you difficult questions about the believability of your faith. You will not always have the answers; none of us do, and that's okay. But you must respond as best you can—which sometimes will mean doing some research so you can come back with a more informed answer. Most importantly, we *must* encourage the questions. If we care about the growth of the kingdom of God, if we are passionate about the spiritual vitality of our churches, if we are concerned about the persevering faith of our younger generation, then we ought to be amply motivated to become equipped apologetically and become involved in apologetic ministry in our circles of influence.

Is apologetics a worthless enterprise? Would the apostle Paul consider it a colossal waste of time? Is it unbiblical to pursue rational arguments for the truth of our faith? On all counts, no. Rather, Christian apologetics, the endeavor to explain and defend the Christian faith, is commanded by God in the Bible, exampled in both the Old and the New Testaments, and desperately required in our post-Christian Western context.

## Recommended Resources for Further Exploration

Beilby, James. *Thinking about Christian Apologetics: What It Is and Why We Do It.* Downers Grove, IL: IVP Academic, 2011.
Groothuis, Douglas. *Christian Apologetics: A Comprehensive Case for Biblical Faith.* Downers Grove, IL: IVP Academic, 2011.

www.reasonablefaith.org—Reasonable Faith ministry (William Lane Craig)

www.apologetics315.com—The internet's best apologetics "clearing-house"

www.str.typepad.com—Stand to Reason apologetics ministry (Greg Koukl)

# CHAPTER 3

# Why Truth?

## The Existence and Nature of Truth

*I am the way and the truth and the life.*
Jesus, John 14:6

*Truth is what your contemporaries let you get away with.*
Richard Rorty

*Truth is like an elastic band: you can only stretch
it so far before it snaps back in your face.*
Tawa, Brian, Josh, and Trevor—at Salisbury
Composite High School, 1993

*A proposition is true just in case it corresponds to
reality, when what it asserts to be the case is the case.*
J. P. Moreland

C hristian apologetics involves "the rational defense of the
Christian worldview as objectively true, rationally compelling

and existentially or subjectively engaging."[1] If I desire to defend the objective truthfulness of the Christian faith, it makes sense that I first embark on a defense of truth itself. A generation or two ago, such an endeavor would not have been necessary. I could count on most everyone, outside of a minority of scholars in the humanities and social sciences, to agree that there is such a thing as real truth. It is all the rage today, however, to question or outright reject the existence of truth. For most people today, truth is seen as being relative to an individual or society. You have your truth; I have mine. That's true for you, but it's not true for me.

Such clichés are varieties of relativism, which, roughly put, holds that truth or knowledge is not absolute, but rather is conditioned by and relative to historical and cultural contexts. Relativism first gained prominence in aesthetics, or the philosophy of art, where it became popular to believe that beauty is strictly in the eye of the beholder. According to aesthetic relativism, there is no such thing as real beauty or true excellence in art; it is all a matter of one's personal response to works of art. Relativism then picked up steam in the realm of ethics, where it became popular to proclaim that right and wrong are socially conditioned or individually determined. According to ethical (or moral) relativism, there is no such thing as real right and wrong, objective good and evil; it is all a matter of one's personal opinion or social consensus.

Relativism soon became ascendant in the realm of religion, where it became popular to hold that religious beliefs are the product of personal or social choices. According to such religious relativism, there is no such thing as true or false religious doctrines; it is all a matter of finding the religious beliefs that work for you and provide fulfillment and meaning. Finally, relativism became (for some)

---

[1]  Groothuis, *Christian Apologetics*, 24 (see intro., n. 1).

a totalitarian claim that applied to all realms of human inquiry and discussion, such that it became popular to believe that truth itself is a matter of personal affirmation. According to this full-blooded relativism (the subject of this chapter), there is no such thing as objective truth or falsity; it is all a matter of personal conviction. Once again, you have your truth; I have mine.

In such a climate of relativistic subjectivism, I seek to defend the Christian faith as (among other things) objectively true. Given our culture's rampant relativism, defending Christianity's truth requires establishing that truth exists—real, objective truth, rather than a personal relativistic truth. I will thus set out in this chapter to defend the existence of objective truth. First, I will outline the historical steps that led us to the postmodern flight from truth. Second, I will survey the consequences of embracing relativism regarding truth and suggest that the majority of people are not really willing to accept those consequences. Third, I will seek to demonstrate that relativism is not only mistaken but cannot even possibly be a correct understanding. Finally, I will identify and define the nature of truth. Having established the existence and nature of truth, we will then be able to proceed to a consideration of how we can pursue truth.[2]

## The Postmodern Flight from Truth

In 2 Samuel 11, a terrifying and tragic sequence of events finds King David, elsewhere described as "a man after [God's] own heart"

---

[2]   The relativism regarding truth under consideration in this chapter is not the same as skepticism regarding truth. Relativism claims that there is no objective truth: you have your perspective, and I have mine, but neither is or can be objectively correct. Skepticism, on the other hand, may acknowledge the existence of objective truth, but claims that we cannot grasp truth (or at least we cannot know what is actually true). Relativism has to do with the metaphysics (existence) of truth, while skepticism has to do with the epistemology (knowledge) of truth.

(1 Sam 13:14), committing adultery with the wife of Uriah, one of his finest soldiers, while Uriah is off fighting David's war. King David sleeps with Uriah's wife, Bathsheba, impregnates her, seeks (unsuccessfully) to cover up his sin by having Uriah sleep with his wife, and ultimately orders Uriah's indirect execution on the battlefield. By the time you come to the end of the chapter, you are left with the perplexed question, How on earth did David end up here? How did he go from God's anointed king, Israel's mighty warrior and righteous psalmist, to self-seeking adulterer and murderer?

Similarly, the past few centuries (or so) of Western civilization have seen the transition from a Christendom marked by embrace of God as the good, the true, and the beautiful to a post-Christian society marked by skepticism regarding God and relativism concerning the nature of goodness, truth, and beauty. Many Christians, when they come to this side of the story of the West, are left with the perplexed question, How on earth did we end up here?

The response in both cases is "one step at a time." David made a series of successive decisions that resulted in an outcome far larger than any of the individual choices. So, too, Western thought has been through a series of successive processes, claims, and realizations that have resulted in an outcome that far outweighs them all.

It began with Enlightenment modernism and the quest for certainty in knowledge. The Enlightenment period (ca. 1650–1900) saw the displacement of religious authority (God, Scripture, church) in favor of autonomous human reason. Early moderns felt that the truth was out there to be apprehended, but they rejected the medieval Christian notion that truth was most accurately and reliably accessible via God's self-revelation in Scripture. Instead, humanity needed to apply reason and inquiry (often through the scientific method) to arrive at a true understanding of reality.

Enlightenment modernism pursued the holy grail of knowledge: a rational certainty that was available to all people and was independent of external authority. The ideal Enlightenment human applied objective (i.e., neutral, not influenced by preexisting prejudices or commitments) reason to arrive at objective (i.e., absolute, not person-specific or culturally-conditioned) truth. The Enlightenment held this goal to be fully achievable so long as humanity could free itself from the shackles of medieval superstition and religious oppression.

It is generally conceded that the Enlightenment dream died around the time of the Great War of 1914–1918, wherein a generation of enlightened modern Europeans objectively slaughtered one another in service of objective truths. The two events (World War I and the close of the Enlightenment) are not causally related to each other, and there were numerous other influences. Nonetheless, the early twentieth century marked the beginnings of a transition from Enlightenment modernism into postmodernism. Two philosophical insights contributed to the death of the Enlightenment dream of neutral rational certainty based on autonomous human reason.

First, philosophers and social scientists became increasingly aware of the existence and influence of worldview. A worldview, roughly put, is "the conceptual lens through which we see, understand, and interpret the world and our place within it."[3] Each person possesses a worldview, and one's worldview is initially formed unconsciously (or subconsciously), primarily based on one's most significant influences (family, peers, educators, media). A person's worldview exerts a great degree of power over every aspect of that person's intellectual and social life—including how one assesses

---

[3] Tawa J. Anderson, W. Michael Clark, and David K. Naugle, *An Introduction to Christian Worldview: Pursuing God's Perspective in a Pluralistic World* (Downers Grove, IL: IVP Academic, 2017), 8.

and interprets evidence and arguments and what one perceives as potentially true explanations for events. For example, in the 2017 movie *Wonder Woman*, Diana (princess of the Amazons) interprets the characters involved in World War I as evidencing the involvement of Ares, the Greek god of war. Steve Trevor, the American spy, cannot even comprehend the possibility of an ancient (and presumably mythical) god existing, let alone endeavoring to perpetuate the current armed conflict. Diana's worldview includes gods and goddesses. Steve's does not. And this worldview difference causes them to interpret events and data in very different ways.

Second, this growing awareness of the existence and influence of worldview led philosophers to conclude that there is no such thing as a view from "nowhere"; that is, the Enlightenment goal of autonomous human reason unencumbered by preexisting beliefs and commitments was an impossible dream. Instead, observers came to increasingly recognize that all human beings are heavily biased by their worldviews, such that they do not see the world in the same way at all. The radical and unavoidable influence of pretheoretical worldview presuppositions led, then, to an abandonment of the goal of neutral, unbiased human subjects coming into direct contact with true reality and arriving at certainty in their knowledge. Given worldview influences, we could not see the world in the same way. If we could not see the world in the same way, we could not even agree on what facts needed to be accounted for and interpreted. If we could not agree on what the facts were, then we could not build further knowledge upon those facts. And so the Enlightenment dream of autonomous human reason reaching neutral rational certainty died.

As the twentieth century progressed, the Enlightenment dream was replaced with a new reality—postmodern relativism. Postmodernism, while a diverse and multifaceted movement, always involves a rejection of modernism, particularly modernism's emphasis upon objective, obtainable truth. Postmodernism professes that truth (in aesthetics, ethics, religion, and everything else) is in the eye of the beholder(s)—a matter of personal or social belief. In its mildest forms, postmodernism is merely skepticism—claiming that there might be a true reality out there, but we human beings are hopelessly unable to gain access to it. In its stronger forms, postmodernism claims that there is no true reality out there at all; there is only what we human beings construct for ourselves. For mild postmodernism, the truth is unattainable. All we can do is believe. For strong postmodernism, the truth is what we make it to be, at least in our own minds; our minds construct our own truth.

The popular professions of postmodernism in contemporary Western society sound like the strong variety: you have your truth, and I have mine; that's true for you, but not for me. Truth is a personal construct, and if I hold this to be true, then for me it actually *is true*. There is no objective truth; there is only what I hold to be true and what you hold to be true, with no way to oppose or adjudicate. There is no objective beauty; there is only what I find beautiful and what you find beautiful. There is no objective morality; there is only what I find morally good and what you find morally good. There is no objective religious truth; there is only the religion that works for me and what works for you.

What can we say about this postmodern relativism? First, we can acknowledge and applaud the postmodern critiques of Enlightenment modernism, with its fruitless quest for objective certainty gained through autonomous human reason. Second, we can agree that worldviews exert strong influence over each and every human being, and that we cannot fully avoid the impact of our unconsciously formed conceptions of life, the universe, and everything. But that does not mean that we should descend into the hopeless relativism that postmodernism embraces and advances. To see why, let us look at the implications (or consequences) of relativism and then see why relativism cannot possibly be correct.

## The Implications of Relativism

An 1895 poem by Mary Lathrap ("Judge Softly") encourages the reader to "walk a mile in his moccasins before you abuse, criticize, and accuse." Before judging another person, it is wise to learn the full circumstances of that person's situation. In philosophy, we talk of trying philosophical positions on for size or walking a mile in a philosophy's shoes. The idea is similar: we want to see where a philosophical position *leads* before committing ourselves to its embrace. If a philosophical tenet leads directly to an unavoidable conclusion that is absurd or clearly false, that is a strong mark against the truthfulness of the philosophy and a reason to be rationally wary.

If postmodernists are correct, and there is no objective truth to obtain, what would follow? What are the logical entailments of relativism? What rational consequences result from embracing a thoroughgoing relativism?

First, if relativism is correct, there are no facts that can be known and agreed upon by all. So it would follow that Christians cannot argue that Jesus's death and resurrection are historical facts. Again, if there are no facts (as facts would require objective truth), then one could not hold as a scientific fact that all life-forms on earth have evolved from a single common ancestor through an unguided process of random mutation and natural selection. Similarly, one could not hold as a historical fact that the Holocaust occurred, or that Caesar crossed the Rubicon, or that George Washington was the first president of the United States, or that overuse of fossil fuels is causing climate change, or that the earth orbits around the sun, or that Beethoven wrote "Ode to Joy." All of these claims require the existence of objective truth, real obtainable facts, and if relativism is correct, then there is no truth, hence there are no facts, hence none of these claims is objectively true.

Second, if relativism is correct, then when people disagree on issues ("facts") such as those mentioned above, there is no independent way to adjudicate the disagreement and arrive at an understanding of who is right and who is wrong. After all, there is no objective "right" and "wrong"; there is only "my truth" and "your truth." If your truth is your truth, then any evidence that I might use to disprove your position can be deemed irrelevant. Determining whose perspective is correct requires both independent standards of obtaining truth *and* the existence of truth—both of which are ruled out by the logical consequences of relativism. Such consequences result in the triumph of tone-deaf tribalism—championing one's own beliefs (or the beliefs of one's "tribe" or group) as the truth with a willful refusal to consider alternative viewpoints, reasons, and evidence. Argument, in the traditional philosophical sense of presenting reasons and evidence with the intent to persuade others to abandon their false views to adopt your correct view, is subsequently worthless—hence the common postmodern phrase "There's no point arguing about this."

Third, if relativism is correct, then education is dead; all that remains is indoctrination or propaganda. After all, there are no objective truths to convey, no historical realities to teach, no scientific laws to promulgate, and no ethical standards to inculcate. If there is no truth, then teachers cannot seek to help students grow in knowledge and wisdom; all they can do is seek to mold students into their own image. If there is no truth, then one cannot teach; one can only indoctrinate. If there is no truth, then one cannot disseminate information; one can only spread propaganda.[4]

Fourth, if relativism is correct, then it is impossible to grow in knowledge. I would like to think that I know more now than I did when I was fifteen, twenty, even thirty years old. I would like to think that I have a better, more accurate, more comprehensive grasp of the world. But, given relativism, I do not "know more" now than I did then. I might have more beliefs, in terms of counting things that I think are true, and that might correspond to possessing "more truths" in the subjective, relative sense of "my truths." But I cannot have a more accurate understanding of reality, because there is no such thing, given relativism, as an accurate (i.e., objectively true) understanding of reality.

All four of these outcomes—there are no facts; disagreements cannot be mediated; education is dead; we cannot grow in knowledge—are, I contend, unavoidable logical entailments of postmodern relativism. That is, if one holds relativism to be correct, if one believes that there are no objective truths, then these four outcomes are straightforward consequences.

## Defeating Relativism

If relativism is correct, if there is no objective truth, then very serious consequences must be faced. The moccasins of relativism are not very comfortable, and they lead to places that are difficult (perhaps

---

[4]    Remember that we are talking about postmodern relativism, not just moral relativism or religious relativism. That is, the relativism that I am addressing here claims that there is no objective truth at all; there is only your perspective and my perspective. One could, say, reject postmodern relativism and accept that there are mathematical, scientific, and historical truths but still reject the existence of objective moral truths. Such a position would be moral relativism and will be addressed in Chapter 5.

impossible) to safely navigate. The absurd implications of relativism may be sufficient reason to reject the position. In the end, however, relativism turns out to be mistaken—not only mistaken but clearly and necessarily mistaken. We will look quickly at two compelling reasons why relativism cannot possibly be correct: first, virtually no one holds to it consistently; second, relativism is self-defeating.

I am convinced that virtually all professing relativists are not authentic relativists. That is, they do not really think relativism is correct. Their skin-deep commitment to relativism becomes quite clear when you begin identifying the logical consequences that relativism entails. Virtually every professing relativist whom I have met believes that there are true facts about the world, even if some people do not believe those facts to be true. For example, the professing relativist who thinks that humanity is causing global warming will strongly criticize climate-change skeptics as "deniers" who refuse to face "the truth" about what is happening to our environment and weather patterns. Relativists with whom I have interacted think it is possible to argue and persuade someone to change his or her mind on a perspective. Thus a professing relativist presents scientific evidence to persuade others that Darwinian evolution is true. Virtually every postmodernist I've read believes that education is not only possible but also essential and that teachers need to strive to present objective facts to their students. Virtually all relativists I talk to think they are smarter and more knowledgeable now than they were five years ago.

In other words, most relativists are only pseudo-relativists, or faux-relativists, or skin-deep relativists. Relativism is a trendy self-identifier; it differentiates you from the "imperialistic modernists" who believed not only that absolute truth existed, but also that *they* possessed the absolute truth and had the right to force it upon others. When antimodernistic professing relativists are faced with the inevitable consequences of sincere relativism, they almost always reject those consequences. Rejecting the content of those consequences, however, requires rejecting the relativism that spawns the consequences! Consider two illustrations.

Imagine that I profess to be an orthodox Christian. One of the logical entailments of biblical Christianity is the belief that Jesus Christ died for our redemption from sin and rose again. A consequence of my professed religion, then, would be the statement "Jesus died for our sins and rose from the dead." If I were to protest, "No, I do not believe that is the case at all," then it would be fair to conclude that I am not really a Bible-believing Christian.

Imagine instead that I profess to be a Marxist-Communist. One of the logical entailments of Marx's communistic theory is the belief that private property should be abolished and class distinctions erased. A consequence of my professed political philosophy, then, would be the statement "No private citizen should be allowed to accumulate more material possessions than any other citizen." If I were to protest, "No, I do not believe that is the case at all," then it would be fair to conclude that I am not really a Marxist-Communist.

Ditto for relativism. Merely professing to be a relativist does not make one a relativist, any more than pretending to be the president of the United States makes me president. If a professing relativist rejects the clear logical entailments of relativism, then it is fair to conclude that this person is not really a relativist after all. And this is, I contend, precisely the situation in which we find ourselves. Many—perhaps most—everyday people in Western society would claim to embrace relativism: my truth is my truth, your truth is your truth; that's true for you but not for me; etc. But the vast majority of those same everyday people reject all of the logical entailments of postmodern relativism!

If even professing relativists are not consistent relativists, there are some serious problems with relativism. Relativism not only is unlivable, but it also turns out to be self-defeating or what philosophers call self-referentially absurd. Consider the statement "There is no absolute truth; that is, there is nothing that is true for all people at all times in all places." Ask the question, is that true? That is, is it *true* that there is no absolute truth? Does it hold for all people that there is nothing that holds for all people? Is it the case for all people in all places at all times that there is nothing that is the case for all people in all places at all times? Or is relativism merely the opinion of the author? If it is the opinion of the speaker, why should I accept it? If, on the other hand, it is true that there is no truth, then the relativist has admitted that there is, in fact, something that is true for all people at all times in all places.

The assertion that all truth is relative is itself an objective truth claim; it purports to be true and binding upon all people. But objective truth is the very thing that relativism denies! Therefore, relativism regarding truth is *self-referentially absurd* or self-defeating. If it is true that there is no truth, then relativism is false, because there is at least one thing that is true—namely, the relativist claim itself. If it is false that there is no truth, then relativism is false and not worth further consideration. If the relativist tries to squirrel out of the dilemma and suggest that the claim "There is no absolute truth" is "neither true nor false," then the relativist has resorted to speaking nonsense. Either the relativist claim is understood to apply to everybody or it is not so understood. It has to be one or the other.

So despite the tremendous popularity of relativist clichés and the hordes of postmodernists who self-identify as full-blooded relativists, we find that relativism is entirely unlivable (i.e., virtually no one consistently accepts the logical consequences of relativism) and self-defeating (i.e., if it is held to be true, then it demonstrates itself to be false).

## What Is Truth?

What, then, is truth?

> "What is it you have done?" [the governor] asked.
>
> [The accused] said, "My kingdom is not of this world. If it were, my servants would fight to prevent my arrest by the Jews. But now my kingdom is from another place."
>
> "You are a king, then!" said [the governor].
>
> [The accused] answered, "You are right in saying I am a king. In fact, for this reason I was born, and for this I came into the world, to testify to the truth. Everyone on the side of truth listens to me."
>
> "What is truth?" [the governor] asked. (John 18:35–38)

Pontius Pilate asked Jesus of Nazareth a most pressing question: "What is truth?" You can perhaps see the wheels turning in Pilate's head: his Jewish subjects claim their religious traditions to be Truth based on the self-revelation of Almighty Yahweh, while his Roman overlords worship a vast pantheon of anthropomorphic but powerful deities. The competing religious truth claims are difficult to adjudicate. So what is this thing called truth? First, an affirmation, then three important distinctions.[5]

We have already seen that relativism does not work; the claim that truth is in the eye of the beholder fails spectacularly. It makes more sense, then, to understand truth to be objective. Traditionally a majority of philosophers have embraced what is known as the correspondence theory of truth—simply meaning, to say that something is true is to say that the statement matches up with (corresponds to) the way that reality actually is. Thus, if I say, "The earth revolves around the sun," my statement is true if and only if objective reality is such that the earth actually rotates in an orbit around the sun.

What is true is true for all people at all times in all places, whether they know it or not, believe it or not, and like it or not. In other words, if something is true, it is the case for all people. If it is true that the earth revolves around the sun, then it is the case, it corresponds to reality, it holds, that our solar system is structured in such a fashion that planet Earth orbits the sun; and that holds—it is the case, it corresponds to reality—for all people in all places at all times, regardless of their personal opinions (i.e., regardless of what *they believe to be true*).

For example, consider the statement "God exists." The statement is either true or false; it either matches reality or it does not. Either God exists or God does not exist. If God does exist, then millions of atheists are wrong. They cannot simply object, "Well, I do not believe that God exists; therefore, God does not exist *for me*." Someone's refusal to believe something has no bearing upon its truthfulness or lack thereof. Truth is true regardless of someone's believing it.

---

[5]   This brief section draws heavily upon my work in chap. 3 of Anderson, Clark, and Naugle, *Introduction to Christian Worldview*, 70–72.

If, on the other hand, God does not exist, then stating that God exists is somewhat like stating that leprechauns exist—amusing but meaningless. It is insufficient to insist, "Well, for me, God exists; so it is true *for me* that God exists." That is akin to me insisting that it is true *for me* that leprechauns exist; or that it is true *for me* that I am the president of the United States. Any reasonable person would respond that my self-delusions do not result in a relativistic truth; rather, they result in me believing something that is false.

The truth, then, is not person-dependent, nor is it relative to an individual or group. What is true is true, full stop. A few distinctions, however, have to be drawn. It is these distinctions, I think, that are often muddled and result in the types of confusions that lead people to *think* that they are relativists when in fact they are not.

First, opinion, unlike truth, is relative to the individual. "Chocolate is the best flavor of ice cream" is a statement of opinion. The sentence *sounds* like a truth claim. On the surface, it seems to be claiming that something (i.e., chocolate ice cream is the best) is objectively true of the real world. It is sometimes assumed that because "chocolate ice cream is the best" and "two plus two is equal to four" possess the same grammatical structure, they must also be statements of the same type. In reality, however, the first statement is a profession of personal preference; the second makes an objective mathematical truth claim. Opinion is not the same as objective truth, even when we use the language of truth when expressing our opinions. In this sense, it can indeed be "true for me" that chocolate is the best, while that statement is not "true for you." But that does nothing to demonstrate that there is no objective truth about reality. All it shows is that people's opinions are, in fact, their own opinions!

Second, however, the claim that "I prefer chocolate ice cream to vanilla ice cream" *is* an objective truth claim, and, as such, is either true or false (true, in my case). The sentence *is* expressing a personal opinion (I *prefer* chocolate), but the structure of the sentence makes it a propositional truth claim rather than a statement of subjective opinion. It is either true or false that I prefer chocolate. The truth of the statement depends on the individual making the statement, which explains why many people mistakenly conclude that such statements demonstrate the accuracy of relativism; after all, the truth of "I prefer chocolate" depends on who *I* is. Indeed, the truth claim is relative in the sense that its truthfulness depends on the identification of *I*. Once *I* is identified, however, the statement becomes either objectively true or objectively false. There is no support for the relativist on this front.

Third, beliefs are subjective, relative to the individual, and prone to error and falsehood. Thus, the belief that God does not exist may in fact be wrong (as I believe it is). That does not make the *truth* (of God's existence) relative; rather, it makes an atheist's belief (about God's nonexistence) *false*. In the fifteenth century, when the majority of scientists believed that the sun revolved around the earth, they were *objectively wrong* in their beliefs. The truth was that the earth revolves around the sun; they just did not know it. The truth did not change between the fifteenth and eighteenth centuries; scientific understanding changed. Belief changes; opinion changes; our understanding of *what* is true changes. What does *not* change, however, is truth itself. Truth does not depend on my beliefs or your beliefs; what is true is true regardless of what you and I believe. Truth is an objective reality that holds regardless of what you believe.

## Conclusion

What does this question of relativism and truth have to do with Christianity and apologetics? At the heart of it, Christianity is a religion that makes several objective truth claims about reality (e.g.,

God exists; the universe is created; Jesus of Nazareth performed supernatural miracles; Jesus was raised from the dead on the third day after his crucifixion). It is not a religion of personal preference or subjective opinion: Christianity depends on historical and theological truths. The Christian faith is either true for all people in all places at all times (whether any individual person accepts it or not, believes it or not, and likes it or not), or the Christian faith is false for all people in all places at all times (whether any individual person accepts it or not, believes it or not, and likes it or not). Later chapters in this book will articulate and rationally defend some of the specific truth claims of Christianity: the existence of God, the reliability of the New Testament, and, most important, the deity, death, and bodily resurrection of Jesus Christ.

All of these claims are objective truth claims about reality. They are not personal beliefs that Christians prefer to hold as matters of opinion; rather, we claim that these beliefs reflect the truth of the real world. They are either objectively true, or they are objectively false. They are not merely matters of opinion.

The question then becomes: Do we have good reasons for believing Christianity to be true and other perspectives to be false? That is the burden of the rest of this book! In chapters 4–6, I will lay out reasons to believe that God exists—a transcendent being along the lines of the God of the Christian Bible. Then in chapters 7–9, I will provide reasons and evidence to accept the central truth claims of Christianity specifically. I hope you will join me for that part of the journey, as we ask, Why God? and then, Why Jesus?

### Recommended Resources for Further Exploration

Anderson, Tawa J., W. Michael Clark, and David K. Naugle. *An Introduction to Christian Worldview: Pursuing God's*

*Perspective in a Pluralistic World.* Downers Grove, IL: IVP Academic, 2017.

Beckwith, Francis J., and Gregory Koukl. *Relativism: Feet Firmly Planted in Mid-Air.* Grand Rapids: Baker, 1998.

Copan, Paul. *True for You, but Not for Me: Deflating the Slogans That Leave Christians Speechless.* Minneapolis: Bethany House, 1998, 2009.

Groothuis, Douglas. *Truth Decay: Defending Christianity against the Challenges of Postmodernism.* Downers Grove, IL: InterVarsity, 2000.

Kelly, Stewart E. *Truth Considered & Applied: Examining Postmodernism, History, and Christian Faith.* Nashville: B&H Academic, 2011.

Kelly, Stewart E., and James K. Dew Jr. *Understanding Postmodernism: A Christian Perspective.* Downers Grove, IL: IVP Academic, 2017.

# PART 2

# WHY GOD?

So far, we have seen that it is essential for contemporary Christians to provide solid reasons and evidence in support of their beliefs—both for their own sake and for the sake of people who do not yet believe Christianity to be true. We have also seen that there is, and must be, such a thing as objective truth. There is a reality external to us. To say something is true is to say that it matches up with the way reality actually is.

It is time now to use those foundational understandings to build a reasonable case for the Christian faith. I will proceed in the time-honored fashion of *classical apologetics*. A classical apologist first seeks to show that there are good reasons to believe that a transcendent divine being (God) exists and then strives to establish that Christianity specifically is the most reasonable form of theism to embrace. In short, I will present arguments first regarding God (part 2) and, second, regarding Jesus Christ (part 3).[1]

---

[1] To qualify: I will seek (in part 2) to show that it is reasonable to believe that God exists; that there is good evidence pointing toward God's existence; and that God's existence is certainly plausible (and even probable). It is not my goal to prove "beyond a shadow of a doubt" that God exists: I don't think such a thing can be done (with God or with virtually anything else of any interest). Similarly, I will seek (in part 3) to show that it is reasonable to believe that Christianity specifically is true, that there are good reasons to believe that Jesus was God in the flesh and rose from the dead.

Once upon a time, it was not terribly necessary to engage in the first of these two tasks, particularly in the Western world. The vast majority of Europeans and North Americans accepted the existence of God until well into the 1800s; arguments for God's existence, then, were interesting but irrelevant. The situation is different today. It remains true that the majority of North Americans are theists, believing in the existence of a divine being roughly equivalent to the monotheistic God of the Bible. But in many European countries, theism is a distinctly minority belief. A 2010 Eurobarometer poll shows that the proportion of the population that affirms, "I believe there is a God," is 18 percent of the population in Sweden, 33 percent in Finland, 27 percent in France, 44 percent in Germany, and 37 percent in England. Even in the United States, the largest bastion of Western Christianity, the percentage of atheists (those who actively deny the existence of any type of divine being) has risen from a negligible amount in 1970 to 12 percent in 2017.[2]

Even among those who *do* believe in God, it is frequently assumed that the only reasons one could have for such belief are personal or experiential; that is, religious and nonreligious people alike seem generally agreed that belief in God is based on personal preference or opinion, family background or cultural teaching, or a personal religious experience. Oddly enough, that perspective itself is as recent as is the trend toward nonbelief! In the 1800s, when virtually all Westerners admitted belief in the divine, the vast majority of them would also have recognized that there were strong reasons supporting their belief. Those reasons (known as theistic arguments) may not have been necessary—after all, everybody already believed in God—but they existed nonetheless. Today, when those

---

[2]    All survey numbers courtesy of "Demographics of Atheism," Wikipedia, accessed August 26, 2020, https://en.wikipedia.org/wiki/Demographics_of_atheism.

arguments are more desperately needed, the majority of Christians and non-Christians alike are sadly oblivious to their existence!

This section seeks to rectify that situation. Over the next three chapters, I will provide an introductory look into strong reasons to believe in the existence of a personal, moral, powerful, creative God.

In Chapter 4, I will highlight scientific evidence that points to God's existence. First, I will outline the *kalām* cosmological argument, which insists that the beginning of the universe requires the existence of a creator who is outside of both time and space. Second, I will outline a version of the design (or teleological) argument, which posits that the apparent fine-tuning in the universe is best explained by the existence of a transcendent divine mind.

Chapter 5 will turn to logical arguments for the existence of God. First, I will outline the ontological argument, which suggests that the very conception of God's nature necessitates God's existence. Second, I will turn to morality and show that the existence of objective morality points to the existence of a transcendent, personal, moral lawgiver.

Chapter 6 will turn to human nature and experience to provide anthropological clues for God's existence. We will look at evidence from religious experience, transcendent desire, human appreciation of beauty, consciousness and free will, and human reason—all of which, I will argue, are best explained by the existence of a transcendent divine being (God).

The force of these theistic arguments, I think, will be to demonstrate that it is reasonable to believe that God exists.

**Chapter 4. Science:** Evidence for God's Existence

**Chapter 5. Reason:** Logical Arguments for God's Existence

**Chapter 6. Humanity:** Anthropological Clues for God's Existence

# CHAPTER 4

# *Science*

## Evidence for God's Existence

*The whole point of religious faith, its strength and
chief glory, is that it does not depend on rational
justification. The rest of us are expected to defend
our prejudices. But ask a religious person to justify
their faith and you infringe "religious liberty."*
Richard Dawkins, *The God Delusion*[1]

*What is really pernicious is the practice of teaching
children that faith itself is a virtue. Faith is an evil precisely
because it requires no justification and brooks no argument.*
Richard Dawkins, *The God Delusion*[2]

In his best-selling book *The God Delusion*, Richard Dawkins
identifies some of the most widespread reasons that atheists
object to religious faith generally and Christianity specifically. One
of the greatest sins of religious faith, in Dawkins's mind, is rooted
in the very nature of faith as he understands it. Faith, for Dawkins,

---

[1]  Richard Dawkins, *The God Delusion* (Boston: Houghton Mifflin, 2006), 45.
[2]  Dawkins, 347.

is believing in something despite having no positive reason for such belief (or, even worse, believing in something despite having positive reasons *not to believe it*).

Sadly, many Christians provide ample ammunition for critics and skeptics, blithely embracing a blind or irrational faith divorced from reason, evidence, and argumentation. For many Christians, it is sufficient to have had a personal experience with God that results in a vibrant and healthy relationship with Christ; they see no reason to pursue additional reasons to believe in the reality of the God whom they clearly experience. I do not want to be critical of such religious believers: I think it is a responsible position to take, internally. However, when someone takes that mentality and presents it outside the walls of the church, it becomes entirely insufficient as a public and cultural witness. Perhaps an analogy would help.

Imagine that you traveled to London and received the unexpected pleasure of an invitation to tea with the queen at Buckingham Palace. Naturally, you accept the invitation and enjoy a delightful outing filled with scintillating conversation and delicious treats. When you come back home, you share your royal tea experience with your neighbor, an expat Brit. Let's call him Richard. Richard is skeptical of your story, filled though it is with precise detail.

"Well, really, old fellow, you *can't* expect me to believe such a thing as you having tea with Queen Elizabeth. Everybody knows that the queen has been too ill to participate in public events. Furthermore, the royal family isn't about to invite some backwoods knuckle-dragger from across the pond into their home palace in London. I simply cannot believe such a wild tall tale."

How should *you* respond? Certainly, when it comes to your own *knowledge*, your memory and experience are sufficient to justify you in your certainty that you indeed did have tea with the queen of England at Buckingham Palace (although you might consider the possibility that someone played a practical joke on you!). But to convince your skeptical neighbors and friends, wouldn't it be nice to have some additional evidence or reasons to present? If you had pictures from your tea and the monarch's signature on your menu, or something of that sort—well, that might help to convince skeptics like Richard that the queen really did host you for tea.

In other words, your own experience may be sufficient for you to *know* that you had tea with the queen, but it is not sufficient to *show* to skeptical Richard that you had tea with the queen. Similarly, I contend, your own experience of and relationship with God might be sufficient for you to *know* that God exists, but it is not sufficient to *show* to someone else that God exists. Your skeptical neighbor is going to need more; Richard needs you to provide some positive reason that he, too, should believe, even though he has not had your experience. Thankfully, there are all sorts of additional reasons to believe that God exists.

In chapters 5 and 6, we will consider a range of arguments. In this chapter, we are going to focus on arguments for God's existence that draw on contemporary science. For many people in the Western world today, science (the hard sciences: biology, chemistry, physics) is the primary (or perhaps only) route to secure knowledge. Given the prominence of contemporary science, then, it is helpful to construct reasons to embrace God's existence that are built upon insights from modern scientific discoveries. Cosmological and design arguments do just that!

## Cosmological Arguments

A cosmological argument draws upon the nature of the universe (Greek: *cosmos*) to point toward the existence of a powerful transcendent Creator. There is not *one* cosmological argument, but rather a diverse family of cosmological arguments. We will focus our attention on one version—the *kalām* cosmological argument.

### Aquinas's Cosmological Argument

Before turning to *kalām*, though, let us consider one well-known and venerable cosmological argument that comes from the thirteenth-century Catholic philosopher and theologian Thomas Aquinas. In short form, Aquinas's argument (from cosmic causation) looks like this:

1. There is an order of causes in the world.
2. Nothing can be the cause of itself.
3. Therefore, everything that is caused is caused by something other than itself.
4. There cannot be an infinite regress of causes.
5. Therefore, there must be a first, uncaused cause.
6. The first uncaused cause is transcendent to time, space, matter, and energy.[3]

Aquinas first notes that there is an order of causes in the world. Unscientifically put, things cause other things to occur. When I drive up to a railroad crossing and a train is crossing the tracks, I intuitively recognize that the train car that I first see is being pulled along by the car in front of it. That car, in turn, is being caused to move by the car in front of it, and so on. This point is a fairly straightforward observation shared by virtually everybody.

---

[3] Thomas Aquinas, *Summa Theologica I*, Q. 2, art. 3. Full text of Aquinas's masterpiece is available online: https://www.newadvent.org/summa/1002.htm#article3, accessed August 26, 2020.

Second, Aquinas argues that nothing can be the cause of itself. It is, again, self-evident that the train car I first see cannot be the cause of its own motion.

Third, it then follows that all caused things are caused by something else. This conclusion follows logically but is also intuitively known. Try this experiment at home: sit a baby or toddler (aged six to eighteen months) in the center of a room and hide behind a wall or door. Roll a large red ball through the room in front of the child and observe her reaction. Invariably, after tracking the motion of the ball itself, she will look the other direction—the direction the ball *came from*. Why? Intuitively the baby already knows that everything that is caused is caused by something other than itself. The ball could not have propelled itself across the room. Someone or something had to send the ball along the floor, and the baby is instinctively trying to identify the originating cause of the event.

Fourth, there cannot be an infinite regress (past chain) of causes. This is the key and most-disputed premise in Aquinas's argument— and, as we will see, in the *kalām* argument as well. Aquinas draws upon mathematical and philosophical reason in this step and argues that it is impossible to obtain an actual infinite number of anything, including causes, in the real world. As a test case, try counting from 1 to infinity. Can't do it? Me neither. Why not? Because it is an impossible task. We can certainly count forward unendingly, unceasingly—never reaching an end point in our numerical sequence. But what we cannot do is obtain infinity. Regardless of how long (or fast) we count, we will never get there. Similarly with respect to a chain of causation. We can imagine, looking into the future, causes proceeding unendingly. But we cannot attain an actually infinite series of causes, because that task is impossible.

I have used images about moving forward *toward* infinity, and we can see the impossibility of actually counting to infinity (or attaining an actually infinite series of causes). But note that the problem is even more apparent when we consider *the past*. I challenged you to try counting from 1 to infinity. You couldn't even do that! But now try something harder. Try counting from negative infinity to negative 1. Ready, set, go. But wait a minute. How do you actually *start* counting from negative infinity toward *anything*? Do you see the problem? There's nowhere to start! This is the real problem, Aquinas notes, with trying to embrace an infinite regress of causes. You cannot have the chain extend backward to infinity, because infinity is not an obtainable number; there is nowhere for the causal chain to have begun.

Picture it this way. We can at least *imagine* jumping into a bottomless pit, even though we know we could not do that in actuality. (That's like starting at 1 and counting to infinity.) But we cannot even *imagine* jumping *out* of a bottomless pit, because there would be no conceptual (or actual) starting point. So Aquinas acknowledges that there simply cannot be an infinite chain of past causes leading up to the present.

Fifth, it follows that there must be a first, uncaused cause. Interestingly, Aquinas draws this segment (steps 4 and 5) of his argument from the ancient Greek philosophers Plato and Aristotle, who both argue to "an uncaused cause" and "an unmoved mover" in their philosophical investigations of the cosmos. If there cannot be an infinite series of causes (*a* is caused by *b*; *b* is caused by *c*; *c* is caused by *d*; etc., to infinity), and if everything that is caused must be caused by something other than itself, then there must be some point at which the causal chain originates with a first, uncaused cause; that is, there must be something (or someone) that serves as the precipitating cause for other things in the universe. But this precipitating cause must itself be uncaused. Why? Because if it were caused, then it would have to be caused by something other than itself (see steps 2 and 3), and we would need to continue extending the causal chain accordingly. So the precipitating cause of all other causes in the universe must itself be uncaused.

Sixth, consider the characteristics that this first, uncaused cause must possess. The uncaused cause must be transcendent to time, space, and energy. Why? Because time, space, and energy are all components of the causal chain in the cosmos, so whatever is sufficient to precipitate the causal chain must be transcendent to (above, beyond, outside of) them. Therefore, the first uncaused cause seems to be atemporal (outside of time), immaterial (outside of space and matter), and immensely powerful (perhaps omnipotent). In other words, Aquinas says, this unmoved mover sounds an awful lot like the God of traditional Western monotheism (including Christianity).

So the very existence of causation in the cosmos points strongly to the existence of God.

### The Kalām Cosmological Argument

The *kalām* cosmological argument was first articulated by Muslim philosophers such as al-Kindi (ninth century) and al-Ghazali (eleventh century). In the late twentieth century, the Christian philosopher William Lane Craig revived, developed, and popularized the argument.[4]

The basic structure of the *kalām* argument is straightforward:

1. Everything that begins to exist has an external cause.
2. The universe began to exist.
3. Therefore, the universe has an external cause.

---

[4]  William Lane Craig, *The Kalām Cosmological Argument,* Library of Philosophy and Religion (Eugene, OR: Wipf & Stock, 2000); Craig, *Reasonable Faith: Christian Truth and Apologetics*, 3rd ed. (Wheaton, IL: Crossway, 2008).

A simple argument structure. But how can we determine whether the argument is successful; that is, whether the conclusion of the argument is true? In philosophy, we pursue *sound* arguments: arguments that combine *valid structure* with *true premises*. A valid argument is structured in such a way that the truthfulness of the conclusion flows logically from the truthfulness of the premises; that is, if the premises are true, the conclusion would also be true. Consider this simple argument:

1. If it is raining outside, the driveway will be wet.
2. It is raining outside.
3. Therefore, the driveway will be wet.

It is easy to see that (all other things being equal), if the two premises (steps 1 and 2) are true, then the conclusion (step 3) is also going to be true. Therefore, the argument is valid. Here's an example of an *invalid* argument form:

1. If it is raining outside, the driveway will be wet.
2. The driveway is wet.
3. Therefore, it is raining outside.

In this case, the fact that the driveway is wet does not logically lead to the conclusion that it is raining. There are all sorts of other reasons that the driveway could be wet: it rained earlier; my kids are washing the car; a ginormous elephant is peeing on our driveway . . . .

The *kalām* cosmological argument is structured in a way that is clearly valid: if the two premises are true, the conclusion would logically follow from them.[5] Remember that we are pursuing a *sound* (successful, strong) argument, which combines valid structure with true premises. *Kalām* clearly has valid structure: the success of the argument, therefore, hinges on the truthfulness of the premises. So *are* the premises of the *kalām* cosmological argument true?

Here, a quick word of caution is in order before examining the premises more closely. In Chapter 2, I defended the existence of objective truth: if something is true, it is true for all people in all places at all times. If, then, the premises of an argument are true, they are

---

[5]   For those who want a little bit more logic, we could put *kalām* in a couple of valid logical formats. The argument can be worded in a valid logical structure known as *modus ponens*.

1. If P is true, then Q is true (e.g., if Lincoln was assassinated, then Lincoln is dead).
2. P is true (e.g., Lincoln was assassinated).
3. Therefore, Q is true (e.g., therefore, Lincoln is dead).

In this argument form, we understand that whenever the antecedent (P—Lincoln was assassinated) is true, the consequent (Q—Lincoln is dead) must also be true. Thus, if the antecedent is true (which in this case it clearly is), then the consequent must also be true. With *kalām*, we could then understand the wording thus:

1. If the universe began to exist, then the universe had an external cause.
2. The universe began to exist.
3. Therefore, the universe had an external cause.

Alternatively, *kalām* can be phrased in the form of a categorical syllogism:

1. All M are P (e.g., all dogs are mammals).
2. All S are M (e.g., all Chihuahuas are dogs).
3. Therefore, all S are P (e.g., all Chihuahuas are mammals).

We understand that when one category (Chihuahuas) is encompassed by another category (dogs), which in turn is encompassed by a yet-larger category (mammals), then the first category is subsumed within the third category. Hence, with *kalām*:

1. All things that begin to exist are things that have an external cause.
2. All things identical to the universe are things that began to exist.
3. Therefore, all things identical to the universe are things that have an external cause.

In each logical presentation, the conclusion is functionally the same: the universe has an external cause. Furthermore, the structure of the argument is clearly valid; if the premises are true, the conclusion follows.

*objectively* true. But when we assess arguments, we cannot demand 100 percent certainty in the truthfulness of the premises under consideration. Instead, we are looking for premises that are much more likely to be true than false, and/or premises that are much more probable than their alternatives. Again, an illustration might help to make this clearer.

Imagine that a man is accused of murdering his wife. Police respond to a 911 call from the wife, who is worried that her irate husband is going to stab her to death. When they arrive on the scene, police find the husband standing over the wife's dead body with a bloody steak knife in his hand. The victim has been stabbed fifteen times, with the wounds matching the knife held by the husband. The husband's skin is found underneath his dead wife's fingernails, implying a struggle. On the scene, the husband immediately confesses to the crime of passion.

But when the trial comes, the man's enterprising defense lawyer offers up an alternative scenario, in which aliens from Optima Prime abducted the husband, sent an alien body double, which killed the wife, and then when police arrived, transported their crew member back to the ship and sent the husband back. Clearly this is a farfetched scenario and highly unlikely to be true. But we cannot say that it is absolutely impossible. Therefore, we cannot conclude with 100 percent certainty that it is true that the husband stabbed his wife to death.

Our inability to establish 100 percent certainty is irrelevant. The questions are whether there is good reason to believe that the premises are more likely to be true than false, and whether there is any good alternative to the premises on hand. In our imaginary court case, the husband will almost certainly be convicted, as there is no reasonable doubt regarding his guilt. Lack of 100 percent certainty will not (should not) prevent us from drawing conclusions and acting accordingly. So, with the *kalām* cosmological argument, do we have good reason to believe that the premises of the argument are true?

*Everything that begins to exist has an external cause.* The first premise of the *kalām* cosmological argument asserts that "everything that begins to exist has an external cause." We know from both intuition and scientific investigation that this premise is true.

First, consider your intuition (what I consider to be common-sense knowledge informed by experience). We know intuitively that nothing that comes into existence can be the cause of its own existence. After all, before a thing comes into existence, it does not exist in order to be able to cause anything, including its own existence. Take a couple of examples.

I was born into the world on October 30, 1975. I was conceived roughly nine months prior—although I was such a large baby it might have been slightly more than nine months, I suppose. At some point in 1975, then, I (as a human being) began to exist—much to my parents' joy and my older siblings' chagrin. Is it possible that I caused my own existence? Clearly not. Before I was conceived, I did not exist. If I did not exist, then I could not cause anything. Therefore, I was caused by something outside myself—in this case, by my parents (in the natural, old-fashioned manner, I suspect).

Consider the Dell laptop on which I am currently typing. It was manufactured (I think) in 2016 in an electronics factory. Therefore, my computer began to exist in 2016. Clearly the components of my laptop were in existence prior to the manufacturing of the laptop itself. Fair enough. Those components, plus the labor and machinery that went into the production process, serve as the external causes of my laptop's existence. Could my laptop have caused itself to come into existence? Again, clearly not. Before the laptop was made, it did not exist. If it did not exist, then it could not cause anything to occur, including its own existence. Hence, my laptop was caused by something outside of itself, and we know it could not have been otherwise.

So we have quite powerful intuitive knowledge that everything that begins to exist has an external cause.

Second, the very basis of modern scientific investigation is built upon the belief that everything that begins to exist has an external cause. Science seeks for causal explanations for things and events—a search that makes sense only because of the scientific tenet that things and events in the natural world all have external causes. When a "shooting star" streaks across the sky, the poets among us may reflect and offer a psalm glorying in the rare experience. The scientist is driven to pursue the cause of the shooting star—was it a satellite, space debris, an asteroid, a meteorite, or something hitherto unknown? The scientist is never content with saying, "Well, the shooting star just happened: it did not have a cause."

Indeed, imagine how odd it would be if we rejected this first premise of the *kalām* cosmological argument. We would have to believe, contrary to both intuition and science, that things can come into existence without any external cause. We've already seen that the notion of self-causation is nonsense; the other alternative, it would seem, is to hold that things that come into existence might have no cause whatsoever. Imagine what that would look like:

Question: "Alethea, where did that mangy cat in the living room come from?" Response: "Nowhere, Dad, it just appeared out of nothingness!"[6]

Question: "Sir, where did you get that $1 million in unmarked $100 bills?" Response: "Officer, it's the strangest thing. The bills just appeared in my duffel bag as I was driving down the road."

---

[6] My older daughter, to whom this book is dedicated, has a love and compassion for stray cats that far outstrips mine—partly due to my allergies, partly due to her big heart.

Question: "Tommy, did you punch Billy in the face?" Response: "No, ma'am, honest, I didn't." Question: "Well, then, Tommy, what caused Billy's black eye and bloody nose and concussion?" Response: "Nothing, ma'am, nothing at all. Those things just happened."

In all three cases, the explanation is clearly insufficient. "Nothing" cannot cause a black eye or the sudden appearance of $100 bills or a stray cat. Indeed, "nothing" cannot cause *anything*, because nothing is the absence of all things and therefore possesses no causal power—indeed, nothing possesses no attributes of any kind, including causal attributes, because it is . . . that's right, *nothing*.

So, from both science and intuition, we know that everything that begins to exist has an external cause.[7]

At this point, a skeptic may be eager to protest: But if everything that begins to exist has an external cause, and you're going to argue that God caused the universe to exist; well, then, what caused God? The question is understandable and sensible but is based on one (or both) of two simple misunderstandings.

First, the skeptic might be misunderstanding the premise itself. The *kalām* cosmological argument does not claim that everything *that exists* has an external cause, but rather that everything *that begins to exist* has an external cause. That small distinction in language makes a large philosophical difference. God, in any classical conception, is a divine being who never begins to exist but has always existed. In this understanding, God would not require

---

[7] There is a lot more to say, but room is limited. For example, a skeptic might object that quantum vacuums give us examples of things (quantum particles) being spontaneously generated and extinguished in a vacuum (i.e., condition of nothingness). However, note that a quantum "vacuum" is not equivalent to nothingness, but rather is a rich sea of fluctuating subatomic energy—hence, quantum particles that are created in that scenario still have an external cause. More responses and counter-responses are available—that is part of the fun of more in-depth study!

an external cause, and neither would he be self-caused; he would always have existed.[8]

Second, the skeptic might be misunderstanding what philosophers, regardless of their personal religious beliefs, understand about God. Atheistic philosophers, like Christian philosophers, understand that *if* God exists, then God would be a necessarily existing being; that is, a being that/who did not come into existence and was not caused by any external cause. Classical conceptions of God, again, hold that God has always existed; therefore, God never began to exist. As such, the God of the Western tradition (if such a being exists) would be exempt from the first premise of the *kalām* cosmological argument.

The first premise of *kalām*, then, seems clearly true. How about the second premise?

***The universe began to exist.*** There are two sources of support for this premise—logical and scientific.

When talking about Aquinas's cosmological argument, we saw that it is logically impossible to attain an infinite number of anything—including past events. But if the universe did not begin to exist, then it would have to have an infinite past. If the universe had an infinite past, then the universe would need to have had an infinite number of past points in time, starting from negative infinity and reaching to the present day. The universe, in essence, would need to have jumped out of a bottomless pit. With nowhere to begin, we could not have reached the present time.

---

[8] Interestingly, the majority of mainstream cosmologists in the late nineteenth and early twentieth centuries believed that the universe had always existed and thus did not require an external cause. Those cosmologists understood that if something (in their case, the universe; in our case, God) did not begin to exist, then its existence did not need to be explained with reference to some external entity. In other words, the idea of something, whether God or the universe, existing without beginning to exist is pretty widely accepted by most everyone.

Until the twentieth century, the logical argument for the beginning of the universe was the only nonreligious argument on the table. It was (and remains) sufficient.[9] Thinkers of all worldviews and disciplines understood that a contingent entity such as the universe could not be self-existent or eternal and thus needed to have a beginning. Religious Scriptures such as Gen 1:1 ("In the beginning God created the heavens and the earth") were understood by Christians to be divine revelation in concord with human reason.

In the modern Western age, however, secular scientists and philosophers have questioned that long-held consensus. Late in the nineteenth century, many astronomers and other scientists embraced a steady-state model of the universe, according to which the universe had always existed in roughly the same way it now exists.[10] The laws and constants of nature, the size and shape of the universe—all of these were understood to have been the same for eternity past. Their conclusion of the steady-state universe was based on scientific observations and inferences. Consider the consistency we observe in the universe:

1. Earth's seasons proceed with regularity, four seasons to a terrestrial year.
2. Earth's orbit around the sun is constant, moving in the same direction with the same speed and rotation.

---

[9]   My point here is that we do not need supporting scientific evidence to establish the truth of the premise "the universe began to exist." I am about to point to corroborating evidence from contemporary cosmology, but this is unnecessary—helpful, but unnecessary.

[10]   The most famous and strident defender of the steady-state model of the universe was Sir Frederick Hoyle, for whom the model was a happy means of denying divine creation of the universe. For his most mature (i.e., last), sophisticated defense of the eternal steady-state model, see Fred Hoyle, Geoffrey Burbidge, and Jayant Narlikar, *A Different Approach to Cosmology: From a Static Universe through the Big Bang towards Reality* (New York: Cambridge University Press, 2000), esp. 197–228.

3. The force of gravity is constant (relative to mass and distance) throughout the universe.
4. The appearance of stars and constellations in the night sky is regular and predictable, having been well known since the ancient Greeks.
5. The melting and boiling point of water (relative to pressure) is constant.
6. Days last for twenty-four hours.
7. The Texas Rangers have never won the World Series.

Okay, so perhaps the last one isn't quite like the others. But it is relatively easy to see how, given observational science alone, astronomers could have come to the conclusion that the universe had always existed the way that it exists today. Philosophers, of course, wish that such scientists had considered the absurdity of an actually infinite past.

The scientific evidence that has come in during the twentieth century, however, has entirely overturned previous suggestions of a steady-state universe, establishing as a scientific consensus beyond reasonable doubt that our physical universe began to exist. Known as the big bang model, the contemporary consensus understanding is that our universe began to exist at a point in the finite past, exploding into existence from a singularity—an infinitesimally small point in space with incomprehensible density and mass. In essence, big bang cosmology holds that the universe came into existence with no prior physical state or cause; that is, our space-time universe *began to exist*. A number of scientific discoveries have led to the cementing of the big bang model, including red shift and entropy.

Red shift describes the change in the light wavelengths emitted by stars over a period of time. American scientist Edwin Hubble (after whom the famous Hubble telescope was named) discovered in 1929 that stars and even galaxies are moving away from the earth *and from one another*. The implications of Hubble's discovery of red shift (which confirmed earlier predictions made by scientists such as Albert Einstein, George LeMaître, and Alexander Friedmann) was that the entire fabric of the universe was expanding like the surface area of an ever-inflating balloon. Astronomers then traced back the current expansion of the universe and inferred that at some point in the finite past, all stars and galaxies occupied the same tiny point in space (the "singularity").

Entropy is the gradual wearing down of the physical universe. Entropy is often understood to be the disorderliness or chaos of a physical system but technically represents the unavailability of a physical system's energy. Scientific observation notes that the level of entropy in a closed physical system always increases, such that the usable energy within that system is always decreasing. So, for example, stars in the universe eventually run out of combustible hydrogen and burn out either quietly or spectacularly (e.g., as a supernova). Applying entropy (also known as the second law of thermodynamics) to the universe as a whole, scientists acknowledged that the total amount of usable energy in the universe is declining, such that the universe will eventually burn itself out. A natural conclusion of the law of entropy is that if the universe had an infinite past, then the universe would have run out of usable energy by now. After all, given a finite amount of usable energy, an infinite amount of time would have exhausted that finite amount of usable energy, and we would (should) find ourselves in a dead universe by now. But clearly we have not yet run out of usable energy (although I am awfully tired some days)—thus, the universe cannot have an infinite past, but rather must have an origin point in the finite past.

From red shift, entropy, and other scientific discoveries, it is clear that the universe began to exist, and that the second premise of the *kalām* cosmological argument is much more likely to be true than not.[11]

***Therefore, the universe has an external cause.***

> For the scientist who has lived by his faith in the power of reason, the story ends like a bad dream. He has scaled the mountains of ignorance, he is about to conquer the highest peak; as he pulls himself over the final rock, he is greeted by a band of theologians who have been sitting there for centuries.
>
> Agnostic astronomer Robert Jastrow,<br>*God and the Astronomers*[12]

> In the scientist's version of Genesis, as in the Bible, the world begins with the dazzling splendor of the moment of creation. . . . Many details of the scientific account differ from those in the Bible . . . but the essential feature is

---

[11] Again, there is much more to say. Some scientists recognize the clear theistic overtones of the big bang model of the universe and strive mightily to avoid it. Mainstream scientists have advocated for alternative models: an oscillating universe (Frederick Hoyle), imaginary time (Stephen Hawking), chaotic inflation, etc. It is worth reading advocates of these models, as well as their critics. Two quick points: (1) the science is above my ability to understand fully, let alone explain competently; (2) each alternative to the big bang model is pilloried mercilessly by critics from all worldviews, whether they embrace big bang or advocate their own unique alternative. The inability of big bang skeptics to agree on a workable alternative is evidence, I think, of the strength of the big bang model of the universe and the desperation of critics to avoid the theistic implications of the big bang, which is clearly the current consensus model.

[12] Robert Jastrow, *God and the Astronomers*. 2nd ed. (New York: Norton, 1992), 107.

the same in both stories: There was a Beginning, and all things in the Universe can be traced back to it.

Robert Jastrow, *The Enchanted Loom*[13]

If it is true that everything that begins to exist has an external cause, and if it is also true that the universe began to exist, then it follows necessarily that the universe has an external cause. So scientific discoveries, commonsense intuition, and logic combine to demonstrate that the universe has an external cause.

Some critics (Dawkins again) will note that the *kalām* cosmological argument does not prove that Christianity is true, nor does it even establish that there is one God as Western traditions argue. Fair enough. Certainly *kalām* should not be asked to do more than it is able. Cosmological arguments are successful in demonstrating that there is some (thing or person) external cause for our physical universe. But that logic does not yet establish the God of the Bible.

But we should ask: What sort of "cause" for the universe could exist that is external to the space-time universe? As Thomas Aquinas noted, the cause of the universe would need to be timeless, spaceless, and incredibly powerful. There is not a terribly long list of candidates that suitably satisfy those conditions; indeed, the cause of the universe sounds very much like the traditional understanding of the God of the Bible. So even if the *kalām* cosmological argument does not establish that Christianity is true or that the God of the Bible exists, it does show that the universe has an external cause and that external cause has characteristics that closely resemble the God of the Bible. In other words, it gets us a good way in the right direction!

---

[13]  Robert Jastrow, *The Enchanted Loom: Mind in the Universe* (New York: Simon & Schuster, 1981), 15–16.

## Design Arguments

A design argument, also known as a teleological (Greek: *telos*, function, end, or design) or fine-tuning argument, works from apparent design or fine-tuning in the universe to point toward the existence of an intentional transcendent designer. Much as with cosmological arguments, there is not *one* design argument, but rather a diverse family of such arguments. We will consider just one such design argument, which is structured as follows:

1. The apparent fine-tuning of the universe is due to necessity, chance, or intelligent design.
2. The apparent fine-tuning of the universe is not due to necessity or chance.
3. Therefore, the apparent fine-tuning of the universe is due to intelligent design.

This argument, like the *kalām* argument, is structurally valid, such that if its premises are true, its conclusion follows. The form of this argument is known technically as a disjunctive syllogism, more colloquially as an either-or. In a disjunctive syllogism, the first premise notes that either *x* or *y* is true (or *x* or *y* or *z*). In many disjunctive arguments (such as ours), the *or*s under consideration are potential explanations for some phenomenon. The argument proceeds by eliminating one side of the disjunct (the *either*), such that only one is left (the *or*). If *x* is not true (or is not the correct explanation), then the only other option, *y*, must be true (or be the correct explanation).

Like all valid arguments, this design argument will be successful (sound) only if its premises are true. So let us take a look at the two premises in our argument.

## The Apparent Fine-Tuning of the Universe Is Due to Necessity, Chance, or Intelligent Design

> A common sense interpretation of the facts suggests that a super intellect has monkeyed with the physics, as well as the chemistry and biology, and that there are no blind forces worth speaking about in nature.
>
> Atheist astronomer Fred Hoyle, "The Universe: Some Past and Present Reflections"[14]

There are two primary contentions in our first premise: (1) there is apparent fine-tuning in the universe, and (2) there are three possible explanations for that apparent fine-tuning.

The first contention has been firmly established by twentieth- and twenty-first-century scientific discoveries and is fairly widely acknowledged in the scientific community. In short, the universe is precisely calibrated so as to allow for the possibility of life. Whether this fine-tuning is the result of physical necessity, random chance, or intelligent design is beside the point; it is universally acknowledged that if the laws and constants were not almost exactly what they are, there could be no life anywhere in the universe, let alone advanced human life on earth.[15]

---

[14]  Fred Hoyle, "The Universe, Past and Present Reflections," in *Annual Review of Astronomy and Astrophysics* Volume 20 (1982), 17. Full text of Hoyle's article is available online at https://www.annualreviews.org/doi/pdf/10.1146/annurev.aa.20.090182.000245.

[15]  The best recent work on fine-tuning is coauthored by two physicists, one agnostic, the other theistic. Geraint F. Lewis and Luke A. Barnes, *A Fortunate Universe: Life in a Finely Tuned Cosmos* (Cambridge: Cambridge University Press, 2016). Lewis and Barnes present fairly technical scientific evidence for the precise calibration of physical and chemical features of the universe. For more accessible treatments of cosmic fine-tuning, see Christian theist Hugh Ross, *The Creator and the Cosmos: How the Latest Scientific Discoveries Reveal God*, 4th ed. (Covina,

There are three layers of fine-tuning in the universe that bear mentioning: macroscopic (fine-tuning of the laws and constants that govern the universe writ large), terrestrial (fine-tuning related to the placement and structure of the planet Earth), and microscopic (biological and chemical fine-tuning related to life on earth, particularly human life).

***Macroscopic fine-tuning of the universe for life.*** Many scientists, including Hugh Ross, have closely examined the fine-tuning of the universe and its suitability for life. Ross relates more than two dozen different laws and constants that are precisely arranged in order for life to exist in the universe. We will briefly examine just one of them—the cosmological constant.[16]

The cosmological constant represents the force that acts against the force of gravity to govern the rate of expansion of the universe. The cosmological constant has to be precisely fine-tuned, such that it is large enough to overcome the force of gravity to enable the universe to expand, but not so large that the universe expands too rapidly. If the cosmological constant were even slightly smaller than it is, the early expansion of the universe would not have been rapid enough to have overcome the force of gravity. The universe would have collapsed back in upon itself almost instantly after the big bang.[17] From that beginning point of the universe, matter "explodes" apart, with atoms flying away from one another with

CA: RTB Press, 2018); or agnostic multiverse theorist Paul Davies, *The Goldilocks Enigma: Why Is the Universe Just Right for Life?* (Boston: Mariner, 2006).

[16] In what follows throughout this chapter, I am not claiming to be a scientist or an expert in these scientific matters. I am entirely indebted to scientists across the worldview spectrum for what little scientific understanding I possess. Hugh Ross, Robin Collins, Paul Davies, Luke Barnes, Geraint Lewis, Stephen Hawking, and Richard Dawkins, among others, have informed this section of the chapter.

[17] The value of the cosmological constant is, to me, almost incomprehensibly small to begin with. According to Wikipedia's suggestion, its value is approximately $1.1 \times 10^{-52} \text{m}^{-2}$.

great force. The force of gravity, however, draws matter together ("What goes up must come down," because, for example, the mass of the earth draws matter back to its surface). Without the force expressed by the cosmological constant, all of the matter in the universe would have been drawn back together by the force of gravity, and we would not have the expansion of the universe at all. The cosmological constant, therefore, must be at least sufficiently large that it permits atoms to exist independently, stretching the spatial boundaries of the universe.

If, on the other hand, the cosmological constant were even slightly larger than it is, the expansion rate would far outstrip the force of gravity, and the universe would have expanded much more rapidly, so that galaxies and stars would not have been able to form. The scientific understanding is that at the universe's birth, the only atoms that existed would have been hydrogen atoms (the lightest element in the universe). Given a higher cosmological constant, those hydrogen atoms would have been quickly freed from gravity's pull, and we would have had a universe composed of nothing but hydrogen—clearly a universe that would not permit any form of life, let alone human life, on earth. So the cosmological constant is precisely calibrated at just the right value to permit an expanding universe that nonetheless contains heavier elements (helium, oxygen, carbon, etc.) that are necessary for life.

The cosmological constant is just one of the universal physical constants that must be precisely configured for life to be possible anywhere in the universe. Others include the strong and weak nuclear force constants, the electromagnetic force, the gravitational force constant, the entropy level of the universe, the mass density of the universe, the speed of light, the initial uniformity of radiation caused by the big bang, the average distance between galaxies, the decay rate of the proton, the mass excess of the neutron over the proton, and the ratio of the mass of exotic (dark) matter to ordinary matter. All of these universal constants are required to be finely-tuned for life to be possible. The fact that all of them are precisely fine-tuned "cries out for a philosophical or theological explanation."[18]

*Terrestrial fine-tuning of the earth for life.* There are also laws and constants that are necessary for life to be possible on a particular planet within a particular galaxy somewhere in the universe. For a planet to be hospitable to life, it must possess a molten core, be protected by an atmospheric shield, travel in an elliptical orbit an appropriate distance from a star of suitable strength and size, with suitable moons orbiting the planet, within a solar system with more distant planets and/or asteroid belts to absorb cosmic asteroid/ meteorite events, in a suitable portion of an appropriate galaxy. Ross documents more than a hundred such parameters of varying degrees of probability. Space does not permit a discussion of these parameters here, but Ross concludes that the possibility of all parameters being met in any single planet is 1 in $10^{160}$ and that, accordingly, it is virtually impossible to expect that there would be even *one* planet anywhere in the universe that meets all of the criteria necessary for life to emerge.[19]

*Microscopic fine-tuning for life on earth.* In addition to macroscopic and terrestrial fine-tuning, there is also fine-tuning on the microscopic scale, which makes human life on earth possible. The unique chemical composition of water ($H_2O$) facilitates the

---

[18]   John Jefferson Davis, *The Frontiers of Science & Faith: Examining Questions from the Big Bang to the End of the Universe* (Downers Grove, IL: InterVarsity, 2002), 133.

[19]   Ross, *Creator and the Cosmos*, 175–99. For more excellent work on terrestrial fine-tuning, see Guillermo Gonzalez and Jay W. Richards, *The Privileged Planet: How Our Place in the Cosmos Is Designed for Discovery* (Washington, DC: Regnery, 2004); Peter D. Ward and Donald Brownlee, *Rare Earth: Why Complex Life Is Uncommon in the Universe* (New York: Copernicus, 2000).

existence of life even in colder regions of the planet. Water is the only molecule that is denser (heavier per cubic inch) as a liquid than as a solid. As such, water freezes from the top down rather than from the bottom up; and rivers and lakes can continue to have flowing liquid water even while the surface is frozen. If water, like other compounds, were denser as a solid, frozen water would sink (the weight of a cubic inch of ice would be heavier than that of a cubic inch of water; the ice would move downward), and rivers and lakes in northern and southern climates would freeze through in their entirety during winter. As a result, there would be no liquid water available in those environments and life would die off. It is fascinating that water, probably the most essential molecule for the existence of life, should bear this unique chemical feature.

When we consider the makeup of our universe, then, we see that there is a wealth of data that shows the exquisite fine-tuning of our universe and our earth for the existence of human life. In addition to the physical and cosmological factors that we have considered, numerous aspects of biological life appear to be fine-tuned for the existence of human life on earth.[20]

When you combine the macroscopic, terrestrial, and microscopic layers together, the evidence for fine-tuning is comprehensive and undeniable. Scientists and philosophers of all backgrounds and beliefs accept that the universe certainly has the *appearance* of having been fine-tuned for the existence of life. Note the somewhat grudging admissions of three nontheists:

An honest man, armed with all the knowledge available to us now, could only state that in some sense, the origin of life appears at the moment to be almost a miracle, so

[20] See, e.g., Michael Behe, *Darwin's Black Box: The Biochemical Challenge to Evolution*, 2nd ed. (New York: Free Press, 2006).

many are the conditions which would have had to have been satisfied to get it going.[21]

The collection of felicitous "coincidences" in physics and cosmology implies that the Great Designer had better set the knobs carefully, or the universe would be a very inhospitable place . . .

Scientists have long been aware that the universe seems strangely suited to life, but they chose mostly to ignore it. It was an embarrassment—it looked too much like the work of a Cosmic Designer.[22]

The laws of science . . . contain many fundamental numbers, like the size of the electric charge of the electron and the ratio of the masses of the proton and the electron. . . . The remarkable fact is that the values of these numbers seem to have been very finely adjusted to make possible the development of life. . . . Most sets of values would give rise to universes that, although they might be very beautiful, would contain no one able to wonder at that beauty.[23]

Thus the existence of apparent fine-tuning in the universe is an accepted established fact. The first part of premise 1 (the fact

---

[21] Francis Crick, *Life Itself: Its Origin and Nature* (New York: Simon & Schuster, 1981), 88.

[22] Paul Davies, *The Cosmic Jackpot: Why Our Universe Is Just Right for Life* (Boston: Houghton Mifflin, 2007), 146, 151. Davies proceeds to argue that the fine-tuning only appears that way because our universe is just one bubble in an extravagant multiverse.

[23] Stephen Hawking, *A Brief History of Time*, updated and exp. 10th anniversary ed. (New York: Bantam, 1996), 129–30.

of apparent fine-tuning) is clearly true. What about the second part of the first premise: the apparent fine-tuning of the universe *is due to either necessity, chance, or intelligent design*? Why, one might ask, am I limiting the possible explanations to these three options? Couldn't there be other possibilities?

In a word, no. Necessity, chance, and design are the only three apparent options on the table; that is, some people advocate physical necessity, others random chance, and others intelligent design, as the explanation for apparent fine-tuning—but one simply cannot find any other potential explanations. If someone were to set forth an additional reasonable option, then of course we would need to consider it—but in the absence of such suggestions, we work with the three options on the table.

Premise 1, then, stands fully intact: the apparent fine-tuning of the universe is due to necessity, chance, or intelligent design.

### *The Apparent Fine-Tuning of the Universe Is Not Due to Necessity or Chance*

How about those first two options: necessity and chance? Could some combination of physical necessity or random chance account for the apparent fine-tuning that we perceive in the universe? Let us consider them in backward order.

***The failure of random chance.*** In a post-Darwin world, random chance is frequently the go-to explanation for perceived design or fine-tuning in the universe, whether on a biological level or a cosmic scale. Many twentieth- and twenty-first-century thinkers, then, employ chance as the best explanation for the macroscopic, terrestrial, and microscopic fine-tuning that we observe. On this theory, we (humans on earth) are just cosmically lucky—hence Paul Davies's famous book title, *The Cosmic Jackpot*. The book argues that *our* universe is tremendously fortunate in just happening to have the right conditions for life to emerge and evolve.

But random chance ends up being a spectacularly bad explanation! Remember from the previous section that there are a number of physical laws and constants that have to be precisely calibrated for there to be life *anywhere in the universe*, let alone on planet Earth. Hugh Ross identifies more than two dozen physical constants; Martin Rees isolates six.[24] Let's give the defender of random chance the best possible chance (pardon the pun) to succeed, by considering just six universal constants. On pure random chance, what are the odds that each of those six constants would be precisely what it needs to be for life to be possible on earth?

To help illustrate the question, consider a standard sound board, say in a local church (or pub or concert hall, whatever you like). Each dial on the sound board represents one of our universal constants—so we'll have to make it a six-channel sound board. If you've ever run sound, you know that it is important to have your channels mixed precisely to have perfect sound in the venue. I know that in our church, the sound guys like to leave the dials set for our usual music team, so that minimal adjustment is needed on a weekly basis. If a kiddo gets into the sound booth and randomly twirls the dials, it causes considerable grief for our sound team, who then has to recalibrate the balance.

So we have a six-channel sound board, with each of the six channels representing one of our universal constants—let's say, gravitational constant, strong nuclear force, weak nuclear force, cosmological constant, electromagnetic constant, and the ratio of matter to dark matter. Each dial has to be precisely what it is for life to exist in the universe. Just for fun, let's say their values have to be

---

[24] See Ross, *Creator and the Cosmos*; Martin Rees, *Just Six Numbers: The Deep Forces that Shape the Universe* (New York: Basic, 2000).

4, 3, 6, 7, 5, and 2. What is the probability that, by random chance, each of those dials would be just what it needs to be? Well, that's a pretty easy question to answer.

The chance that you'd have the gravitational constant come out at exactly 4, given a dial with ten settings from 1 to 10 (whole numbers only), would be exactly 1/10 or 10 percent or 0.1. The chance that strong nuclear force would be exactly 3 is also 1/10 or 10 percent or 0.1. What is the probability that they would *both* be precisely what they need to be? As we add necessary components, we multiply our probabilities: the chance that they would both come out just right randomly is 1/100 or 1 percent or 0.01. As we add additional universal constants (dials), the improbability increases exponentially: 0.001 for three, 0.0001 for four, 0.00001 for five, and 0.000001 for all six.

The probability that all six dials would be exactly where they need to be if we have just randomly spun the dials is 1 in a million (1/1,000,000 or 0.0001% or 0.000001, or $1 \times 10^{-6}$). Now, if one wants to be technical, one in a million odds are not impossible odds; that is, it is *possible* that one could spin all six dials in the sound booth and just happen to have them all come out exactly right.[25] But the question isn't whether it is *possible*; the question is whether it is a reasonable or realistic explanation. And we can already see intuitively that the answer is no. But the odds get worse.

We have been considering the possibility that random chance will get the outcome we need for all six dials, where the possible values on the dials are limited to whole numbers between 1 and 10. But when it comes to our universal constants, we have a far greater possible range of values. To get the possible range of values, we take the smallest known constant (in this case, the gravitational constant)

---

[25]    In perhaps the only good line from the terrible movie *Dumb and Dumber*, "So you're saying there's a chance."

and the largest known constant (in this case, the strong nuclear force), and take those values as the minimum possible range of values for the universal constants. Although the units used to express the constants can differ, we are looking at a possible range in values of something like from 1 to $1 \times 10^{40}$. That is, instead of 10 being the highest number on our sound board dials, our dial has all of the whole numbers from 1 up to 1 followed by forty zeroes. That's a lot of zeroes and a lot of possible numbers on the dial!

When you add that in, the possibility that we could get the universal constants we have, precisely calibrated, just by random chance, then even for Rees's minimal six constants, our odds are now 1 in $10^{240}$. To put that in context, there are fewer than $10^{240}$ subatomic particles in the universe. Spinning the dials randomly and getting precisely this outcome is less likely than going to Long Beach in California and picking up the one pink grain of sand among the uncountable nonpink grains; less likely than randomly firing a gun in the air and happening to hit the bull's-eye of a target on the surface of Jupiter.

Is it possible that we arrived at the physical laws and constants we have simply by random chance? Yes. But is that a reasonable explanation for the apparent fine-tuning of the universe? Clearly not.

***The failure of physical necessity.*** The belief that chance is the best explanation for the apparent fine-tuning in the universe is highly irrational. How about physical necessity?

For decades, physicists have been pursuing their GUT—not an ever-expanding midsection but a grand unifying theory (or a "theory of everything") that would tie together other known physical laws and constants in the universe. The goal is to provide a physical explanation for why the forces of gravity, electromagnetism, strong nuclear force, and weak nuclear force, for example, have to be precisely what they are in relationship to one another. Unfortunately, to date, no such GUT (or ToE) has been offered.[26] Furthermore, it seems clear to scientists and nonscientists alike that the physical constants in the universe could logically have been very different from what they actually are. So if someone is to suggest that the universe *must* have the physical constants that it does (e.g., the cosmological constant or the force of gravity), then that person should present strong evidence for the claim. In the absence of such evidence, it is reasonable to conclude that physical necessity fails as an explanation for the apparent fine-tuning of our universe.

*The failure of chance + physical necessity.* If chance alone cannot account for apparent fine-tuning, nor can physical necessity on its own, perhaps the combination of chance and necessity could do the trick! In this vein, many observers suggest that our universe is just one of billions (or more) of parallel universes, all existing as part of a vast multiverse (multiple + universe). According to multiverse theorists, each separate universe is governed by a different set of randomly determined physical laws and constants. Even if the initial likelihood of having our six physical constants being set "just right" for life was only 1 in $1\times10^{240}$, given the existence of billions upon billions of universes, eventually one would turn up with the right set of laws and constants for life to exist. In this scenario, we combine random chance (each separate universe has randomly generated physical laws and constants) with physical necessity (there are billions of such universes) to arrive at the inevitability of a life-permitting universe. We just happen to live in one such universe!

---

[26]  Some have suggested that string theory, or M theory might provide just such a GUT. But (1) there are multiple competing versions of string theory, none of which has gained broad general acceptance; and (2) most of the competing string theories still provide for multiple (billions) of ways for the universe to be constructed, the vast majority of which would not be suitable for life of any sort. For more, see Craig, *Reasonable Faith*, 162–63.

Multiverse theory has become increasingly popular in the non-Christian scientific community[27] and has gained some traction among prominent Christian physicists and philosophers.[28] Non-Christian multiverse theorists suggest that the multiverse would show that apparent fine-tuning in our universe can be reasonably understood to arise from a combination of chance and physical necessity and thus does not point toward intelligent design. For two primary reasons, their suggestion fails.

First, multiverse theory is speculative and unproven. There is a lack of strong evidence supporting the existence of multiple parallel universes alongside our own. Indeed, given some versions of multiverse theory, such parallel universes would be impossible for us to detect even if they did exist. It seems wiser to consider multiverse theory to be more science fiction than hard science at this point in time.

Second, even if a multiverse *did* exist, it would not undermine our design argument. If we are a part of a vast multiverse, we would need to have a suggestion as to the nature of that multiverse and an explanation as to the origin of the multiverse.

Supporters of multiverse theory would need to ascribe characteristics to the multiverse. What is the multiverse like? Various

---

[27] See Alex Vilenkin, *Many Worlds in One: The Search for Other Universes* (New York: Hill & Wang, 2006). Other prominent multiverse theorists include Max Tegmark, Paul Davies, and Alan Guth.

[28] See, e.g., Don N. Page, "The Everett Multiverse and God," in *God and the Multiverse: Scientific, Philosophical, and Theological Perspectives*, ed. Klaas J. Kraay (New York: Routledge, 2015), 45–58. Klaas Kraay, Robin Collins, and Timothy O'Connor contribute to the same volume as theists who are open to multiverse theory. Theorists like Page suggest that the existence of a multiverse would serve to further magnify the greatness, creativity, and power of the Lord God—not only has he created an intricate, beautiful, expansive universe; he has created countless billions of diverse universes, each with its own mathematical, scientific, and physical beauty.

pictures have been proposed: it is like a bubble bath, with individual "bubble" universes; it is like a universe-generating machine, burping out individual universes, like the cannonballs in Super Mario World; it is a mysterious, inexplicable, beginningless, spaceless, immaterial, incredibly powerful entity.

The first two suggestions—the bubble bath and the universe-generating machine—lead to further difficulties. If the multiverse is a gigantic bubble-universe bath, we are left with the question, where did the bubble-universe bath come from? The same problem plagues the universe-generating machine picture: Where did the machine come from? Or who designed the universe-generating machine? The inability of multiverse theorists to answer those questions pushes more supporters to the third option: multiverse as a mysterious, beginningless, spaceless, immaterial, incredibly powerful entity. But what does that multiverse sound like—other than a covert description of some sort of God?

### Therefore, the Apparent Fine-Tuning of the Universe Is Due to Intelligent Design

If there are three possible options on the table (the apparent fine-tuning of the universe is due to chance, necessity, or intelligent design), and the first two options have failed, then we are left with intelligent design as the best explanation.

We are familiar with intelligent design as the best explanation for many apparently fine-tuned features of the world in which we live. William Paley's classic essay argues that a reasonable person, stumbling across a watch in a forest for the first time (with no previous knowledge of what a watch is), would easily conclude that the watch has been crafted by an intelligent designer.[29] Each of us knows

---

[29] William Paley, "The Watch and the Watchmaker," in *Readings in Philosophy of Religion: Ancient to Contemporary*, ed. Linda Zagzebski and Timothy D. Miller

the difference between a beach with ripples and patterns caused by waves and a beach with ridges that spell out "John loves Mary." If I see a bowl-shaped set of mud, twigs, and leaves in a tree branch and hear "cheep-cheeps" from it, I reasonably conclude that a bird has crafted a nest. Each of us knows the difference between Mount St. Helens or Mokoliʻi,[30] on the one hand, and the pyramids or the Mount Rushmore carvings, on the other hand. A bowl of alphabet soup can contain a random assortment of letters; a dictionary requires an intelligent designer. In short, humans are accustomed to concluding that some things are best explained as being the product of intelligent design rather than chance or physical necessity. Mokoliʻi is best explained with reference to the random workings of waves, wind, rain, and geological activity; Mount Rushmore is best explained with reference to human agency and design.

If both chance and necessity fail as explanations for the apparent fine-tuning of our universe at the macroscopic, terrestrial, and microscopic levels, we are reasonable in appealing to intelligent design as the best explanation for that apparent fine-tuning. In other words, the apparent fine-tuning of the universe is most reasonably understood as pointing to the *actual, intentional* fine-tuning of the universe! The question then becomes: What would an intelligent fine-tuner of the universe have to be like? Clearly it could not be some governmental agency or multinational corporation. Rather, the universe's intelligent designer would need to be something like the traditional Christian conception of God: a transcendent, powerful, creative, and wise being.

---

(Malden, MA: Wiley-Blackwell, 2009), 28–30. The argument was first published in Paley's *Natural Theology* (1802).

[30]   Mokoliʻi is a beautiful island off the east coast of Oahu that resembles the traditional hat worn by Chinese farmers in the eighteenth and nineteenth centuries.

Transcendent—above and beyond the universe (or multiverse, if you so prefer) that exists.

Powerful—able to bring new things into existence.

Creative—possessing the imagination to create vast domains of space filled with innumerable physical objects.

Wise—knowing how best to create a world capable of sustaining intelligent life.

Such a design argument may not conclude that the God of Christianity exists, but it does (like the cosmological argument) point us quite strongly in that direction.

## Conclusion

In this chapter, we have taken a brief look at two contemporary scientific arguments for the existence of God. The *kalām* cosmological argument suggests that because the universe began to exist, and all things that begin to exist have an external cause, therefore the universe has an external cause. The design argument we examined suggests that because the apparent fine-tuning of the universe cannot be reasonably explained by chance and/or physical necessity, therefore the fine-tuning is best explained by intelligent design. The cosmological argument points to the cause of the universe being timeless, spaceless, and incredibly powerful. The fine-tuning argument points to the designer of the universe being transcendent, powerful, creative, and wise.

Does this (cosmology and design) prove beyond a shadow of a doubt that God exists? No, I don't think so. But it does suggest that it is more reasonable to believe that God exists than it is to deny God's existence. At the very least, these two signposts, considered on their own, should make belief in God eminently reasonable and respectable. There are certainly good reasons to believe that God does exist. In the next two chapters, we will consider more such arguments, from reason and human nature respectively.

### Recommended Resources for Further Exploration

Craig, William Lane. *The Kalām Cosmological Argument.* Library of Philosophy and Religion. Eugene, OR: Wipf & Stock, 2000.

Davies, Paul. *The Cosmic Jackpot: Why Our Universe Is Just Right for Life.* Boston: Houghton Mifflin, 2007.

Gonzalez, Guillermo, and Jay W. Richards. *The Privileged Planet: How Our Place in the Cosmos Is Designed for Discovery.* Washington, DC: Regnery, 2004.

Lewis, Geraint F., and Luke A. Barnes. *A Fortunate Universe: Life in a Finely Tuned Cosmos.* Cambridge: Cambridge University Press, 2016.

Ross, Hugh. *The Creator and the Cosmos: How the Latest Scientific Discoveries Reveal God.* 4th ed. Covina, CA: RTB Press, 2018.

Ward, Peter D., and Donald Brownlee. *Rare Earth: Why Complex Life Is Uncommon in the Universe.* New York: Copernicus, 2000.

# CHAPTER 5

# *Reason*

## Logical Arguments for God's Existence

Colin McGinn, in his interview "Faith & Reason" with Bill Moyers, says,

> There are no, I think, intellectual arguments for the
> existence of God at all. The whole history of twentieth-
> century theology, of course, has conceded that point,
> because the whole history of it is the necessity of faith.
> You don't need faith if you have reason; if God can be
> proved by reason, by the ontological argument or the
> cosmological argument or the argument from design, faith
> is not necessary to underpin the belief in God. . . . So
> you're meant to believe, for example, that God exists as a
> matter of faith. You believe in an existential proposition:
> God exists. And you believe it on faith, independently
> of evidence or argument. To anybody who is devoted to
> rationality, that has to sound very strange.[1]

---

[1]    Bill Moyers, "Faith and Reason: Colin McGinn and Mary Gordon," season 1, episode 1. PBS, June 30, 2006. McGinn's interview can be viewed at https://www.pbs.org/video/bill-moyers-faith-reason-colin-mcginn-mary-gordon/#:~:text=Two%20

In Chapter 4, we considered two types of arguments that use contemporary scientific evidence (among other things) to point toward the existence of God. The *kalām* cosmological argument, if successful, points toward the existence of a timeless, spaceless, powerful, transcendent being beyond the physical universe. The fine-tuning argument shows that the apparent design of the universe is best explained by the existence of a transcendent, powerful, creative, and wise being beyond the physical universe. In the face of even just these two contemporary arguments, it is difficult to sustain Colin McGinn's claim that "there are no . . . intellectual arguments for the existence of God." McGinn might just mean that he is unpersuaded by the arguments that exist; but it is quite inaccurate to claim, as he does, that there are simply *no arguments* at all for the existence of God! Arguments are there—even if not definitive—that increase the probability of God's existence and show that it is reasonable to believe that God does exist.

In addition to the reasonable scientific arguments presented in the previous chapter, there are also logical arguments that point to God's existence—arguments that do not look to the claims or consensus of contemporary scientists, but rather take a logical look at reality and conclude that God exists. In this chapter, we will explore two such families of logical arguments—ontological arguments and moral arguments.

---

provocative%20authors%20Mary%20Gordon,journey%20from%20belief%20to%20disbelief.; the relevant part of the interview begins at 15:20. The transcript of Moyers's interview with McGinn can be read at https://www.pbs.org/moyers/faithandreason/print/faithandreason102_print.html.

## Ontological Arguments

The ontological argument is unique in the history of theistic arguments. Unlike other theistic arguments, the ontological argument depends on no empirical evidence or observations. It is what we call an a priori argument, an argument that does not depend on any external data or investigation.[2]

The ontological argument is also the toughest of the theistic arguments to understand. It is difficult to wrap your mind around and comprehend, and thus it is also hard to use in productive conversation with others. That being said, there are some types of people for whom this is the most persuasive type of argument—particularly those with a mathematical or logical bent to their mind.

### *Anselm's Ontological Argument*

The classic ontological argument comes from Anselm, the archbishop of Canterbury in the eleventh century. Anselm's argument goes through five premises to arrive at the conclusion that God must exist.

1. God is understood as that than which nothing greater can be conceived; even "the fool" (atheist) thinks that God, should God exist, is "that than which nothing greater can be conceived."[3]

---

[2]    *A priori* simply means "before (considering) the facts"; *a posteriori* means "after (considering) the facts." A priori knowledge, then, is known by pure reason, without any consideration of empirical investigation; a posteriori knowledge is arrived at via exploration of the external world.

[3]    For our purposes, I will use Anselm's "that than which nothing greater can be conceived" as synonymous with contemporary philosophy's "greatest conceivable being." GCB is a little shorter and more efficient than TTWNGCBC.

2. A thing exists either (a) in the understanding alone or (b) in the understanding and in reality. It is "greater" to exist in reality than it is to exist only in the understanding.
3. If God exists only in the understanding, then he is not "that than which nothing greater can be conceived," since he would be greater if he existed in reality as well.
4. But God is by definition that than which nothing greater can be conceived.
5. Therefore, God must exist not only in the mind, but in reality as well.[4]

***God is understood as that than which nothing greater can be conceived.*** Anselm begins with the recognition that everyone believes that God, should God exist, is the greatest conceivable being. This premise is actually the key premise in the argument, and Anselm notes that even "the fool" (i.e., the one who does not believe in God) has this conception of God as being "that than which nothing greater can be conceived." The atheist, of course, believes that this God does not exist. But, says Anselm, even the atheist agrees that God, should God exist, is the greatest conceivable being—possessing maximal power, goodness, presence, knowledge, love, and so forth.

***A thing exists either in the understanding alone or in the understanding and in reality.*** There are two ways, Anselm says, for something to exist. It can exist only in one's mind, in one's conception, but not in the "real world." Unicorns, leprechauns, the tooth fairy, elves, and orcs would be examples of things that exist in our understanding alone but not in reality. We can understand and

---

[4]   Helpful versions of Anselm's ontological argument can be found in many places. This one, though slightly edited, comes from Groothuis, *Christian Apologetics*, 188 (see intro., n. 1).

conceive of such things. But things can also exist not only in one's mind, but also in reality. Horses, Irishmen, comets, computers, and hockey would be examples of things that exist not only in our understanding, but also in reality.

*It is greater to exist in reality than it is to exist only in the understanding.* Existence, Anselm holds, is a "great-making property." If God is that than which nothing greater can be conceived, then it is greater for God to exist in reality than to exist solely in the understanding or imagination. A thing is greater (in magnitude) if it exists in the real world than it is if it exists only in the understanding.

*If God exists only in the understanding, then he is not the greatest conceivable being.* If it is greater to exist in reality than only in the understanding, then if God exists only in the understanding, God would not be "that than which nothing greater can be conceived." After all, we can conceive of this being existing not only in the understanding, but also in reality. And it would be greater for this maximally great being to exist in reality, not merely in the understanding. So if God exists only in the understanding, he would not be that than which nothing greater can be conceived, because we could conceive of one greater—namely, this being also existing in reality.

*God is by definition that than which nothing greater can be conceived.* But we have already articulated that God is understood as that than which nothing greater can be conceived. That is, both those who believe in God and those who do not believe in God have historically agreed that the conception of God includes God being this greatest conceivable being. And if God is understood to be that than which nothing greater can be conceived, then God must exist not just in the understanding, but also in reality.

*Therefore, God must exist not only in the mind, but in reality as well.* To be "that than which nothing greater can be conceived,"

God must exist in reality, not just in the understanding. Therefore, God exists.

When people hear Anselm's ontological argument for the first time, it frequently sounds like some sort of verbal trick—a game played with language but having no bearing on reality. It seems that Anselm is trying to do something to confuse us into confessing God's existence. There are, accordingly, a number of traditional critiques of Anselm's argument. We will briefly consider three of them.

The first comes from internet atheists who make fun of the ontological argument by saying that we can use the same argument form to imagine *anything* into existence. I once saw an online atheist call-in show where one of the hosts said that the ontological argument goes like this: "I can conceive of a pink polka-dotted unicorn; therefore, a pink polka-dotted unicorn must exist." Frankly, that is a terrible misunderstanding of Anselm's argument.

It is the particular nature of the thing being conceived that is important in the ontological argument. A pink polka-dotted unicorn is in no way "that than which nothing greater can be conceived," and thus there is nothing about its conception in the mind that entails that it should also exist in reality. The pink polka-dotted unicorn is not the greatest conceivable thing (it is not even the greatest conceivable unicorn!), so it does not have to exist in reality as well. The ontological argument only works, in Anselm's formulation, with the conception of God—because God is understood to be "that than which nothing greater can be conceived." There is only one thing that is (or even can be) that than which nothing greater can be conceived! Therefore, we should not *expect* the argument to work with anything else. So this objection simply misses the point.

I want to stress something here. It is not a bad thing to fail to understand the ontological argument. A *lot* of people do not understand it. I heard the ontological argument for the first time as a college freshman; it took me about fifteen years of hearing and reading about the argument before I started to understand it. As such, I have mixed feelings when I successfully teach an accurate understanding of the ontological argument to my students. On the one hand, I am pleased that I have helped them understand something that I struggled for years to comprehend. On the other hand, I wonder what is wrong with me that it took me so long to wrap my mind around it! At any rate, there is no shame in not understanding the ontological argument. But to fail to understand it and then to propagate a terrible misunderstanding of it is inexcusably childish. If you do not understand it, then just confess that the argument makes no sense to you and move on. There is no shame, no harm, in that.

A second criticism of Anselm's argument comes from a contemporary of his named Gaunilo, who asks, what about that island than which no greater can be conceived? If I can conceive of the greatest conceivable island, does that mean the island must also exist in reality? It is an interesting suggestion, to be sure! In response, Anselm notes, wisely, I think, that there is no consensus as to what a "greatest conceivable island" would be like. You might have a conception of what you think a greatest conceivable island would be, but there is nothing saying that others will share that conception. You might think that the island should be 75 degrees Fahrenheit, two square miles in size, with 150 palm trees. Someone else might think it should be considerably warmer and larger, with more variety (and number) of trees. Someone else might think it should be much cooler with fewer trees. What color should the sand be? Should there be rocky cliffs or not? Should the coastline be reef-protected lagoons or open to the ocean with wild crashing waves? You get the point. We do not have a shared conception of a greatest conceivable island.

What makes Anselm's argument work, in Anselm's mind, is that there is such a shared conception of a greatest conceivable being—"that than which nothing greater can be conceived." It is a being with maximal power, maximal knowledge, maximal goodness, maximal love—the traditional "omnis" of God (omnipotence, omniscience, omnipresence, omnibenevolence). These are the characteristics of that than which nothing greater can be conceived, and the Christian and the atheist alike share this picture of God. The atheist thinks that such a being does *not* exist, while the Christian contends that such a being does exist—but the conception of the being is shared. The same is *not* true with any other potential "greatest conceivable."

A third traditional objection to the ontological argument comes from the early modern philosopher Immanuel Kant in his *Critique of Pure Reason*. Kant says that Anselm's argument requires that existence function as a predicate; that is, that existence is like tallness or youngness, in that it adds something meaningful and descriptive to the entity under consideration. Kant thinks that this is mistaken—he believes existence is *not* a predicate. That is, Kant claims that to say that something "exists" does not add anything to the notion of the thing in the first place.

Here, though, it seems that Kant is misguided. Kant is saying, for example, "I can understand the concept of a unicorn. To say that a unicorn 'exists' does not add anything." I think, however, that anyone who reads fairy tales to their kids understands that this is false! I am fascinated by things like elves, hobbits, dwarves, Rivendell, rings of power, and anything else associated with Tolkien's Middle Earth! But I also understand that there is a difference between those things residing only in books/film and those things existing in reality. Think of watching Harry Potter movies with your kids; after episode 1, your daughter asks, "Do unicorns and wizards really exist?" Your response, according to Kant, should be, "Well, sweetheart, they're in the book, aren't they? If it's in the book, existing in reality doesn't add anything to it." That kind of misses the point. We understand intuitively that existence *is* a predicate, that to say something exists clearly adds something to the thing under consideration. Thus, it *is* the case, that it is greater for a good thing to exist in reality than for it to exist only in the understanding.

So as we set these three objections aside, it seems that Anselm's ontological argument works! If you begin with a shared conception of that than which nothing greater can be conceived, you arrive at the necessary existence of that being in reality as well.

### Plantinga's Ontological Argument

A twentieth-century version of the ontological argument that comes from American philosopher Alvin Plantinga. Plantinga's version depends on what we call possible worlds philosophy or (more formally) modal logic. A possible world is a technical term that points to a maximal state of affairs that describes reality. It is the way things could be or could have been. For example, there is a possible world in which I am not writing (or have not written) this book. There is a possible world in which my parents stop after three children, and thus I am never born. There is a possible world in which Germany won World War II. There are possible worlds where aliens exist (the Marvel Universe depends on that possibility!) and possible worlds where they do not. There is a possible world in which I have chicken for lunch, another possible world in which I have steak. These are all things that are logically possible, and all logically possible things can be conceived of as existing in some possible world. As such, the only things that do not exist in any possible world are logically impossible things—such as married bachelors or square circles.

So possible worlds are a way that reality *could* be. Only one possible world actually exists, and that is our actual (or real) world, the world or timeline that we live in. But we can all understand that things *could be* different than things *actually are*—that notion is the basis for superhero shows, time-travel movies, and body-swapping plots. So there are these possible worlds that are out there conceptually; our world (colloquially called the actual world) is one of these possible worlds.

With that philosophical understanding of possible worlds in our tool belt, let's turn to Plantinga's five-step ontological argument.

1. It is possible that a maximally great being exists.
2. If it is possible that a maximally great being exists, then a maximally great being exists in some possible world.
3. If a maximally great being exists in some possible world, then a maximally great being exists in every possible world.
4. If a maximally great being exists in every possible world, then the maximally great being exists in our actual world.
5. If a maximally great being exists in our actual world, then a maximally great being actually exists.[5]

***It is possible that a maximally great being exists.*** That is, it is possible that God exists. God's existence is not logically contradictory. There are, we should note, a few nontheistic philosophers who argue that the characteristics traditionally ascribed to God—omnipotence, omniscience, omnipresence, and omnibenevolence—somehow result in a logical contradiction. Most frequently, their suggestion is that the presence of evil in the world

---

[5] Again, there are numerous helpful articulations of Plantinga's modal ontological argument for God's existence. This version comes from Craig, *Reasonable Faith*, 184–85 (see chap. 4, n. 4).

shows that God cannot be both all-powerful and all-good. I will deal with that claim in Chapter 10. For now, we will set it aside and note that virtually all people agree that the idea of God is not a logical contradiction. Whether or not one believes that God actually *does* exist, God's existence seems to be logically possible. There is nothing incoherent about the notion of God's existence.

*If it is possible that a maximally great being exists, then a maximally great being exists in some possible world.* Remember that a possible world is just a maximal state of affairs, and all things that are logically possible will exist in at least some possible world. Anything that is not logically impossible can be conceived of as existing in some possible world.

*If a maximally great being exists in some possible world, then a maximally great being exists in every possible world.* But here's the thing—we understand God to be a maximally great being. If that being exists in some possible world, then it (he?) must exist in *every* possible world. Why? Well, if a maximally great being did not exist in all possible worlds, but only in one or some possible worlds, then it would not be a maximally great being after all.

Think of this. For a maximally great being to exist in one possible world but not in others, that would suggest that God, this maximally great being, depends on the circumstances, the context, of that possible world in which God exists. If these features were not realized, as they may not in other possible worlds, then God would not exist in other possible worlds. Thus God would be a dependent being, or a contingent being, dependent on the circumstances that exist in that possible world in which he conceivably exists.

But if this maximally great being is dependent on those conditions, then this is not a maximally great being after all. There would be a greater being—namely, a being that does not depend on any particular circumstances existing in some possible world, but rather who (which?) exists in all possible worlds. That kind of being would be greater. So if God is understood to be a maximally great being, then if God exists in some logically possible worlds, God must exist in all possible worlds; otherwise God would be contingent and not the maximally great being.

*If a maximally great being exists in every possible world, then a maximally great being exists in our actual world.* This is perhaps the most straightforward premise in Plantinga's argument. Recall that our actual world is just one of the logically possible worlds that exists, even if these other worlds exist only in our conception. If a maximally great being exists in all possible worlds, then by default, God exists in this actual world.

*If a maximally great being exists in our actual world, then a maximally great being (God) actually exists.* And, naturally, if a maximally great being exists in our actual world, then it is simply true to state that a maximally great being exists. That is, beginning with the logical possibility of God's existence, with God understood as a maximally great being, we arrive at the actuality of God's existence in our world.

Note, again, that this argument does not apply or work for *all* things. A leprechaun, for example, is a logically possible being. Thus, it is fair to say that it is possible that a leprechaun exists (premise 1). If it is possible that a leprechaun exists, then it follows that a leprechaun exists in some possible world (premise 2). But we cannot carry the argument forward. There is no reason to think that because a leprechaun exists in some possible world, it must therefore exist in every possible world (premise 3). There is nothing within the conception of a leprechaun to imply or require that it not be contingent or dependent on certain states of affairs.

Even if some enterprising Irishman wanted to insist that he conceives of leprechauns as being maximally great, such that their existence in some possible world would guarantee their existence in every possible world, the argument would still not work. Why not? Because that enterprising Irishman has a unique understanding of leprechauns that is not shared by anybody else. The argument cannot get off the ground without a mutual conception of the being in question.

What gives Plantinga's argument force is the first premise: the universal recognition that if God exists, God is a maximally great being. A maximally great being cannot be contingent or dependent on any other set of circumstances. If this is the case, then this maximally great being exists in all possible worlds (if it exists in any). The atheist's only way out, again, is to suggest that God's existence is impossible, because the very idea of God involves a logical contradiction.

So that gives us two versions of an ontological argument for the existence of God. The question now is this: is it a successful argument? The argument has a valid structure, such that the conclusion flows naturally from the premises—if the premises are true, then the conclusion is going to be true as well. Furthermore, it seems that the premises are in fact true. So the argument is sound; it "works," logically speaking.

But is the ontological argument going to persuade anybody? You tell me! If people are willing and able to evaluate the logical structure and content of the argument, then it may be persuasive. But it is not going to be rhetorically persuasive for most people. Let me, however, share stories about two atheistic philosophers and their encounters with the ontological argument.

First, I mention Bertrand Russell, the most prominent philosophical atheist in the English-speaking world in the first half of the twentieth century. The story is told that Russell, in his relative youth, came out of a store with a bag of groceries, only to come to a sudden stop on the sidewalk. He dropped his bag of groceries to the ground and exclaimed: "The ontological argument is sound!" Remember, for a philosopher to call an argument "sound" means that they recognize it has valid form and true premises, such that the conclusion of the argument is also true. Russell, in effect, was acknowledging that the ontological argument successfully proves the existence of God. Did Russell renounce his atheism? No. As the story goes, he went home, smoked a cigar, and got over it.[6] In other words, Russell briefly acknowledged God's existence but then swept that recognition under the rug. What I find fascinating, though, is the acceptance, short though it was, that the ontological argument works and shows God's existence.

Second, I note Colin McGinn, a late-twentieth-century Scottish-American philosopher. McGinn was interviewed by Jonathan Miller for a BBC program on atheism, faith, and reason. McGinn, as seen earlier, insists that there are no good arguments for the existence of God. After briefly describing the ontological argument to Miller, McGinn states that the argument is "totally unconvincing to everybody who hears it. . . . There is something gone wrong with that." Miller then asks McGinn to explain where the argument goes wrong. McGinn's response is fascinating: "Well the difficulty is nobody has ever managed to pinpoint exactly what's wrong with it."[7] Notice what happened here. He claimed, first, that there are no intellectual arguments for the existence of God, but then acknowledged that he has no way of refuting the ontological argument. Its conclusion is that God exists, so clearly the argument has to be

---

[6]  Russell's story is recounted by a fellow British atheist, Richard Dawkins, in *The God Delusion*, 81–82 (see chap. 4, n. 1).

[7]  Colin McGinn, "The Atheist Tapes," with Jonathan Miller. Episode 1, 2004. McGinn's interview can be seen in full at https://www.youtube.com/watch?v=-GUFt006eQE; the relevant exchange occurs at 12:30–14:45.

flawed, but he does not know what is wrong with it. (Incidentally, the purpose of arguments is to persuade someone of something they do not currently accept. If one's objection to the ontological argument is that they don't like the conclusion, then perhaps they ought to swallow their pride and accept the soundness of the argument!)

So here you have two philosophical atheists who recognize the strength of the ontological argument for the existence of God. Will it persuade most people? Probably not. But if someone is willing to trace through the logical structure of the argument and is able to process the possible-worlds concepts, then one can see that the argument is tremendously strong.

But if you struggle to follow the contours of the ontological argument, be encouraged! You are in good company. In the end, I think the ontological argument is the strongest by sheer force of logic, but it is probably the weakest persuasively or rhetorically.

## Moral Arguments

I gotta tell you, the longer you live, the more you look around, the more you realize . . . something is wrong here. War, disease, death, destruction, hunger, filth, poverty, torture, crime, corruption, and the Ice Capades. Something is definitely wrong.

Comedian George Carlin[8]

Human beings of all stripes seem to be inescapably interested in moral questions: Is there anything that is truly right and wrong in the world? Is there objective good and evil? If so, what is the standard

---

[8]   George Carlin, "You Are All Diseased: As Seen on HBO." Cited in James S. Spiegel, *The Making of an Atheist: How Immorality Leads to Unbelief* (Chicago: Moody, 2010), 62.

or foundation of morality? How should I live? How should other people live? These major questions (and others like them) occupy the realm of ethics.

Traditionally, there has been a close relationship between ethics and religion; a majority of humans have derived their answers to ethical questions from their respective religious worldview. The relationship is so close that some suggest that the existence of morality points toward the existence of a transcendent, personal, benevolent deity. In the remainder of this chapter, I propose a simple three-step argument for the existence of God—the argument based on morality.

1. If God does not exist, then objective moral values and duties do not exist.
2. Objective moral values and duties do exist; that is, it is false that objective moral values and duties do not exist.
3. Therefore, God exists; that is, it is false that God does not exist.

The structure of the moral argument is a straightforward *modus tollens* form, where the falsity of the consequent (the *then* in an if-then argument) logically requires the falsity of the antecedent (the *if*) as well. For example, consider: if it is raining outside, then the ground will be wet. That statement seems to be clearly true. What if we then note that the ground is not wet? That addition easily establishes that it is not raining outside.[9]

Modus tollens arguments like the moral argument for God are accepted by all to be valid in structure, meaning that if the premises (statements 1 and 2) are true, then the conclusion (statement 3) must

---

[9]    More formally, the second statement should be "It is not the case that the ground is wet," and the conclusion would be "It is not the case that it is raining outside."

also be true. Like all arguments, then, the interesting conversation revolves around the two premises. In the moral argument, two key claims are being made: there is such a thing as objective morality (premise 2); and objective morality can be sufficiently explained only by (grounded in) the existence of God (premise 1).

### Objective Moral Values and Duties Do Exist

The first crucial contention is that there is such a thing as objective morality—moral values and duties that are binding upon all people in all places at all times, whether people recognize it or not. Until the twentieth century, a belief in moral objectivism was virtually universal. There were occasional moral skeptics, such as Protagoras ("Man is the measure of all things"), but nearly all Westerners accepted the existence of objective moral values and duties. The rise of postmodern philosophy, combined with the decline of Christian belief, led to the rapid rise of moral relativism.

Today, therefore, the existence of a moral law is not universally embraced in contemporary society; indeed, you might not believe that there is such a thing as an objective or universal moral code! Surveys fairly consistently show that a majority of Westerners reject the existence of objective morality in favor of some flavor of moral relativism (roughly: moral standards of right and wrong are dependent on individual or cultural standards, such that there is nothing that is morally right or wrong for all people in all places at all times).

A 2001 (post-9/11) Barna survey found that 64 percent of American adults claim that "moral truth is always relative to the person and their situation," with only 22 percent professing belief in moral absolutes.[10] A similar 2016 Barna survey found that 44

---

[10] Barna Research, Culture and Media, "Americans Are Most Likely to Base Truth on Feelings," February 12, 2002, https://www.barna.com/research/americans-are-most-likely-to-base-truth-on-feelings/.

percent of American adults believe that moral truth is "relative to circumstances," while 21 percent profess to "have not given it [moral truth] much thought"; 35 percent, meanwhile, affirmed objective morality.[11]

Moral relativism is widespread in contemporary society. The moral relativist believes that there are no objective moral values and duties, but rather that right and wrong are different for different people. Moral relativism comes in two flavors, cultural or individual.

Cultural relativism holds that standards of right and wrong, good and evil, are determined by one's culture or society; different cultures have different contexts and histories and thus arrive at different understandings of what is morally acceptable and unacceptable. What's more, the cultural relativist holds that there is no objective standard to which those different moral standards can be compared; right and wrong can be different for different cultures or different times.

Individual relativism, or subjectivism, holds that standards of right and wrong, good and evil, are set by the individual human being. Different people see the world differently and choose to act in different fashions. What is "right for me" might be "wrong to you" and vice versa. Moreover, there is, again, no objective standard to which those different personal moral codes can be compared; right and wrong can be different for different people.

Both individual and cultural relativism are plagued by numerous flaws that render the positions highly implausible. Here are a handful of such problems with relativism.

First, if cultural relativism is correct, then it is impossible to criticize the moral standards of another culture or to hold one culture

---

[11] Barna Research, Culture and Media, "The End of Absolutes: America's New Moral Code," May 25, 2016, https://www.barna.com/research/the-end-of-absolutes-americas-new-moral-code/.

to be morally superior to another. As C. S. Lewis noted, "If no set of moral ideas were truer or better than any other, there would be no sense in preferring civilised morality to savage morality, or Christian morality to Nazi morality. In fact, of course, we all do believe that some moralities are better than others."[12]

Given cultural relativism, we cannot criticize the beliefs or actions of the Taliban, al-Qaeda, the Nazis, or contemporary white supremacists. Their beliefs and practices are not objectively morally wrong; they are merely different from ours. Because moral relativism denies the existence of an objective standard to which we can compare different moral systems, it provides no way to establish that one culture is "morally better" than another. We cannot decry the practice of suttee (widow burning) in Hindu India or temple prostitution or female genital mutilation or selling children as brides to older men. Such practices cannot be morally wrong; they are just different. And if that culture is acting in accordance with its understanding of moral right and wrong, then its practices are perfectly justifiable, even if we happen not to like them.

But we do not *act* as if other cultures are merely different from our own; instead, we criticize and even condemn some beliefs and practices, demonstrating that, despite our professions, we *do* think that some moral values and duties apply to all people in all places at all times.

Second, if individual relativism is correct, then it is similarly impossible to criticize the moral standards of other people or to hold some individuals to be moral examples or moral heroes. One may believe in treating people with compassion and gentleness, while another may believe in raping and pillaging. Who is to say that one of them is morally wrong? Given relativism, I can recognize that other

12  C. S. Lewis, *Mere Christianity* (1952; repr., San Francisco: HarperSanFrancisco, 2001), 13.

individuals in our society have different moral standards than I do, but I cannot insist that my standards are right and theirs are wrong; there is no objective wrong, there is only different. Again, note that this is *not* the way that people actually behave (and believe). We do in fact vigorously point out moral wrongdoing in other people. Note Lewis: "Whenever you find a man who says he does not believe in a real Right and Wrong, you will find the same man going back on this a moment later. He may break his promise to you, but if you try breaking one to him he will be complaining 'It's not fair' before you can say Jack Robinson."[13]

Third, if moral relativism is correct, then we face the "reformer's dilemma." Given relativism, there is no such thing as moral progress for either cultures or individuals. If there is no objective standard of right and wrong that applies to all people in all places at all times, there can be only moral *change*, not moral progress (or regress). So when the United Kingdom abolished slavery throughout the British Empire in 1833, it was not a mark of moral improvement in the country. Similarly the legalization of gay marriage in the United States in 2015, the outlawing of foot binding in China in 1912, the desegregation of schools in the American South in 1954 (and following), granting women the right to vote in democratic elections—all of these cultural moves were merely moral changes.

In the same way, in this scenario, if individuals change their minds on some moral question, it can never be said that they have come to embrace a morally superior position or have come to a knowledge of moral truth. When a former slave-ship captain such as John Newton abandons his slaving practices and begins fighting for the abolition of the slave trade, he has not made any moral improvement in his life; he has merely changed his mind.

---

[13]   Lewis, 6.

But does this logic reflect what we actually think about moral changes? Don't you think it is possible to make moral progress (or regress) as an individual and as a culture? Don't you think it really is better to abolish slavery than to legalize slavery? Don't you think individuals have improved their moral condition if they come to recognize that all human beings are created equal in dignity and worth?

There are other significant shortcomings of moral relativism, but this should suffice for our purposes. It seems that although many people might *profess* to be moral relativists, the way the vast majority of us think and act about ethics demonstrates that we believe in the existence of an objective standard. Why, then, do so many people claim to be moral relativists? I see two most likely explanations.

1. They don't think about morality very often or deeply.
2. They recognize that different people (and cultures) have wildly different moral beliefs and practices.

Recall the second Barna survey I mentioned from 2016. In that survey, 44 percent of Americans professed moral relativism, while 21 percent admitted to "have not given [moral truth] much thought." Moral relativism is an easy position to embrace if you have not given moral questions much thought. It sounds tolerant, sensitive, and even culturally cool. As soon as you rationally begin to examine the position, however, moral relativism crumbles quite quickly. I suspect that the vast majority of professing moral relativists, if they took the time to critically assess their own beliefs, would abandon relativism and acknowledge that they believe objective moral values and duties do exist.

The more compelling reason to accept moral relativism is the recognition of moral diversity in the world. Diversity of belief, however, is no indication that there is no objective truth with respect to the question at hand. For example, there might be a variety of scientific beliefs about what caused the origin of our universe. Does that mean that there is no objectively true answer? Clearly not! So why would we assume any differently in the moral sphere? It seems wiser to acknowledge that people (and cultures) can be quite mistaken in their moral beliefs, just like we can be mistaken in our scientific or historical beliefs.

Two additional notes. First, although it is true that cultures have different moral beliefs and practices, it seems these differences are often overly exaggerated; there are more similarities than there are differences. Indeed, many of the differences are related to the application of objective moral principles. For example, cultures may differ in how one practically ought to treat elderly parents in the community, but all cultures apparently value respecting one's elders. Second, some differences in moral practice do not stem from different moral values and duties, but rather from different factual beliefs. For example, virtually all cultures seem to share an aversion to eating the remains of deceased relatives. The Hindu prohibition against eating beef stems from their conviction that a deceased relative could have been reincarnated in a cow. You may find that belief quite mistaken, but the resulting difference in moral practice is not the result of a moral disagreement; it is a disagreement about matters of fact.

The bottom line is that our actual practice and beliefs show that we believe very deeply in the existence of objective moral values and duties. Think of it: if there are no objective moral values and duties, that means there are no moral requirements for human beings; there is no set of actions that are mandatory, no set of acts that are forbidden. If there are no objective moral values and duties, then it is meaningless to say that Ted Bundy *ought not to have* raped and murdered scores of college girls. If there are no objective moral values and duties, it is meaningless to say that ISIS fighters act wickedly when they cut off the heads of Christian civilians in Syria. We could very meaningfully say, "I really hate that rapists rape," or, "I really wish that ISIS would quit killing people." But we all mean much more than that. We believe that some actions are objectively wrong and others are objectively right, regardless of what some people believe and practice.

In conclusion, nearly everybody accepts the existence of objective moral values and duties. Do you? If so, then you accept the first key claim of the moral argument for God: objective moral values and duties do exist.

## *If God Does Not Exist, Then Objective Moral Values and Duties Do Not Exist*

The second claim in the moral argument is that objective moral values and duties require the existence of a transcendent, personal, good Creator—that is, God. My argument is if there is no God, there can be no objective standard for moral values and duties.

The fundamental insight behind this premise is that the existence of objective moral values and duties that are binding upon all people in all places at all times is dependent on a transcendent source for those moral truths. The best candidate for such moral truths is a transcendent, personal, good divine being—God. If no such being exists, then there can be no such thing as objective moral values and duties. If God does not exist, objective moral values and duties do not exist either.

Many thoughtful atheists have admitted that this is the case. William Provine, the late professor of the history of biology at Cornell University, claimed that the implications of atheistic evolution are stark but clear: "There are no gods, no purposive forces of any kind. There is no life after death. . . . There is no ultimate foundation for ethics, no ultimate meaning in life, and no free will for humans, either."[14]

Similarly, Richard Dawkins writes, in *A River Out of Eden*,

In a universe of blind physical forces and genetic repli-
cation, some people are going to get hurt, other people
are going to get lucky, and you won't find any rhyme
or reason in it, nor any justice . . . there is, at bottom,
no design, no purpose, no evil and no good, nothing but
blind, pitiless indifference.[15]

Lest you accuse me of cherry-picking atheists who are lousy philosophers (or not philosophers at all), here is Bertrand Russell from his 1903 essay "A Free Man's Worship": "Brief and power-less is Man's life; on him and all his race the slow, sure doom falls pitiless and dark. Blind to good and evil, reckless of destruction, omnipotent matter rolls on its relentless way."

C. S. Lewis noted that these considerations were partially responsible for his rejecting the atheism that he had embraced as an Oxford professor:

My argument against God was that the universe seemed
so cruel and unjust. But how had I got this idea of *just* and
*unjust*? A man does not call a line crooked unless he has
some idea of a straight line. What was I comparing this
universe with when I called it unjust? If the whole show

---

[14]   William Provine, "Opening Speech," in "Darwinism: Science or Naturalistic Philosophy?" A Debate between William B. Provine and Phillip E. Johnson, Stan-ford University, April 30, 1994. Video of the debate can be accessed at https://www.youtube.com/watch?v=m7dG9U1vQ_U; this line comes from the tail end of his open-ing speech, 41:15–41:50.

[15]   Richard Dawkins, *River Out of Eden* (New York: Basic Books, 1996), 133.

was bad and senseless from A to Z, so to speak, why did
I, who was supposed to be part of the show, find myself
in such violent reaction against it? . . . Of course I could
have given up my idea of justice by saying it was nothing
but a private idea of my own. But if I did that, then my
argument against God collapsed too—for the argument
depended on saying that the world was really unjust, not
simply that it did not happen to please my fancies. Thus,
in the very act of trying to prove that God did not exist—
in other words, that the whole of reality was senseless—I
found I was forced to assume that one part of reality—
namely my idea of justice—was full of sense.[16]

Thus, for atheists like Provine, Dawkins, Russell, and (for-
merly) Lewis, an acknowledgment of objective moral values and
duties would subsequently lead to an acceptance of the existence
of God. Given that objective morality cannot exist without God, if
there is such a thing as objective morality, then God must exist.

But not all atheists agree that God is required to sustain the
existence of objective moral values and duties. Indeed, there is a
veritable cottage industry of philosophers seeking alternative foundations for objective moral truth. Let us briefly examine two of the
most popular and prominent theories: social contract theory and
evolutionary ethics.

*Social contract theory.* Some suggest that morality is a social
construct, particular to individual human societies. Moral standards
are established to enable survival and promote human flourishing.
Individuals freely choose to enter into a contract with one another in
a society, thereby accepting certain standards of belief and behavior.

---

[16] Lewis, *Mere Christianity*, 38–39.

The social contract is then objectively binding upon all members of that society, providing a standard for moral values and duties that transcends the individual. Under this model, ethical standards can change over time and between cultures. The social contract in my society right now will be different from the social contract in seventeenth-century Germany, and that's okay. There is nothing fixed, universal, or absolute in human morality. Thus if you do not like the morality of your social contract, you should move to a different one or fight to have your own social contract changed, as did Jack Kevorkian, Martin Luther King, and William Wilberforce. Why do I find it fascinating that some philosophers (my favorite example is the Frenchman Jean-Jacques Rousseau) hold social contract theory to be a sufficient ground for objective morality? Because at the root, social contract ethics is not an explanation of universal objective moral values and duties, but rather a denial of them! Let me explain.

First, social contract theory denies the universality of ethics. Social contract ethics are, by definition, not universal, but local. So although social contract ethicists promote their theory as an explanation for the universality of human ethics, it simply is not and cannot be so. Moral standards that are binding in one social contract do not apply to all people in all places at all times; they merely apply to these people in this place at this time. Hence, such moral standards are not objective, but relative to culture; that is, social contract ethics is merely an example of cultural relativism!

Second, social contract theory denies the objectivity of ethics. Different social contracts are not by definition good or bad; they are merely different. More frightening, that means that Hitler's genocidal ethic was not wrong; it was an acceptable German social contract. Further, it was wrong for the Allies to prosecute war criminals at the Nuremburg trials; after all, those men and women were doing what was considered right and good within their social contract.

Again, this is a denial of universal human sensibility, which holds that some things, even if acceptable under a particular social contract, are objectively immoral (wrong).

Social contract theory simply cannot account for the existence of a universal, objective moral standard. It is not embraced as a wide-ranging human ethical system, except at the popular level where it has not been thoroughly thought through. Ironically, years ago when I taught that theory at a local university, two Christians rose up to defend social contract theory as an adequate foundation for objective moral values and duties, only to be immediately corrected by a non-Christian in the group, who pointed out the inherent relativism of social contract ethics! One need not embrace the existence of God in order to recognize that social contract theory is unable to ground an objective morality.

*Evolutionary ethics.* Can evolutionary ethics fare any better than social contract theory? According to evolutionary ethics (also called sociobiology or evolutionary psychology), morality develops as animals gain cognitive and relational capacities. Robert Trivers developed the notion of "reciprocal altruism" in the 1970s to explain why selfish creatures driven by evolutionary impulses would cooperate with other creatures, even when doing so seemed to jeopardize their immediate self-interest.[17] The idea, ably articulated by E. O. Wilson, Richard Dawkins, and others, identifies the long-term communal interests of species like human beings to work together, to trust one another, and to put others ahead of oneself at times. For example, it is better as a whole for people to risk their lives running into burning buildings to save others. After all, down the road it might be oneself *inside* the burning building needing someone else to risk their life running in to save you. Similarly, it makes sense

---

[17]    See Robert Trivers, *Natural Selection and Social Theory: Selected Papers of Robert Trivers* (Oxford: Oxford University Press, 2002), 3–55.

to care for helpless babies and aging parents. Why? Because down the road, we will likely need our own children to care for us. If our children have seen us care for our elderly parents, they will be more likely to take care of us too.

As these types of reciprocal altruistic insights accumulate, human societies codify these relationships into moral codes: "Thou shalt honor thy father and mother." It then goes better for society if these moral codes are enforced by some type of implicit or explicit moral police—some even attribute the rise of religion to the need for moral enforcement. Our moral values and duties, then, have evolved over time. But once in place, evolved ethical values and duties are objectively binding upon members of that species or community.

Unfortunately, evolutionary ethics suffers from several significant problems. Here are three of the most glaring.

First, at best, evolutionary ethics would seem to be *descriptive*, not *prescriptive*. That is, the theory could adequately explain how human beings experience morality, but it seems incapable of establishing a binding moral code. At worst, evolutionary ethics presents moral values and duties as illusions imposed on us by a blind, purposeless process of random mutation and natural selection.

Second, evolutionary ethics is similarly unable to move beyond *is* to *ought*. At best, evolutionary ethicists can *exhort* us to cooperate on the basis that this will achieve our own long-term benefit and *warn* us that failing to cooperate *may* cost us in the long run. But sociobiology cannot tell us how we *ought* to act. Indeed, the enlightened elite in evolutionary ethics are best advised to keep the masses uninformed and adhering to some type of moral standard that ensures the preservation of the species, while they live in accordance with selfish interests and desires. Evolutionary ethics demonstrates the utilitarian value of acting cooperatively in the interests of all members of society. But it fails to provide an evolutionary basis for abandoning one's own selfish interests, particularly if one can do so without affecting the overall moral actions of the rest of society.

Third, and most problematically, evolution is incapable in principle of arriving at a truly objective standard for moral values and duties. Why? Because the one constant in evolution is change. Evolution is an unceasing process of random mutation and natural selection, wherein organisms and populations are undergoing constant change. If evolution is the source of social moral values and duties, then those social moral values and duties are likewise subject to constant change. But objective moral values and duties are, again, binding for all people in all places at all times.

All attempts to ground objective morality without God suffer from the same fatal flaw. They fail to account for the real nature of the moral law. All naturalistic theories fail to explain the existence of an objective, external standard of right and wrong. If morality is an evolutionary product, then morality itself is subject to evolution. What is right today may be wrong tomorrow. What is wrong today may be right tomorrow. What is right for me may be wrong for someone else who is either more highly evolved or closer to being an amoeba. Ethical standards are, ultimately, relative. There is no standard by which we may judge thoughts and actions.

Therefore, if there is no God (transcendent, personal, good being), then there are no objective moral values and duties. It is exceedingly difficult (if not impossible) to ground objective morality within the natural world.

***God and objective moral values and duties.*** Indeed, an objective moral standard by definition must exist externally to us. As such, it requires an external source—a moral source that is beyond (transcendent to) our human existence. In other words, an objective moral standard requires something very much like our Christian understanding of God. There is no good without God.

Please note: I am *not* claiming that one must believe in God in order to be a good person or to act in accordance with the moral good. I think belief in God is pretty much irrelevant to moral belief and behavior. My eldest sister (by her own profession) does not believe in God, but from my perspective she is an upstanding moral citizen. My argument is not that you must believe in God in order to act morally. My argument, instead, is that if there is no God, then there is no such thing as objective good and evil. Therefore, if God does not exist, then neither my sister nor I am an objectively good (or bad) person, because there is no objective standard by which you can judge our moral beliefs and behavior.

For something to be "good" requires the existence of a standard of "goodness." That standard cannot be provided by nature, natural selection, evolution, or the cosmos, even when those terms are capitalized. Christian theism, unlike social contract theory and evolutionary ethics, is able to account for our moral intuitions and beliefs.

God serves as the standard for objective moral values and duties, and he reveals that standard both in created human conscience and self-revelation in the Bible. According to traditional Christian theology, God is transcendent, personal, and good (omnibenevolent). Being transcendent to the physical universe and human beings, God is capable of serving as an objective standard. Being a (tri-)personal deity, God is capable of possessing moral qualities and agency. Being good, God is a trustworthy moral compass, capable of establishing an objective moral standard that we ought to embrace and follow.

### Therefore, God Exists

We have seen that both of the primary contentions of the moral argument for God are true. There is good reason to reject moral relativism and instead accept that there are objective moral values and duties. There is good reason to reject ethical theories such as social contract theory and evolutionary ethics and instead accept that objective moral values and duties can be sufficiently explained only by and grounded in the existence of a transcendent, personal, good being. Therefore, there is good reason to think that God—a transcendent, personal, good being—actually exists.

## Conclusion

We began this chapter with Colin McGinn's claim that there are no intellectual arguments for the existence of God. I trust that you can see that McGinn is demonstrably mistaken in a way that should be somewhat embarrassing. We have looked briefly at two rational arguments for the existence of God—ontological and moral. It may be that you do not find either type of argument airtight. Take heart. I do not find them airtight either. But then again, I do not find any argument—in philosophy, history, or science—to be absolutely airtight! The important question is whether the premises of the argument are highly likely to be true and more likely to be true than false. If this is the case, then you ought to consider the significance of the conclusion!

You might also note that ontological and moral arguments for God's existence do not lead necessarily to the God of Christianity; again, you would be right! But these arguments are not intended to arrive at the God of Christianity. Rather, the goal at this point is more modestly to arrive at (1) the existence of a maximally great being, possessing all power, knowledge, goodness, and presence; and (2) the existence of a transcendent, personal, good being. If we can arrive successfully at the existence of such a being, we will have made great progress, and we can move on (in chaps. 7–9) to look at reasons to believe Christianity specifically is the most reasonable form of theism to embrace.

## Recommended Resources for Further Exploration

Craig, William Lane. *Reasonable Faith*. 3rd ed. Wheaton, IL: Crossway, 2008.

Groothuis, Douglas. *Christian Apologetics: A Comprehensive Case for Biblical Faith*. Downers Grove, IL: IVP Academic, 2011.

Lewis, C. S. *Mere Christianity*. 1952. Reprint, San Francisco: HarperSanFrancisco, 2001.

# CHAPTER 6

## *Humanity*

### Anthropological Clues for God's Existence

*I . . . had an experience. I can't prove it, I can't even
explain it, but everything that I know as a human
being, everything that I am tells me that it was real.
I was given something wonderful, something that
changed me forever. A vision of the universe, that
tells us undeniably, how tiny, and insignificant and
how . . . rare, and precious we all are! A vision that
tells us that we belong to something that is greater than
ourselves, that we are NOT, that none of us are alone.*

Ellie Arroway[1]

I n chapters 4 and 5, we looked in some depth at four different
types of arguments for the existence of God, four separate clues
that point toward a theistic universe. In Chapter 4, we focused

---

[1]  Ellia Arroway, played by Jodie Foster, in the 1997 Sci-Fi blockbuster "Contact," directed by Robert Zemeckis, screenplay by James V. Hart and Michael Goldenberg. Arroway is transported to an alien planet (dimensionally, not physically), and reports her personal encounter with alien life forms to a skeptical Senate committee. She is heartbroken and despondent when most refuse to take her personal testimony at face value.

on contemporary scientific evidence and arguments through cosmological and design arguments. In Chapter 5, we focused on reason and logic through ontological and moral arguments. Now we will turn our attention inward and consider four clues from human nature and experience that point toward God: religious experience, transcendent desire, free will, and reason.

The late philosopher Ronald Nash introduced me to the distinction between the Outer World and the Inner World. The Outer World is the realm of sensory experience and physical reality—the things we see, touch, hear, smell, and taste. The Inner World is the realm of personal experience and psychological reality—the things we feel, think, reflect upon, and intend. The evidence and arguments we looked at in Chapter 4 (cosmology, design) are examples of the Outer World. Arguably, the ontological and moral arguments in Chapter 5 are representative of the Inner World.

But in this chapter, we consider more explicitly the Inner World and ask the question, what do human experiences, desires, and capacities tell us about the nature of reality? It is my contention that when we evaluate the full range of the Inner World, we see clues that point us in the same direction as the arguments from the past two chapters—toward acknowledging the existence of a transcendent, personal Creator of the universe. In my estimation, each argument in this chapter is more suggestive than conclusive. But put together, they inform our understanding of life, the universe, and everything.

## Religious Experience

O my God, what must a soul be like when it is in this state! It longs to be all one tongue with which to praise the Lord. It utters a thousand pious follies, in a continuous endeavor to please him who thus possesses it.

Teresa of Avila

While he [a fellow worshiper] was describing the change which God works in the heart through faith in Christ, I felt my heart strangely warmed. I felt I did trust in Christ, Christ alone, for salvation; and an assurance was given me that he had taken away my sins, even mine, and saved me from the law of sin and death.

John Wesley, *Journal,* vol. 6

A quick glimpse at human history shows us that the vast majority of people in all civilizations have been highly religious. Even today, despite the advance of secularism in Western nations, religious belief and practice are the standard in human societies.

It is not just religious belief and practice that are common in human history, however. In addition, religious believers in diverse times and places have claimed personal encounters with divine reality; that is, they say they have experienced the presence and power of God personally in their lives. Sometimes the religious experience includes audible or tactile elements; other times the religious experience is primarily inward. Either way, there have almost certainly been billions of religious people over the centuries who have had profound religious experiences in which they have encountered or experienced divine reality. For example, a 2009 Pew Forum survey found that nearly half (49 percent) of American adults claim to have had a "religious or mystical experience."[2] What, if anything, can this

---

[2] See Pew Research Center, "Many Americans Mix Multiple Faiths," December 9, 2009, https://www.pewforum.org/2009/12/09/many-americans-mix-multiple-faiths/.

prevalence of religious experience tell us? I suggest the following six-step argument.

1. If some person $S$ seems to experience some entity/thing/ event $E$, then (all other things being equal) $S$ should believe that $E$ probably exists/occurred (principle of credulity).
2. If some person $S$ testifies to some experience/event $E$, then we (other people) should accept, prima facie, the truthfulness of $S$'s claim (principle of testimony).
3. Millions (perhaps billions) of people profess to have had a personal experience of encountering divine reality in their lives.
4. (From premise 1) Therefore, these millions (or billions) of people are justified in believing that divine reality exists.
5. (From premise 2) Therefore, we (other people) should accept, prima facie, the existence of the divine reality experienced by millions (or billions) of people.
6. Therefore, it is likely that a divine reality exists.

There are three primary claims being made in the first three premises, which then lead to three conclusions.

First, the principle of credulity claims that we should generally take our personal experiences to be trustworthy and reliable. For example, back in Chapter 4, I imagined having tea with the queen of England. I noted there that, if I hoped to convince my skeptical friend that I dined with the queen, then it would be helpful to be able to provide additional empirical evidence (photographs, videos) of the event.

But let's say I didn't have those pieces of evidence. All I had, instead, was my own recollection. My skeptical friend might not believe me (we'll come back to him in a moment), but how about me? Should I believe that the event occurred? Should I believe that the queen of England exists and that we had tea together? The principle of credulity says yes, indeed, I should take my personal experience seriously and consider it to be a trustworthy source of knowledge about what happened and/or exists.

The words "all other things being equal" are, however, important. If someone is able to present counterevidence, suggesting that it is impossible that I had tea with the queen, then I ought to take that into consideration and perhaps even allow it to overturn my acceptance of my personal experience and memory. For example, if I claim to have had tea with the queen on April 2, but my friend provides documentary evidence that (1) I was in Biloxi, Mississippi, on April 2 and (2) Queen Elizabeth was in Brussels, Belgium, on April 2, then probably I need to reconsider my claim! Without such counterevidence, however, it is appropriate, even necessary, to take our experiences and memories to be trustworthy. (Imagine if you were skeptical of everything that you think you remember and everything that you think you experience! Would you ever kiss your spouse again?)

Second, the principle of testimony claims that we should, prima facie, generally take other people's testimonies to be true. The Latin phrase *prima facie* means "before considering the [or other] facts," with the idea of "all other things being equal." So unless we have good reason not to, we should accept the truthfulness of other people's testimonial claims. For example, if my wife comes home from Aldi and claims to have seen our neighbor at the store, I should take her word for it.[3]

---

[3] But what if it is not my wife but some random stranger? Does the principle of testimony still apply? That is a tougher question. Without delving into the complex of arguments lurking in the background, it seems that we can safely say three things.

Again, there may be other facts to consider that lead me to be skeptical of someone's testimonial claims. If I was having coffee with my neighbor during the time my wife says she saw him at the store, then I have good reason to overrule my prima facie trust and reject her story. There may also be person-specific considerations. If the testifier is a known prankster (or just plain dishonest), then that might provide sufficient reason to reject that person's testimonial claims. But, barring such reasons (what Alvin Plantinga calls "defeaters"), we should generally take people's claims at face value and accept their truthfulness.

A skeptic might argue that the principle of testimony is going to lead us to accept false claims that other people make. That certainly is a danger and is a good reason to consider other facts and considerations rather than blindly accepting everything that everybody ever says. But even if we recognize the realistic danger of potentially accepting false claims, the opposite danger is far worse. How have you learned virtually everything you know? Have you not learned it from other people and the testimonies they have brought, whether in the home or in the classroom? Did you doubt everything your

---

First, if the stranger is testifying to something that is not out of the ordinary (beyond our everyday expectation and/or experience), then, yes, we ought to at least tentatively accept the stranger's testimony as being true.

Second, if the stranger is testifying to something that is out of the ordinary, then perhaps we ought to withhold judgment, or even question the truthfulness of the testimony.

Third, if the stranger is testifying to something that is out of the ordinary, and we accordingly suspend judgment, only to find that there are numerous other people (many strangers, some acquaintances) who put forth a similar story, then perhaps we ought to reconsider our withholding of judgment and accept the testimony (at least tentatively) as being true.

Again, however, there is much more to be said. For a brief discussion of some of the issues, see Robert Audi, *Epistemology: A Contemporary Introduction to the Theory of Knowledge*, 3rd ed. (New York: Routledge, 2011), 150–70.

parents or teachers told or taught you? If so, would you ever have learned anything? It seems that the principle of testimony is necessary to learn anything. Furthermore, it reflects the way we act on an everyday basis. The claim seems reasonable.

Third, millions (perhaps billions) of people profess to have had a personal experience with God (or a divine being of some sort). These religious experiences span the spectrum of human religions—Christian, Jew, Muslim, Hindu, Buddhist, New Age, etc. In the panoply of voices who have had religious experiences, my voice is only one. But I have had a handful of transformative personal encounters with what I believe to be the very presence of God.

My most vivid religious experience occurred during my fourth year of college, in the midst of intense uncertainty regarding future plans. During a worship service one October morning in 1996, I felt the (to me) undeniable physical presence of God permeate my body, and I audibly heard the words, "I want you to be a pastor." The occasion was as shocking and unexpected as it was clear and undeniable. I had never entertained any notion of serving in a church (I honestly thought that pastors were born, not made), and I had never experienced God's presence in such a direct physical way. But it was as clear and distinct an experience as I have ever had; the voice was audibly perceptible (to myself, though not to others around me), and I could not deny the meaningful content of the words I heard.

Experiences like mine have been shared by millions of Christians, and similar experiences are reported by followers of other religious traditions as well. So it seems pretty clear that this third premise (millions of people profess to have had a personal experience of encountering divine reality in their lives) is true.

What can or should we conclude based on the principles of credulity and testimony, combined with the widespread nature of personal religious experiences?

Fourth, as a preliminary conclusion, we should note that the millions (or billions) of people who have personally experienced divine reality in their lives are justified in concluding that such a divine reality exists. Thus, for example, it is reasonable for me to believe that God exists, based on (among other things) my vivid personal encounter with God. But how about other people? If someone is currently skeptical that God (or some sort of divine reality) exists, should other people's religious experiences persuade them otherwise? I contend that they should.

Fifth, as a secondary and more significant conclusion, we (other people) should accept, prima facie, the existence of the divine reality experienced by millions (or billions) of people. Someone who does not believe in God should take the combined weight of religious experience testimony seriously and consider the possibility that God exists.

This might sound like a bold and unsustainable claim. But consider the lesson we can learn from the 1997 blockbuster movie *Contact*, starring Jodie Foster, and based on the novel by atheistic cosmologist Carl Sagan. In the movie, Foster plays Ellie Arroway, a scientist pursuing proof that extraterrestrial life exists. Arroway and others receive a radio message that is interpreted as evidence that aliens exist. They then decode plans to build a ship, hoping to establish contact with the alien species.

Arroway enters the ship and has a vivid and undeniable (to her) experience of communicating with aliens from Vega (the original vegans!). Unfortunately the recording equipment fails to bear out the truthfulness of her encounter, and all that is left is her passionate, stirring, and absolutely certain first-person testimony of her alien experience. In the movie, Sagan clearly wants the reader to conclude that the first-person claim of an encounter like Arroway's ought to be sufficient to persuade the open-minded hearer; likewise in the movie, it is only narrow-minded bigots who reject Arroway's testimony.

But note that Arroway is only *one* individual claiming to have had *one* encounter with an alien species. If it is reasonable for Sagan to expect others to be persuaded by Arroway's singular encounter, how much more reasonable is it for religious people like myself to expect Sagan and other skeptics to be persuaded by the combined weight of millions of divine encounters?

But, skeptics might protest, there are independent grounds on which they believe that aliens exist. Granted. By the same measure, I have shared several other independent grounds on which it is reasonable to believe that God exists.

In short, I propose that the experiences of millions (perhaps billions) of people throughout history, wherein they encounter what to them is the undeniable presence of God, should carry significant weight and provide good reason to believe that there is a transcendent, personal divine being. That is, the widespread nature of religious experience is a clue that a divine reality (God) exists.

## Religious Desire

In addition to religious experience, I think that widespread religious desire also serves as a clue pointing to God's existence.

In their time, Blaise Pascal, in his *Pensées*, and C. S. Lewis, particularly in *Surprised by Joy*, popularized arguments from religious desire or yearning. One of Lewis's insights is that (human) creatures are not born with desires unless something exists in reality that is capable of satisfying those desires. "A baby feels hunger: well, there is such a thing as food. A duckling wants to swim: well, there is such a thing as water. Men feel sexual desire: well, there is such a thing as sex."[4]

From Lewis's insight, we can build the following inductive argument:

1. If human beings have a natural desire or yearning for something, then there exists something in the real world that can satisfy that desire.
2. Many (nearly all?) human beings have transcendent desires (a) to know and touch divine reality, and (b) to live on past physical death.
3. Therefore, it is probable that there exists (a) a divine reality to know and touch, and (b) life after death.

First, there are universal human desires—desires that we (virtually) all have that do not have to be taught, but rather seem to be natural. Some are easy to identify: food, drink, and sex. Others are a bit more difficult, but, once identified, they seem clear: community, meaning, and love. With each of these natural universal human desires, we can see that there is something that truly exists and is capable of satisfying the desire.

Second, most human beings evidence religious or transcendent desires—desires to know and touch divine reality (to experience God) and to live on past physical death. Lewis's original claim was more modest; he simply noted that *he* had desires for transcendence, and he drew conclusions on that basis. But I think the bolder claim can be sustained—it isn't just that *I* have these transcendent religious desires, but that *most of us* have these desires! For example, Barna Research reveals that "half of all atheists and agnostics say . . . that

---

4    Lewis, *Mere Christianity*, 136 (see chap. 5, n. 12).

there is life after death," with the majority of those professing that they expect (and hope?) to go to heaven.[5]

Third, therefore, it is reasonable to conclude that there exists a divine reality to know and touch as well as life after death. Nothing on this physical earth seems capable of satisfying our religious desires; therefore, we must look to a transcendent source for such satisfaction. If we are correct in concluding that all of our universal natural human desires are matched by something capable of fulfilling those desires, then it is indeed reasonable to conclude that there must be some sort of a God capable of fulfilling our transcendent religious desires.

A perceptive critic might note that the arguments from religious experience and desire share a common weakness: they do not establish the God of Christianity. The same was true for the clues we explored in chapters 4 and 5. But in those chapters, at least the transcendent being I argued for bore a striking resemblance to the Christian understanding of God. Here the situation seems to be different. Religious experience and desire do not make Christianity any more likely than Hinduism, Shintoism, Jainism, Islam, or Judaism, and so forth. I confess this is entirely true. As my mentor Gary Habermas would say, these arguments do not determine which version of theism is correct.

What they do show, if successful, is that *some version* of theism is more likely to be true than is naturalism or atheism. And, from my perspective at least, it seems that the primary worldview competition in the West is between Christian theism and naturalism (also known as secularism or atheism). Thus, the limited scope of

---

[5]   See Barna Research, Culture and Media, "Americans Describe Their Views about Life after Death," October 21, 2003, https://www.barna.com/research/americans-describe-their-views-about-life-after-death/. I note that this Barna survey is from 2003; I would be interested to know what more contemporary studies show.

the arguments from religious experience and desire are of at least some positive value. But if you are wondering whether Christianity is more likely to be true than are other religions, you'll need to wait for (or turn to) chapters 7, 8, and 9!

## Free Will

> Free will *is* an illusion. Our wills are simply not of our own making. Thoughts and intentions emerge from background causes of which we are unaware and over which we exert no conscious control. We do not have the freedom we think we have. . . . Either our wills are determined by prior causes and we are not responsible for them, or they are the product of chance and we are not responsible for them.
>
> Sam Harris[6]

What did you have for lunch today? If you haven't had lunch yet, what *will* you have for lunch today? And why? Did you choose your lunch, or did your lunch choose you? Perhaps someone served you a lunch that you had no say in—if so, think back to the last meal that you prepared (or ordered) for yourself. Why did you choose to eat what you ate? Was your decision caused by forces beyond your control? Are your motivating desires so strong, or your bio-chemical programming so fixed, that you could not have chosen any differently than you did? Or did you make a legitimate decision and choose to have *this* rather than *that* for lunch?

If you did choose *this* over *that* for lunch, or for any other life event, then you are claiming to possess at least a measure of

---

[6]   Sam Harris, *Free Will* (New York: Free Press, 2012), 5.

*libertarian free will*. Libertarian free will is the power of contrary choice or the ability to make decisions between multiple "live options," meaning options that we could legitimately choose (or not choose). Our daily experience confirms the possession of libertarian freedom; it certainly appears to us that we are making real choices between multiple options that lie before us, and not only at the refrigerator and buffet table. We choose our friends, our television programs, the speed at which we drive, a vacation destination, and our bedtime reading list (thank you for choosing this today!).

Furthermore, libertarian free will seems to be necessary if we believe in moral accountability—the ability to be praised or blamed for our moral actions (or, conversely, the ability to praise or blame others for their moral actions). Think of this: assume for a moment that we do not have libertarian free will, but rather that each of our actions is determined by forces beyond our control. Perhaps, on this view, my actions are caused by my deepest or strongest desires, which in turn are determined by past events and genetic composition; or perhaps my actions are caused in a straightforward biochemical fashion. Either way, I do not make a choice when I act. I act merely in accordance with the way things were predetermined to occur. If this is the case, then is it sensible to *blame* me or *praise* me for my actions? It seems not.

Moral praise and blame seem to require libertarian free will, the ability to choose between multiple live options. We praise individuals when they choose the better of two or more options that lie before them. Conversely, we blame individuals when they choose the worse of two or more options that lie before them. We neither praise nor blame individuals for doing something they could not have avoided doing. It only makes sense to pronounce moral judgments in cases where the moral agents could have acted otherwise than they actually did.

For example, we do not morally blame a new alpha male lion for killing all the cubs in a pride and forcibly copulating with the lionesses. We understand that the lion is acting in accordance with its biological programming. It cannot do otherwise than it does. If humans do not have libertarian free will, then it makes little sense to morally blame (or praise) them for actions they take, since those actions are not the result of a free choice.

But moral accountability is deeply embedded in our individual and social psyche. That is, we do, as individuals and as societies, blame and praise people for things they do, thereby betraying our deeply held underlying belief that people *can* act otherwise than they actually do. Even Sam Harris, who explicitly rejects the notion that we have free will, holds other people morally accountable for praiseworthy or blameworthy beliefs and actions!

It seems, then, that we typically arrive naturally at the conclusion that we possess libertarian free will based on (1) our direct experience of life and (2) our deeply held belief that we and fellow humans are likewise morally accountable for our beliefs and actions. What can we conclude from this? Very simply, that free will points toward the existence of God.

1. Human beings possess libertarian free will to at least some degree, such that it is appropriate to (a) claim that we make legitimate decisions between multiple live options, and (b) attach moral praise and blame to people's beliefs and actions.
2. The world we live in is either (a) the creation of a personal, moral, transcendent being, or (b) it is not.
3. The presence of libertarian free will is exceedingly difficult to explain if the world is not the creation of a personal, moral, transcendent being.

4. The presence of libertarian free will is easy to explain if a personal, moral, transcendent being exists.
5. Therefore, it is more likely than not that the world is the creation of a personal, moral, transcendent being.

The first two premises are, at this point, easy to accept. We have already done the difficult work of arguing for human possession of libertarian free will. The second premise simply notes that either God created the universe, or not. The interesting conversation revolves around premises 3 and 4.

I contend that libertarian free will does not fit neatly into any worldview that does not embrace a personal, moral, transcendent Creator of the world. While there are other worldview options to consider, let's look at just one—atheism or naturalism. In an atheistic worldview, there is no god, no creator of the universe, no spirits, no souls—nothing nonmaterial that exists. On a strong atheistic perspective, human beings are merely highly advanced biochemical machines, which operate according to clear genetic programming. I have already made the argument (chap. 5) that in such a worldview there would be no objective moral values and duties. And if there are no objective moral values and duties, then the notion of moral praise and blame becomes quite inappropriate. We should not "blame" people for doing things that are not objectively wrong any more than we should "blame" people for liking the "wrong" flavors of ice cream.[7]

But on a deeper philosophical level, if we are merely highly advanced biochemical machines, then we do not make any legitimate decisions between multiple live options. Rather, when faced with various options, our programming will consider the options and go

---

[7] Except garlic ice cream; if someone likes garlic ice cream, there's something seriously "wrong" with them! I jest, but only sort of.

in the direction that we are hardwired to choose. That is, libertarian free will is incompatible with an atheistic framework. Granted, there are various atheistic philosophers (John Searle, Colin McGinn) who try to argue that there is some sort of immaterial aspect to human persons that arises from our physical body, such that we are able to make legitimately free choices. But, to the degree that they maintain their strong atheism, philosophers (such as Jaegwon Kim, Richard Rorty, and Paul Churchland) are forced to deny the immateriality and irreducibility of human mind.[8] To the degree that they accept the immateriality and irreducibility of human mind, philosophers (such as Thomas Nagel) are forced to abandon tenets of atheism.[9]

Hence, if the world is not the creation of a personal, moral, transcendent being, then libertarian free will is exceedingly difficult to explain.

On the other hand, if a being along the lines of the God of Christianity created the world, then libertarian freedom is very straightforward to explain. God's nature, combined with his revealed moral law, provides the sufficient foundation for moral praise and blame. And because God is a powerful (omnipotent) and wise (omniscient) being, God would be capable of creating human beings with moral agency, with the ability to make legitimate choices between multiple live options.

So if the world is the creation of a personal, moral, transcendent being, then libertarian free will is easy to explain.

---

[8]  To say that human mind (which would include not only free will but also intentionality, perception, consciousness, and rationality) is "irreducible" is to claim that mind cannot be explained by physical or material things and processes; rather, there is an undeniable, unavoidable nonphysical aspect to mind.

[9]  This is a very brief consideration of a very complex question. For a deep discussion, see J. P. Moreland, *Consciousness and the Existence of God* (New York: Routledge, 2008).

Our experience of making legitimate choices between multiple live options, combined with our deep-seated sense of moral accountability, thus provides indirect evidence that some sort of God does exist.

## Reason

> With me the horrid doubt always arises whether the convictions of man's mind, which has always been developed from the mind of lower animals, are of any value or at all trustworthy. Would one trust in the convictions of a monkey's mind, if there are any convictions in such a mind?
>
> Charles Darwin[10]

As you are reading this book, I hope you find yourself thinking many thoughts. Sometimes I suspect you disagree with claims I make or conclusions I draw. Sometimes I hope you ponder a new suggestion that you have never heard before and ask yourself whether there is sufficient reason to change your mind on a particular issue. Your consideration of arguments and claims that I make involves the use of reason or rational deliberation.

Every time you weigh arguments and consider the strength of evidence for different positions, you are using your powers of reasoning. Each time you deliberate over a math question, you are using your powers of reasoning. When you consider what tool would be best to tackle a particular home improvement project, you are using

---

[10]   Charles Darwin, Letter to W. Graham, July 3, 1881, in *The Life and Letters of Charles Darwin*, ed. Francis Darwin (1897; repr., Boston: Elibron, 2005), 1:285. Cited in Douglas Groothuis, *Christian Apologetics: A Comprehensive Case for Biblical Faith* (Downers Grove, IL: IVP Academic, 2011), 414.

your powers of reasoning. In each case, you are presuming that your powers of reasoning are trustworthy and reliable.

But it seems to me that we should trust our powers of reasoning only if the world (including humans) is created by a transcendent, personal, wise being, like the God of Christianity.

1. Human beings possess trustworthy rational faculties, such that it is appropriate to presume that our reason will lead us to a true understanding of the world around us.
2. The world we live in is either (a) the creation of a personal, wise, transcendent being, or (b) it is not.
3. The presence of trustworthy rational faculties is exceedingly difficult to explain if the world is not the creation of a personal, wise, transcendent being.
4. The presence of trustworthy rational faculties is easy to explain if a personal, wise, transcendent being exists.
5. Therefore, it is more likely than not that the world is the creation of a personal, wise, transcendent being.

Premise 1 is, I hope, straightforward. There seems to be little point in rationally defending the trustworthiness of our rational faculties if, in fact, our rational faculties are not trustworthy. I will presume, then, that we rightly trust our powers of reason. If I am wrong, then this entire book is an exercise in futility (as is all education and any other attempt to rationally teach or persuade anybody of anything).

Premise 2 is likewise straightforward. There are indeed numerous worldviews that reject the existence of a personal, wise, transcendent being who has created the world. But for our condensed purposes, we will again lump them all together.

Premise 3 is the key turn. Let us look briefly at two alternative worldviews and how difficult it is to establish the trustworthiness of reason in them.

First, consider textbook versions of an Eastern pantheistic worldview, some variety of Hinduism or Buddhism. According to such a worldview, the universe is fundamentally One, in that everything that exists is a part of ultimate reality, identified in Hinduism as Brahman. Human beings draw distinctions between things, separating, for example, matter and spirit, illness and health, good and evil. But at the root, those distinctions are not real, but rather are part of the illusion, called *maya*, in which we are trapped. The goal is to escape the cycle of birth, and rebirth and to transcend the illusory distinctions of this world.

The important thing to note in that basic worldview articulation is the notion of maya or illusion. The distinctions that humans perceive and articulate in the world are *not* real; they do not reflect the way the world actually is. And yet those distinctions seem fundamental and reasonable to us. To put it bluntly, our rational faculties drive naturally, even undeniably, toward the conclusion that there are real distinctions in the world. These Eastern worldviews insist that those distinctions are not real. What does that mean about the status of our rational faculties? It would seem that in these Eastern worldviews, our rational faculties are not trustworthy. Therefore, it is exceedingly difficult, I would argue impossible, to explain the existence of trustworthy rational faculties in these forms of Hinduism and Buddhism.

Second, consider an atheistic or naturalistic worldview. Imagine that there is no god and that our world is not created but is the product of random chance and physical necessity. For most naturalists, the origin and nature of human beings are best explained by means of some Darwinian evolutionary process. The key mechanism in evolution is natural selection, in which living creatures are more likely to pass on genetic traits that help specific creatures survive and thrive in their environment. So the crucial factor to consider is survivability or survival value. Does eyesight help creatures survive and thrive? If yes, then eyesight will be successfully passed on to subsequent generations. Does lactose tolerance help humans survive in increasingly agricultural societies? If yes, then lactose tolerance will be selected for survival.

What does that mean for human rational faculties? In short, our rational faculties—things like deliberation, calculation, logical reasoning, weighing of evidence—are primarily directed toward helping us to survive and thrive in our environment. But if our rational faculties are directed toward survival, then they are not primarily intended (or designed) to help us know and embrace truths. Furthermore, our rational faculties can help us to survive even if they do not help us to find truth. But if this is the case, then we can "trust" our rational faculties only in the sense that we can trust them to help us survive in a difficult world; we cannot trust our rational faculties to gain true beliefs. When philosophers think of "trustworthy rational faculties," however, we think of faculties that help us to gain knowledge, to better understand the world around us—not merely to help us survive. So it is exceedingly difficult to explain the existence of trustworthy rational faculties given a naturalistic worldview that embraces evolutionary theory as the explanation for human life and reason.[11]

On the other hand, if a God created the universe and designed human beings in his image, as Christianity claims, then it is tremendously easy to explain our possession of trustworthy rational

---

[11]   For an excellent in-depth presentation of this argument, see Alvin Plantinga, *Where the Conflict Really Lies: Science, Religion, and Naturalism* (New York: Oxford University Press, 2011), 307–50.

faculties. God is a logical, rational being. God has the power and wisdom to create humans with rational faculties that are directed toward gaining knowledge of the world around them. So if you believe that human beings do possess trustworthy rational faculties, then there is some reason to think that a divine being along the lines of the Christian God must also exist.

## Conclusion

In this chapter, we have raced briefly through four clues from human nature that point toward the existence of some sort of God: religious experience, religious desires, free will, and reason. Do any of these arguments establish beyond a reasonable doubt that God exists? No, I don't think so. They are suggestive, not conclusive. But these arguments do show that it is more reasonable to believe that God exists than it is to deny that claim.

Do these arguments, individually or collectively, show that the God of Christianity exists? No, I don't think so. But when you combine the arguments in this chapter with those from chapters 4 (cosmology, design) and 5 (ontology, morality), you have a fairly strong cumulative case for the existence of something very much like the God of Christianity, a transcendent being who is tremendously powerful, creative, wise, good, personal, relational, and rational. That does not *have* to be the God of Christianity, but the arguments are getting us closer.

In the next three chapters, I will explore evidence and reasons that suggest the truthfulness of Christianity specifically. My primary focus will be the person and work, and particularly the supposed resurrection, of Jesus of Nazareth.

## Recommended Resources for Further Exploration

Lewis, C. S. *Surprised by Joy.* 1955. Reprint, New York: Harper-One, 2017.

Moreland, J. P. *Consciousness and the Existence of God.* New York: Routledge, 2008.

Pascal, Blaise. *Pensées.* Translated by A. J. Krailsheimer. New York: Penguin, 1995.

Plantinga, Alvin. *Where the Conflict Really Lies: Science, Religion, and Naturalism.* New York: Oxford University Press, 2011.

Williams, Clifford. *Existential Reasons for Belief in God: A Defense of Desires & Emotions for Faith.* Downers Grove, IL: IVP Academic, 2011.

# PART 3

# WHY JESUS?

H ow do you eat an elephant?"
When I was asked that question, I was quite perplexed. I wasn't sure whether I was supposed to respond by stating the appropriate utensils for the meal (fork and knife?) or my favorite elephant steak seasoning (garlic and herbs?). Turns out I was missing the point.

The right answer, I was told, is "one bite at a time."

A wise mentor used elephant consumption as a teaching moment, an opportunity to help me learn to tackle seemingly insurmountable tasks one step at a time. Since then, I have faced many busy times, encountered numerous onerous obstacles, and dreaded demanding deadlines. Whenever I feel that there is no way I can accomplish all that lies before me, I remind myself, "You eat an elephant one bite at a time."

It seems to me that talking about religion, particularly Christian faith, is similar (in some ways) to eating an elephant. Many people want to try to swallow the whole elephant at once, or worse, want to force-feed the whole elephant to you in one giant bite. So they suggest, for example, that you need to "look at this one incredible undeniable authoritative proof for the truth of Christianity!" Or, on the contrary, they insist that "this single piece of scientific evidence infallibly demonstrates that there is no god."

I think it is a mistake to approach a huge subject so simplistically. Instead, it is important to slow down and look at one question at a time. Worldviews, especially religious worldviews, are massive conceptual and practical frameworks, and the elements of worldviews tend to hang together (or fail to do so). Thus I like a building-block approach to conversations about worldviews. You eat an elephant one bite at a time. You complete a huge task one step at a time. You build a house one brick at a time. I want to show that Christianity is true one argument at a time.

We started that cumulative case argument in Chapter 3 with a defense of objective truth. Then in chapters 4–6, I presented several clues from science, reason, morality, and human nature that support belief in the existence of some personal divine being, that is, God.

But there are religions other than Christianity that believe in some sort of god. So why should you think that Christianity is more likely to be true than any other religion—say, Islam or Hinduism? One could answer that question by comparing religious traditions and beliefs[1] or by showing logical, evidential, or existential shortcomings in other religions.[2] Instead, I would like to take a positive or constructive approach to the task.

I would like to build upon the planks of truth and God that have, I trust, been successfully established in parts 1 and 2. I would now like to provide reasons to think that the New Testament Gospels provide a reliable record of the life, ministry, death, and resurrection of Jesus of Nazareth, and that this accumulated evidence supports the

---

[1]   A good example of that approach can be found in James W. Sire, *The Universe Next Door: A Basic Worldview Catalog*, 6th ed. (Downers Grove, IL: IVP Academic, 2020).

[2]   A good example of that approach can be found in part 3 of Anderson, Clark, and Naugle, *Introduction to Christian Worldview*, 225–322 (see chap. 3, n. 3).

truthfulness of the primary claims of the Christian faith. This project has three steps, each one providing a plank to support the next.

First, we must recognize that our primary sources of information about Jesus of Nazareth are the New Testament Gospels. There are other historical records that reference Jesus as well, but the bulk of our data comes from Matthew, Mark, Luke, and John. Our knowledge of the life and ministry of Jesus is only as secure as the historical reliability of the sources. I will begin this section, in Chapter 7, by providing reasons to believe that the New Testament Gospels are textually and historically reliable, such that they are able to communicate an accurate picture of Jesus of Nazareth.

Second, the identity, actions, and claims of Jesus are of primary importance to the Christian religion. Christianity claims that Jesus is a unique figure: the God-Man, fully divine and fully human. In Chapter 8, I will argue that there is good reason to believe that Jesus thought he was in fact God in the flesh and that his actions and accomplishments verify his divine identity.

Third, the events of Easter weekend are the fulcrum of the Christian religion (and, I would argue, human history as a whole). Christianity claims that Jesus died by Roman crucifixion, that his death was a sacrifice to atone for human sins, and that on the third day Jesus was raised back to physical life by God the Father. In Chapter 9, I will focus on the miraculous claim of Jesus's resurrection, suggesting that the historical evidence provides good reason to believe that Jesus was in fact raised from the dead.

If these arguments are successful, they indicate that the core claims of Christianity are true and that there is good reason to embrace and follow the Christian religion.

**Chapter 7. The Story:** Are the Gospels Textually and Historically Reliable?

**Chapter 8. The Man:** Who/What Is Jesus of Nazareth?

**Chapter 9. The Fulcrum:** Did Jesus Rise from the Dead?

# CHAPTER 7

# *The Story*

## Are the Gospels Textually and Historically Reliable?

I grew up in a pretty average Canadian home and family. Well, I think my family is pretty extraordinary, but you know, we were normal in most ways. I had (and still have) a great mom and dad who loved us four kids. We went to school, were encouraged to excel in everything, to learn and to grow. I took music lessons—violin, then piano, then trumpet. I played soccer growing up, and we played street hockey every day after school until my mom told us it was suppertime, and then time for bed. And, like most Canadian kids, I never went to church. My family was not a churchgoing Christian family. We were a strong, close, loving family, but the Christian faith was not part of our experience. I sometimes jest that we were "good Scandinavian pagans"—but that's an exaggeration. We were more British than Scandinavian and more nonreligious than pagan.

In grade 12, I met Jesus. More accurately, Jesus met me, where I was, and brought me to himself. I was given a Bible, a *New International Version Student Bible*, and began reading in the Gospel of Matthew. There I met Jesus and learned more about the God-Man who had redeemed me and brought me new life. I took the words of the Bible seriously, as God's Words spoken to me (and to all people). I still do today.

As a devout Christian, I acknowledge the New Testament as the inspired and authoritative Word of God—God's revelation of his character, actions, purpose, and calling to his people. The text of the New Testament is central to my Christian faith, as indeed to the faith of all Christians.

This is all fine and good—but what if the *text*, the words of the Gospels, is not what was originally written? What if we cannot trust the text? That is, what if the words that we have in Matthew's Gospel are not an accurate reflection of what Matthew actually wrote but have been radically changed by later scribes and copyists? Furthermore, what if the original text is irrelevant and what we have is simply made-up fairy stories about a man who never existed or at least who never did and said the things that the New Testament says he said and did? Indeed, numerous people today think that the text and story of the New Testament are untrustworthy.

I aim to answer two questions in this chapter. First, can we trust the text? Do we have an accurate record today of what the New Testament authors originally wrote? Second, can we trust the story? Are the New Testament Gospels reliable as historical records? On the one hand, I want to establish that those who wrote the New Testament documents were in a position to give us an accurate picture of what happened in the life, ministry, and death of Jesus of Nazareth. On the other hand, I also want to show that the text that those individuals wrote down has come down to us faithfully over the intervening centuries.

## Can We Trust the Text? The Textual Reliability
## of the New Testament Gospels

When historians ask whether we can trust some ancient text, they are investigating *textual integrity*—the reliability with which an ancient manuscript has been transmitted, copied, and passed down to us through the ages. When it comes to the New Testament Gospels, textual integrity means *the accurate transmission of the words of the New Testament, such that the words we have in our New Testament are a faithful representation of the words originally written by the ancient authors.*

Why is textual integrity important? For many reasons, but the most important is that if we do not have textual integrity, we probably do not have historical reliability.

Imagine with me[1] that I have in my hands the only existing biography of my great-great-great-grandfather Sven Anderson, handwritten in Swedish by his eldest son, Argur, in a series of journals. Argur's account of his father's life would be the best source of information about the famous Sven Anderson (inventor of Swedish meatballs). What a treasure it would be! Naturally, I prepare to publish the account so that the world can acknowledge the genius of my ancestor. But now, imagine that I come across some parts of Sven's biography that strike me as inaccurate or unkind. I don't want to malign Great-Great-Great-Grandfather's memory, so I decide to, well, change a few details here and there. You know, take out the section about Sven beating his wife; change the section about Sven's dispute with his neighbor to make the neighbor look worse.

Whatever the changes I make, they are all made before the account of Sven's life is published. My newly published biography

---

[1] Everything that follows about my great-great-great-grandfather is entirely imaginary, even his name.

of Sven Anderson would still be the only source of information about the life of the great Swede, but it would no longer be an accurate account. The changes that I made would have rendered it historically suspect. The biography is no longer historically reliable, not because of any fault of the original author (Argur Anderson), or of the original handwritten document, but rather because of the ill intentions and actions of myself as a later scribe.

Some critics, most notably the wildly popular Bart Ehrman, insist that this is precisely what has happened with the New Testament: the original Gospels may indeed have been historically reliable. Unfortunately, they have been messed up by copyists and scribes over the centuries. Thus the text we have now does not reflect the original text, and for that reason does not convey helpful, accurate information about Jesus.

> What good does it do to say that the words [of the New Testament] are inspired by God if most people have absolutely no access to these words, but only to more or less clumsy renderings of these words? . . .
>
> I kept reverting to my basic question: how does it help us to say that the Bible is the inerrant word of God if in fact we don't have the words that God inerrantly inspired, but only the words copied by the scribes—sometimes correctly but sometimes (many times!) incorrectly? . . . We don't *have* the originals! We have only error-ridden copies, and the vast majority of these are centuries removed from the originals and different from them, evidently, in thousands of ways.[2]

---

[2] Bart D. Ehrman, *Misquoting Jesus: The Story behind Who Changed the Bible and Why* (San Francisco: HarperSanFrancisco, 2005), 7.

Ehrman is correct: if the words of the Gospels have not been reliably passed on, then we do not have an accurate knowledge of the life and ministry of Jesus of Nazareth. The New Testament Gospels are, by all accounts, the best source of information we have about the life, ministry, death, and resurrection of Jesus Christ. If the Gospels are the result of a long process of textual corruption and alteration, such that the original form of the Gospels is irrecoverable, then our ability to know who Jesus is, what he has done, and what we are to do in response, is irreparably compromised.

So the text of the New Testament matters. The question is, can we trust the text? Do we have good reason to believe that the New Testament has in fact been accurately transmitted?

### The Wealth of the New Testament Manuscript Tradition: Quantity

The New Testament was not originally written in English. It was written in Greek, the common language throughout the first-century Roman Empire. The Greek New Testament was then translated into other languages, Syriac and Latin being among the earliest. Our English New Testaments are translations of Greek originals and other ancient translations from the Greek.

However, *originals* is a misleading word. We do not have the original New Testament. That is, we do not have the handwritten Gospel of Matthew that came from Matthew's pen. What we have, rather, is copies of the originals. The originals are known as the autographs (αυτογραφοι). These documents are long gone, disintegrated in Middle Eastern dust or burned in a Roman or Jewish fire. So we have *copies* of the original autographs. In fact, we have copies of copies of copies of copies of copies of the first copy of the original autographs. The various copies of the New Testament (in whole and in part) are known individually as manuscripts and collectively as the Manuscript Tradition; it is from these copies that our English translations are derived.

The original copies of the New Testament documents were not made by computer, photocopier, or printing press. They were painstakingly handwritten, sometimes by candlelight, often secretly under the threatening cloud of persecution. Sometimes the copies were handwritten as an elder or bishop *read* the Scriptures aloud. Either way, copies were made by hand from a very early date and then circulated among the first Christian communities.

The existing copies of the New Testament documents are known as the Manuscript Tradition. We have an incredible wealth of New Testament manuscripts, especially in comparison to other ancient documents.

For example, the Roman historian Tacitus wrote a history of the first-century Roman Empire, from Tiberius Caesar to Nero (AD 14–68), called the *Annals*. Tacitus lived from AD 58 to 117 and wrote his *Annals* around AD 100, later than all of the New Testament documents. However, there are only three surviving manuscripts of the *Annals*. The oldest contains only the first six books of the *Annals* and was handwritten in a Benedictine monastery in Germany around AD 850, more than seven hundred years after Tacitus originally wrote.

Livy is a slightly earlier Roman historian, born around 65 BC and dying about AD 17. Livy's *History of Rome* chronicled the founding of Rome down to the reign of Augustus Caesar in his own lifetime. Livy's *History* has a stronger manuscript tradition than Tacitus, with twenty-seven whole or partial manuscripts, the earliest of which dates back to the fourth century AD. In terms of ancient texts other than the New Testament, Livy's manuscript tradition is about as good as it gets.[3]

Notice what I am saying here. We have good evidential support for Livy's *History of Rome*. That support consists of fewer than three dozen existing copies of his writing, many of which are partial and contain many textual discrepancies. The earliest manuscript we have of Livy was copied nearly four hundred years after he wrote the original. So Livy's original was copied by someone, then someone else, then someone else—and four hundred years later someone copied the copy that we now have in our possession. There simply aren't a lot of manuscripts, and they are not terribly close to the time of the original writing. But, outside of the New Testament, Livy is as good as it gets.

Furthermore, ancient historians and classicists agree that the manuscript evidence for Livy, Tacitus, and others is sufficiently strong to establish their textual reliability. As Peter Williams notes,

> Much of the study of classical Greek and Latin literature
> is built on a foundation that no one really acquainted with
> Greek and Latin manuscripts doubts, namely, that most
> such manuscripts from the ninth through to the sixteenth
> centuries AD give us a reasonable representation of texts
> as they were in classical Greece or Rome.[4]

If the manuscript evidence for Livy and Tacitus is sufficient to establish their textual reliability, then the manuscript evidence for

---

[3] Certainly there are other ancient authors (Suetonius, Herodotus) who have more copies in their manuscript traditions. But in terms of date, the earliest copy of Livy is fewer than four hundred years after the time of his writing—a very short time span, comparatively speaking.

[4] Peter J. Williams, *Can We Trust the Gospels?* (Wheaton, IL: Crossway, 2018), 111–12.

the New Testament should be sufficient to establish its textual reliability beyond any reasonable doubt!

To date, scholars have discovered more than 5,000 Greek manuscripts of the New Testament (along with tens of thousands of manuscripts in other common ancient languages), the earliest manuscripts being partial copies of individual books dating to less than a hundred years after the originals were written. There are at least ten, and possibly closer to twenty, New Testament manuscripts that date to the second century. Remember, the earliest copies of Livy are nearly four hundred years after he wrote; the earliest copies of the New Testament are within a hundred years of when it was written. Furthermore, we have as many New Testament manuscripts from the first 150 years after its authorship as we have for Livy in the first 1,500 years after his writing!

We have manuscripts containing the entire text of the New Testament from as early as the fourth century. Tell me, how could you possibly tell whether the *Annals* reflect what Tacitus originally wrote? Well, you have to trust the three existing manuscripts, assuming that they agree with one another (which they don't)! In the case of the New Testament, however, we have thousands of manuscripts to compare to one another. Unbiased ancient historians thus have great respect for the textual integrity of the New Testament because they are accustomed to working with other ancient documents that have much poorer textual traditions.

So the first point to be established firmly is that we have, in comparison to other ancient documents, an extreme abundance of manuscript evidence to use in evaluating the textual integrity of the New Testament.

*The Wealth of the New Testament Manuscript Tradition: Quality*
The manuscripts we have, once again, are not the original manuscripts. They are copies of copies of copies.

But there's a funny thing about copying by hand, especially under less-than-ideal conditions. Even with incredible care and attention, it is inevitable that some mistakes will occur. When copying text, it is easy for your eye to skip a whole line and pick up further on; in fact, this phenomenon happens when I am *reading* a text, let alone trying to copy it by hand. It's also easy to err by replacing something unfamiliar with something much more familiar (e.g., replacing "Tawa" with "Tara" in a written copy [curse the iPhone's autocorrect function]). Sometimes scribes could err by attempting to smooth out apparent inconsistencies or difficulties.[5]

However, the vast majority of those scribal errors are pitifully insignificant. Let us look at two brief examples, with help from the United Bible Society's Greek New Testament.[6] The UBS Greek New Testament includes what they call "text-critical apparatus." In a nutshell, the text-critical apparatus lists all of the variant readings of particular verses and tells us in what manuscripts those variants appear. In each case, the UBS provides a rating to the preferred (most likely to be original) wording. That is, there is a reading that textual critics believe is the original reading, what the biblical author wrote, and the letter rating tells us how confident they are about their recovery of the original reading. An A rating means that textual critics are certain "beyond a reasonable doubt" that their identified reading is the original. A B rating means that they are highly

---

[5] The six most common types of copying errors are spelling mistakes, errors resulting from faulty hearing or eyesight, errors of concentration (such as skipping a line), using or omitting a definite article, transposing a word, and substituting a proper name for a pronoun (or vice versa).

[6] Barbara Aland et al., eds., *The Greek New Testament* (Stuttgart, Germany: Biblia-Druck, 1994).

confident, perhaps 85 percent sure, that they have the original reading. A C rating indicates considerable uncertainty, with only perhaps 70 percent confidence that the preferred reading is the original. A D rating is, in my colloquial terminology, indicative of throwing up our hands and admitting that textual critics are very uncertain; the preferred reading may well be the correct one, but it is almost as likely that some variant reading is the original. With those basic tools in our back pocket, let's turn back to a couple of insignificant so-called errors in the manuscript tradition.

First, consider Phil 4:23. My NIV ends the letter with "The grace of the Lord Jesus Christ be with your spirit." The UBS Greek text-critical apparatus notes that some manuscripts end Philippians with "The grace of the Lord Jesus Christ be with your spirit. *Amen.*" The difference is so slight, and the effect on meaning so negligible, that most English translations do not even note the textual variant in their study notes or footnotes. Does it really affect anything whether or not Paul ends his letter to the Christians in Philippi with "Amen"?

Second, consider 1 John 1:4. After citing his own eyewitness status to the ministry of Jesus, does John say he is writing to make *his* or *their* ("our" or "your") joy complete? Again, the manuscripts disagree. Some have "our" ($\eta\mu\omega\nu$); others have "your" ($\upsilon\mu\omega\nu$). Does it matter? Not really. Both are perfectly applicable, and it doesn't affect the message of the passage, let alone the letter.

There are thousands of insignificant copying errors like these in the New Testament manuscripts; indeed, I would suggest that the vast majority of errors and differences in the manuscript tradition are similarly meaningless. Even the most strident opponents of Christianity admit that there are very few scribal errors in the New Testament manuscripts that have any sort of importance or relevance.

Nonetheless, skeptics such as Bart Ehrman insist that if the New Testament Gospels were truly inspired by God, if they were inerrant in the original manuscripts, then God would have preserved them perfectly through time—even avoiding the insignificant mistakes.[7] That is, God would have ensured that his inerrant Word would have been perfectly copied by scribes, such that no errors ever crept into the manuscript tradition. Copyists would have been faithful, never inserting their own thoughts or "correcting" what they understood to be mistakes in the original they were copying from. Scribes would never have made slight mistakes, missing a line or a word here and there, misspelling words elsewhere.

I think this argument is actually quite foolish. Think of what Ehrman is requiring: God would *have to*, on his account, overrule the free will of countless thousands of individuals over centuries, preventing them from committing the copying errors that they would very naturally commit if they were operating under their own power. In other words, God would have to turn scribes into robots; does Ehrman really want God to have done that? Is it even a realistic expectation? No on both counts.

Indeed, we ought to expect that the manuscripts containing copies of the New Testament documents would have a large number of copying errors. Copying manuscripts is a difficult, painstaking, and mistake-prone enterprise. If the New Testament was copied by thousands of people over hundreds of years, we should expect there to be discrepancies between the manuscripts. And this indeed is the case. Thousands of scribal errors can be identified in the New Testament manuscripts. But there's the rub: due to the quality (and quantity) of the New Testament manuscript tradition, we are able to find the

---

[7]  See, e.g., Ehrman, *Misquoting Jesus*, 10–11.

copying errors and correct them, ensuring that, in virtually all cases, we have the original wording of the New Testament.

By comparing New Testament manuscripts, it is almost always relatively easy for textual critics[8] to identify where the mistake was made and what the original reading was. Why? Different scribes copying the same manuscript are almost certain to make mistakes; but they will make *different* mistakes. Hence, where one scribe might miswrite John as Jon, another (perhaps Scandinavian in origin) may write Johan, another (perhaps French) Jean, and another yet Jan. Most of the scribes, however, would correctly transcribe John as John. By comparing existing manuscripts side by side, textual critics are able to ascertain with fair certainty what the original (correct) reading is.

Let's look at some examples in the New Testament where we have differences in the manuscript tradition. Some manuscripts read one way and others a different way. I think our examination will not support Ehrman's thesis that the text of the New Testament is hopelessly corrupted, but will instead provide good reason for trusting the textual integrity of the New Testament.

***Obvious additions: Mark 16:9–20 & John 7:53–8:11.*** Ehrman cites two prominent examples of places in the New Testament where later scribes have obviously inserted a lengthy passage where it did not originally exist.

Mark's Gospel ends fairly abruptly. After the crucifixion and burial of Jesus, Mark 16 recounts the discovery of the empty tomb by three women. An angelic messenger instructs the women, "Go, tell his disciples and Peter, 'He is going ahead of you into Galilee. There you will see him, just as he told you'" (v. 7). Then verse 8

---

8    A textual critic is a scholar whose expertise is in dealing with, analyzing, dating, and comparing ancient manuscripts in the pursuit of identifying the original reading of those manuscripts (whether biblical or otherwise).

reads, "Trembling and bewildered, the women went out and fled from the tomb. They said nothing to anyone, because they were afraid." And there ends the Gospel of Mark, according to the oldest and most reliable manuscripts.

Most English translations (unwisely, in my estimation) continue to print verses 9–20 as the official ending to Mark's Gospel, but they preface the section with an indication that these verses are not in the earliest manuscripts. The scholarly consensus is that verses 9–20 do not belong at the end of Mark's Gospel. If there was originally more after verse 8 (and scholars disagree on whether there was), it has been lost; what we have is definitely not original. This is a clear case where later scribes have added an ending. The ancient scribe who originally inserted the verses was unwilling to allow such an abrupt ending to the Gospel; possibly the scribe knew what we have as verses 9–20 through some other oral or written source and added them as an "appropriate" ending. Either way, Mark 16:9–20 does not belong in Mark's autograph.

Another significant and rather obvious addition is John 7:53–8:11, which also happens to be one of the best-loved Jesus narratives in the Gospels. In this story, a woman caught in adultery is brought before Jesus by a crowd eager to judge and stone her. (No mention of where the guilty male party happened to be; it does, after all, take two to commit adultery.) Jesus rebukes the crowd, inviting the innocent members of the mob to cast the first stones. Ashamed, they each walk away; Jesus implicitly absolves the woman of her wrongdoing and exhorts her to "Go now and leave your life of sin." As with Mark 16, the manuscript evidence for John 8 is clear but also somewhat confused. Many ancient manuscripts do not have these verses at all; others have the story but at a different point in John's Gospel; others still have the story but place it in a different Gospel altogether (Luke). What seems clear, however, is that the story was not a part of the *original copy* of John's Gospel.[9] Textual critics are virtually certain, with both Mark 16 and John 8, that these passages are not in the original. The readings that do not include these verses are given a solid A rating.

Ehrman cites these two passages as reasons to reject the reliability of the New Testament text. However, the cases more appropriately display the value of textual criticism in identifying passages that were not in the original. Furthermore, biblical scholars have long been aware that Mark 16 and John 8 contain obvious additions to the text. Indeed, when Erasmus produced the first modern Greek New Testament in 1516, with only two twelfth-century manuscripts as source material, he nonetheless identified these same two passages as additions by later scribes.

***Verbal dictation errors: Revelation 1:5.*** Revelation 1:5 is a fascinating example of a possible early scribal error based on a *mishearing* of the text. In the NIV, the second half of the verse reads, "To him who loves us and has *freed us* from our sins by his blood . . . [then v. 6:] to him be glory and power for ever and ever! Amen." Most Bibles do not even have this as a textual note, but a small number of manuscripts have a different reading: "To him who loves us and has *washed us* from our sins by his blood" (emphasis mine). The Greek word in question is either *lusanti* (λυσαντι, "to release, to set free") or *lousanti* (λουσαντι, "to wash"). One can easily understand how a scribe could mistake the word; after all, they sound (and read) basically the same.

---

[9]    Please note: this does not mean the story must be false or invented. Indeed, John the Gospel writer insists that not everything that could be told about Jesus is told about Jesus in his Gospel. Therefore, the narrative of Jesus and the adulterous woman could be authentic and historically accurate. However, it is quite clear that it is not part of the original Gospel of John.

My conclusion is that at one point in time, an elder or bishop was reading the text aloud to a group of copyists; one or more of the copyists heard the wrong word and recorded it. Perhaps they felt too shy to raise their hand and ask the elder to identify which word (*lusanti* or *lousanti*) he meant. Perhaps they heard *lousanti* ("to wash") and thought that it fit the context perfectly, so never even wondered whether they might have misheard. Either way, a mistake was the end result. Nonetheless, there are very few manuscripts that read *lousanti* rather than *lusanti*, so textual critics are virtually certain that they have the original wording, *lusanti*.

So Rev 1:5 affirms the role of textual criticism and its ability to identify places where oral misunderstanding *has* occurred and resulted in textual variants. Here our confidence in the textual integrity of the New Testament is heightened, not lessened.

Note also that, *even if* we did not have confidence that we have the original reading of Rev 1:5 (*lousanti*, "to free"), the alternative reading (*lusanti*, "to wash") still fits very neatly with core Christian theology. Christian doctrine holds that Jesus's atoning death on the cross has both *washed us* from our sins (their accompanying guilt and punishment) and *freed us* from our sins (their power/control over our desires and dispositions).

***Heightened Christology?: John 1:18.*** Does John 1:18 read, "No one has ever seen God, but *God the One and Only*, who is at the Father's side, has made him known" (emphasis mine)? Or is it supposed to read, "but *the one and only son*, who is at the Father's side, has made him known"? Textual critics are fairly confident that "God the One and Only" is the correct textual tradition (it earns a B rating in the UBS); Bart Ehrman disagrees.[10] Personally, I'll go with the majority of textual scholars, but just for the sake of argument,

---

[10]    See Ehrman, *Misquoting Jesus*, 161–62.

assume that Ehrman is correct, and that John's Gospel originally read, "the one and only Son," instead. What would this change?

According to Ehrman, a great deal. It demonstrates that some early copyist (very early, in this case) felt it necessary to make divine Christology explicit in John 1. The entire prologue of John (1:1–18) emphasizes the divine nature and origin of Jesus of Nazareth. Verse 18 is kind of like the icing on the cake, emphasizing that Jesus is "God the One and Only." Ehrman says this addition is late, and that originally the divine nature of Christ was only implicit in the verse.

My question is, does it really matter? An understanding of the divine nature of Jesus certainly does not rest on John 1:18 alone. In the general passage, Jesus's divinity is amply evidenced. (1) Verse 1: "The Word was with God, and the Word was God." (2) Verses 2–3: "He was with God in the beginning. Through him all things were made." (3) Verse 12: "To all who did receive him, to those who believed in his name, he gave the right to become children of God." (4) Verse 14: "The Word became flesh and made his dwelling [tabernacled] among us. We have seen his glory, the glory of the one and only Son." Verse 18 certainly adds to the divine overtones. But even if Ehrman is correct in asserting that it originally read, "the one and only Son," the Christology of John 1:1–18 is still incredibly rich and points to the divine nature of Jesus. John 1 is just an example of how the supposedly "significant theological implications" that Ehrman attributes to textual errors are really not important when understood in context. At best, Ehrman shows that some scribes *did* make changes to the text to serve their theological agenda. But if that is the case, then John 1:18 also equally demonstrates that, in cases where that has occurred, textual critics (such as Ehrman) are equally effective at identifying the places where scribes have monkeyed with the text and are able to get back at the original reading. And, in either case, the surrounding passage in John 1 strongly points to what verse 18 emphasizes: Jesus's unique divinity is present regardless of whether or not there is a copying error in verse 18.

***Countering docetism?: Luke 22:43–44.*** Your Bible probably has a textual note concerning Luke 22:43–44.[11] In my NIV, the verses are printed but with a textual note that "some early manuscripts do not have" them. It is most likely that the verses were not in Luke's Gospel originally, but were added in by later scribes to match the emotions of Jesus in the parallel passages of Matthew 26 and Mark 14. Compared to the other Gospels, Luke's Jesus is composed, almost impassionate, as he faces his impending crucifixion.

Critics suggest (somewhat plausibly) that later copyists added these two verses to counter the growing heresy of docetism. Docetism taught that Jesus was the divine Son of God but only *seemed* to take on humanity. Thus when Jesus was on the cross, it was only the human flesh that was put to death; the divine essence of Jesus was unaffected. Luke's Gospel was perceived as being the most susceptible to docetist tendencies, so scribes may have felt the necessity to counter docetism by inserting anguished emotions upon the Savior in Luke 22.

Textual critics are fairly confident that these verses were not present in Luke's original, even though the majority of our manuscript tradition contains the verses. The reason is simple. It is easier to conceive of a copyist *adding* these verses in (to counter docetist tendencies) than it is to imagine a copyist *deleting* these verses.

Let's assume, then, that the verses were not originally there. What is changed, historically or theologically, with that understanding? Absolutely nothing! There is merely the demonstration that some later copyists indeed altered the text, but also the confident understanding that the discipline of textual criticism is able

---

[11]  "An angel from heaven appeared to him and strengthened him. And being in anguish, he prayed more earnestly, and his sweat was like drops of blood falling to the ground."

to discern and correct such incidents. Is the Jesus of the Gospels altered? No. Are the emotions that Jesus experienced and expressed in the garden of Gethsemane somehow eliminated? No, they are eminently present in Mark and Matthew. Again, this textual debate does *not* have any great theological consequence. It exhibits the reasons early scribes might choose to make additions to the text. But, and I want to emphasize this strongly, it also demonstrates how good the process of textual criticism is at identifying places in the text where additions were made.

*Atonement and the Father: Hebrews 2:8–9.* The textual variant contained in Heb 2:9 is so unimportant that most of our New Testaments will not even contain a textual note about it. Indeed, textual critics are as certain as they can be (99+ percent) that they have preserved the correct rendering. Nonetheless, some skeptics seek to make hay with the variants in the manuscript tradition. What precisely is at stake here?

The context of Hebrews 2 is about the nature of Jesus Christ and his relationship to humanity. Calling upon the echoes of Ps 8:4–6, Heb 2:9 reads, "But we see Jesus, who was made a little lower than the angels, now crowned with glory and honor because he suffered death, so that *by the grace of God* he might taste death for everyone" (emphasis mine). The vast majority of manuscripts, including our earliest ones, contain this reading. However, there are a few later manuscripts that, instead of "by the grace of God [χαρι θεου]," read "apart from God [χωρις θεου]." Thus the end of the verse would read that "apart from God he might taste death for everyone." There is, I will admit, a theological difference in meaning with this variant.

However, this is not a significant difference. Both implications—that Jesus died *by the grace of God* and *apart from God*—are at least potentially in accordance with traditional theology. The first one is obvious and undisputed, so skeptics focus on the less-attested variant reading. But what does Mark relate to Jesus crying out from the cross? Mark 15:34: "My God, my God, why have you forsaken me?" As Jesus hangs on the cross, bearing upon himself the accumulation of all human sin, he also takes upon himself the punishment for those sins. Speaking of the atonement being achieved *apart from God* would then emphasize the separation, abandonment, that is felt by Jesus according to his humanity as he hangs, burdened by the guilt of sin, upon the cross. Granted, the variant textual tradition of Heb 2:9 does not present this information in the clearest manner, but, again, remember that this is almost certainly *not* the original reading of Heb 2:9 anyway! The correct reading is that Jesus tastes death *by the grace of God*. Even if we assume (which we need not) that the variant reading is correct, Heb 2:9 can still fit within the scope of orthodox New Testament theology concerning the atoning death of Christ.

***Teaching the Trinity: 1 John 5:7–8.*** First John 5:7–8 contains another fairly evident textual variant. My NIV reads, "For there are three that testify: the Spirit, the water and the blood; and the three are in agreement." Again, the vast majority of manuscripts, including the earliest ones, contain this reading. However, there are some manuscripts that have a longer version, and read, "For there are three that testify in heaven: the Father, the Word and the Holy Spirit, and these three are one. And there are three that testify on earth: the Spirit, the water and the blood; and the three are in agreement." It is quite evident, therefore, that at some point in time a copyist or scribe added in the longer reading to teach Trinitarian theology explicitly.

A skeptic might make a big deal of this issue, insisting (correctly) that 1 John 5 is the only place in the New Testament where the Trinity is explicitly affirmed, and that with the restored original reading, the Trinity is not a New Testament teaching. However, I have taught, preached, and written about the Trinity numerous times, and not once have I turned to 1 John 5:7–8 for textual support. On the one hand, the verses are not part of the original and thus cannot legitimately be used to support Trinitarian teaching. On the other hand, full-blown Trinitarianism is easily defended from numerous other passages of Scripture.[12] So, what skeptics identify as a theologically significant textual variant is, in reality, both known and inconsequential.

***Two highly debated textual variants.*** So far, we have examined textual variants wherein scholars are virtually certain that they have identified the original reading. There are, however, some verses for which scholars are not clear on what the New Testament originally said. Let's take a quick look at two of the approximately forty textual variants that receive a D rating from the UBS textual critics. That is, these are verses where "the Committee had great difficulty in arriving at a decision" regarding the original reading.

First, there are variations of Rev 18:3. Does the original read, "For all the nations have *drunk* the maddening wine of her adulteries," or "All the nations *have been made to drink* the maddening wine of her adulteries," or something similar? This is one of the most disputed textual variants in the New Testament. But what does the textual difference affect? Virtually nothing! In the UBS's chosen variant, the verb is active, insinuating that the nations have drunk the wine of their own accord. In the alternative variant, the passive construction insinuates the drinking of the wine as an ordained punishment. Not a big deal either way.

Second, Matt 23:26 receives a D rating. Is the original reading, "First clean the inside of the cup and dish," or is it "First clean

---

[12]   For three examples of working out the biblical evidence for the triunity of God, see Augustine, *On the Trinity*, various translations; Michael F. Bird and Scott Harrower, eds., *Trinity without Hierarchy: Reclaiming Nicene Orthodoxy in Evangelical Theology* (Grand Rapids: Kregel Academic, 2019); and Malcolm B. Yarnell III, *God the Trinity: Biblical Portraits* (Nashville: B&H Academic, 2016).

the inside of the cup"? Bruce Metzger notes that "the weight of the external evidence [i.e., number of manuscripts] appears to support the longer text."[13] Nonetheless, the presence of the singular pronoun ("The outside of 'it' also will be clean") *autou* (αυτου) in numerous manuscripts points to an original that had only the cup. It appears that scribes sought to harmonize verse 26 with verse 25 by reintroducing *paropsidos* (παροψιδος, "dish"), but this led to a mismatch between the nouns and the pronoun, necessitating the later replacement of the singular *autou* (αυτου, "it") with the plural *auton* (αυτων, "them"). The shorter reading best explains the other manuscript variants. But notice the important thing: the uncertainty of the correct variant reading affects literally *nothing* of substance in the text.

## *Conclusion: The New Testament's Textual Integrity*

New Testament textual critics generally agree that we have recovered 97 percent of the original wording of the New Testament with near certainty. Furthermore, places in the New Testament where textual critics still are not entirely certain which reading in the manuscript tradition truly reflects the original are insignificant. No key Christian doctrines, no key historical truth claims, are affected by outstanding issues in textual criticism. We have a high degree of confidence that the New Testament text as we have it reflects the text originally written by the New Testament authors. The textual integrity of the New Testament is unparalleled in ancient literature. In other words, to answer our original question: yes, we can trust the text of the New Testament.

---

[13] Bruce M. Metzger, *A Textual Commentary on the Greek New Testament* (Peabody, MA: Hendrickson, 2005), 50.

## Can We Trust the Story? The Historical Reliability of the New Testament

The first Bible I was ever given, when I was seventeen, was a red-letter *NIV Student Bible*. I began reading in the Gospel of Matthew, the first book in the New Testament. As I read, I was captivated by the story and the words of Jesus of Nazareth, son of Joseph, called the Messiah or Christ. Everything I read was brand-new to me. I had never heard anything about this Jesus before (except as a frequently invoked cuss word). In my red-letter Student Bible, the words ascribed to Jesus are in red print, reflecting the Christian belief that Jesus said these words or at least something very much like them.[14] And as a young man, exploring the Christian faith for the first time, I absolutely ate it up. Jesus's teaching was powerful; his ministry was both spectacular and compassionate. I wanted to know more about this incredible man, whom Christianity claims is the pivotal figure in all of human history.

But after I committed my life to following Jesus as Lord, I was presented with a troubling question by my friends: what if Jesus never said or did what the Gospels claim he said and did? That is, are those words that appear in my Bible as red-letter words truly the words uttered by Jesus of Nazareth? Or did he say quite different things during his earthly ministry?

In the first half of this chapter, I tried to show that the texts originally written by the New Testament authors have been accurately

---

[14]  Biblical scholars generally agree that the Gospels do not contain the precise words that Jesus uttered, but rather an accurate presentation of what Jesus said, including a faithful rendering of his unique words, style of teaching, and phrasing. See, e.g., Richard Bauckham, *Jesus and the Eyewitnesses: The Gospels as Eyewitness Testimony*, 2nd ed. (Grand Rapids: Eerdmans, 2017); Craig S. Keener, *Christobiography: Memory, History, and the Reliability of the Gospels* (Grand Rapids: Eerdmans, 2019); and Michael R. Licona, *Why Are There Differences in the Gospels? What We Can Learn from Ancient Biography* (Oxford: Oxford University Press, 2016).

preserved throughout time, such that scholars are virtually certain that we have their original wording. But the textual integrity of the Gospels is of little help if what the Gospel writers recorded was not an accurate presentation of the life, words, ministry, and teachings of Jesus of Nazareth.

As a comparison, imagine that I have faithfully preserved and published the handwritten journals of my great-great-great-grandfather Sven Anderson (inventor of Swedish meatballs, remember?). That's all fine and dandy; but what if Sven's journal is itself an embellished, fabricated pack of lies? I will have accurately presented a reliable text, but we would not have a reliable historical record of Sven's life and times.

To be able to learn from a historical source, we must be able to trust both the text and the story. We must have confidence that the historical source has been faithfully preserved and that the original source was both able and willing to provide an accurate picture of its subject matter. If the New Testament Gospels are the most promising historical source of knowledge about Jesus of Nazareth, it is important to assess both the textual integrity of the Gospels *and* their historical reliability.

In the 1980s, a group of scholars known as the Jesus Seminar began publishing their theory that the vast majority of words attributed to Jesus in the Gospels did not originate with Jesus. They argue that the Gospels are unreliable, theologically colored texts. In their view, "the historical Jesus has been overlaid by Christian legend, myth, and metaphysics and thus scarcely resembled the Christ figure presented in the Gospels and worshiped by the church today."[15] According to the Jesus Seminar, only about 18 percent of words attributed to Jesus in the Gospels are his own words; the rest

---

[15] Craig, *Reasonable Faith*, 299 (see chap. 4, n. 4).

are legendary additions.[16] In response to the question "Can we trust the story?" the Jesus Seminar answers with an emphatic no!

The historical reliability of the New Testament Gospels matters. Jesus is unquestionably the center of the Christian faith—the narrative of his life, ministry, death, and resurrection form both the historical and doctrinal core of Christianity. Our knowledge about who Jesus was, what he said, what he did, and what happened to him stems primarily from the New Testament Gospels. Even the Jesus Seminar acknowledges that the canonical Gospels are as good as it gets so far as historical information about Jesus. If Christianity revolves around Jesus, and if our knowledge of Jesus derives primarily from the Gospels, then it is important to know whether we can trust what the Gospels say.

In the remainder of this chapter, I present five lines of argumentation that support the historical reliability of the New Testament, particularly the four Gospels (Matthew, Mark, Luke, and John). I think the evidence shows that we have ample reason to believe that the Gospels contain accurate and reliable eyewitness accounts of the life and ministry of Jesus of Nazareth. All things considered, it is more reasonable to conclude that the Gospels are historically reliable than it is to conclude that they are untrustworthy.

### *The Gospels Claim to Contain Eyewitness Testimony*

The New Testament books, particularly the Gospels, are presented as either eyewitness accounts or accounts derived from eyewitnesses. We'll briefly consider the claims in two Gospels and one epistle.

---

[16] See, e.g., Robert W. Funk, Roy W. Hoover, and the Jesus Seminar, *The Five Gospels: What Did Jesus Really Say? The Search for the Authentic Words of Jesus* (New York: Harper & Row, 1996).

*The Gospel of Luke.* Many have undertaken to draw up an account of the things that have been fulfilled among us, just as they were handed down to us by those who from the first were eyewitnesses and servants of the word. Therefore, since I myself have carefully investigated everything from the beginning, it seemed good also to me to write an orderly account for you, most excellent Theophilus, so that you may know the certainty of the things you have been taught. (Luke 1:1–4)

Notice Luke's emphases.[17] First, he notes that his Gospel account accords with the stories passed down by those who were eyewitnesses. Second, he has carefully investigated the events surrounding Jesus of Nazareth. Third, he presents his Gospel as an orderly, historical account of Jesus's life. Luke does not profess to be an eyewitness of Jesus's life and ministry, but he does claim that he has done his research and consulted those who *were* eyewitnesses.

Furthermore, when talking about the historical reliability of the Gospel of Luke, we cannot separate it from the book of Acts, of which Luke is also the author. In several passages in Acts, Luke slips into the first-person plural, revealing that he accompanied Paul on his missionary journeys. Note, for example, the change in Acts

---

[17] There is considerable academic debate regarding the authorship of the Gospel of Luke (and many other books of the New Testament). Traditional designation of authorship goes back to at least the early second century and unanimously links the Gospel of Luke with the book of Acts, both being written by Luke, a travel companion of the apostle Paul and most likely a medical doctor. For discussions of authorship on Luke and the other New Testament documents, see Craig L. Blomberg and Robert Stewart, *The Historical Reliability of the New Testament: Countering the Challenges to Evangelical Christian Beliefs* (Nashville: B&H Academic, 2016).

16. In verses 1–9, Luke records the events in third person. In verse 7, "they came to the border of Mysia." But after Paul's night vision (dream?) in verse 9, Luke resumes the narrative in first-person plural: "After Paul had seen the vision, we got ready at once to leave for Macedonia." The first-person plural recurs in Acts 16:10–16; 20:5–11; 21:1–26; 27:1–32; and 28:1–16. Luke is an eyewitness of many of the accounts recorded in Acts; furthermore, as an associate of Paul, he would reasonably have had access to the eyewitness accounts of the other apostles—James, John, and Peter in particular. It is reasonable to conclude that Luke's Gospel both claims and contains eyewitness testimony.

***The Gospel of John.*** The Gospel of John is understood to be the latest of the four Gospels, written around AD 95, or sixty-five years after Christ's crucifixion. But the author insists that it is a trustworthy eyewitness account of what truly happened. John 20:30–31 reads, *"Jesus did many other miraculous signs in the presence of his disciples, which are not recorded in this book. But these are written that you may believe that Jesus is the Christ, the Son of God, and that by believing you may have life in his name."*

One page later, John 21:24–25 reads,

This is the disciple who testifies to these things and who wrote them down. We know that his testimony is true.

Jesus did many other things as well. If every one of them were written down, I suppose that even the whole world would not have room for the books that would be written.

Although this passage suggests that the words in John's Gospel may have been written by a disciple's close associates rather than by the disciple himself, they insist unapologetically that the words derive from an original disciple and hence an eyewitness of Jesus's ministry.

While John and Luke make explicit references to the eyewitness content they contain, Mark and Matthew are not so explicit. Nonetheless, early church tradition associates the Gospel of Matthew with Matthew (or Levi), the tax collector called by Jesus as a disciple in Mark 2 and Luke 5; it holds that the Gospel of Mark was written by John Mark as a record of the apostle Peter's remembrances of Jesus's ministry. If traditional authorship is correct (and I think there is good reason to believe it is), then all four Gospels in the New Testament have strong claims to eyewitness status.

***The First Epistle of John.*** The letter of 1 John also contains a striking claim to eyewitness status. The letter opens:

> That which was from the beginning, which we have heard, which we have seen with our eyes, which we have looked at and our hands have touched—this we proclaim concerning the Word of life. The life appeared; we have seen it and testify to it, and we proclaim to you the eternal life, which was with the Father and has appeared to us. We proclaim to you what we have seen and heard, so that you also may have fellowship with us. And our fellowship is with the Father and with his Son, Jesus Christ. (1 John 1:1–3)

The author of 1 John is claiming that his own hands have touched Jesus of Nazareth and his own eyes and ears have seen and heard what Jesus said and did.

Admittedly, all this provides is a *claim* to contain eyewitness testimony.

### The Early Date of the New Testament Gospels

A second reason to accept the reliability of the Gospels is that they were written relatively close to the time of the events they relate. Most scholars agree that Mark is the earliest Gospel and date it between AD 50 and 70. Matthew and Luke were written between AD 60 and 85; John was written between AD 80 and 95. Jesus was crucified in AD 28, 30, or 33; so the longest possible time span between Jesus's death and the writing of the last Gospel is less than seventy years. This means that when the New Testament Gospels were written and began to circulate among early Christian churches, there would still have been hundreds, perhaps thousands, of people alive who themselves had seen and heard Jesus during his earthly ministry. The early date of the New Testament Gospels is important because it establishes the presence of living eyewitnesses who could either confirm or contradict the claims that the Gospels make about the life of Jesus.

Although it is not in the Gospels, the testimony of 1 Cor 15:3–8 is also important historically. Here Paul relates that after the resurrection, Jesus appeared "to more than five hundred of the brothers at the same time, most of whom are still living, though some have fallen asleep" (v. 6). Paul asserts that his claim can be checked with people who were still alive and were the eyewitnesses of what Paul is claiming to have happened. First Corinthians was written in the mid-50s, quite probably after Mark but before the other Gospels. Again, the point is simply that the Gospels and other New Testament documents are early enough to contain authentic eyewitness testimony. They were also written early enough to have aroused opposition and sparked contradictory testimony if the Gospels contained inaccurate reports.

## The Church Has Always Recognized the Eyewitness Status of the Gospels

A third reason to accept the reliability and trustworthiness of the Gospels as eyewitness accounts is that the Christian church universally has acknowledged them as such. From the first century onward, Christians have recognized that Matthew, Mark, Luke, and John are historical records of Jesus's life. There is no debate within the church until the rise of critical scholarship during the Enlightenment (sixteenth century and onward). When the Gospels claim eyewitness status and the church historically recognizes them as reliable and trustworthy, we ought to have strong reasons for rejecting such status.

We have accounts as early as Papias in the first century, and Justin Martyr and Clement in the second century, that affirm the reliable eyewitness accounts contained within the canonical Gospels. Justin Martyr affirmed the reading of "the Gospel" in churches alongside the prophets. By AD 170, Irenaeus of Lyons referred simply and authoritatively to "the Four Gospels," comparing them to the four winds of heaven. Simply put, within about one hundred years, there was an established tradition within Christendom recognizing four, and only four, canonical Gospels as authoritative, reliable sources about Jesus of Nazareth.[18]

---

[18] See, e.g., Eusebius's quotation of Papias, *Interpretation of Our Lord's Declarations, in Eusebius, Ecclesiastical History: Complete and Unabridged, new updated ed., trans.* C. F. Cruse (Peabody, MA: Hendrickson, 1998), 3.39 (pp. 103–6). See also Eusebius quoting Clement of Alexandria, 3.24 (pp. 88–90); and *Documents of the*

Our early testimony is unanimous and affirming: the Gospels are historically reliable. There is a complete and total lack of dissenting opinion; there is no record of anyone early who argued that the Gospels were unreliable accounts, that what they relate *did not* happen. It would be chronological snobbery to insist that we can know better, 2,000 years later, what *really happened* in the first century than the people who were around then. The universal church's recognition of the historical reliability of the canonical Gospels matters.

What about other gospels—accounts of Jesus's life and ministry that are not in our New Testament? Ten years ago, the much-publicized *Gospel of Judas* made headlines around the world. Fifteen years ago, the best-selling book and blockbuster movie *The Da Vinci Code* argued strenuously (and wrongly) that there were more than eighty gospels of Jesus's life, and that the patriarchal, misogynistic Catholic Church whittled them down to four acceptable, censored Gospels. We don't have time or space to dive deeply into the issue,[19] but the early church fathers, from the first century through the fourth, did not recognize any extracanonical gospels as authentic eyewitness accounts. Early church leaders such as Clement, Papias, Justin, and Tertullian quote copiously from Matthew, Mark, Luke, and John, and cite them as authoritative accounts. But they never quote from other gospels—Peter, Philip, Mary, Judas, and so forth. They never mention them as acceptable accounts. They do, however, sometimes cite them as untrustworthy accounts written later

---

*Christian Church*, ed. Henry Bettenson and Chris Maunder, new ed. (Oxford: Oxford University Press, 1999), 29–32; and J. N. D. Kelly, *Early Christian Doctrines.*, rev. ed. (Peabody, MA: Hendrickson, 1978), 29–34.

[19] For more on this, consult two excellent books by Darrell L. Bock: *Breaking the Da Vinci Code* (Nashville: Thomas Nelson, 2004); and *The Missing Gospels: Unearthing the Truth behind Alternative Christianities* (Nashville: Thomas Nelson, 2007).

by people who had no connection with the eyewitnesses to Jesus's ministry. If you glance through some of the other accounts of Jesus's life, you will recognize quite quickly why the early church did not accept them as valid historical accounts of Jesus's ministry.

The church had three primary criteria for documents to be considered canonical: (1) universality (read throughout the ancient church), (2) apostolicity (written by an apostle or the associate of an apostle), and (3) orthodoxy (conforming to the rule of faith handed down by the early church). Matthew, Mark, Luke, and John met those criteria. None of the other gospels did. Imposters wrote in the name of Peter, Paul, Mary, or Philip in the second century (and later) to try to gain acceptance within some circles of the church.

But early Christians were neither naive nor ill-informed. Like the Gospel writer Luke, they sought to establish what they believed on solid historical and evidential grounds. They did not credulously swallow every tale or myth about Jesus—only what was well grounded and well attested by eyewitness testimony. That is why the four canonical Gospels were accepted and others were not.

### The Internal Evidence of the Gospels: Incidental Details and Undesigned Coincidences

A fourth reason to accept the historical reliability of the Gospels is the evidence of the Gospels themselves. That is, the internal evidence of events and details contained within each Gospel strongly supports their status as reliable eyewitness documents. When the police seek an eyewitness account of what happened at a crime scene, they often look for incidental details that witnesses are able to provide. They also seek independent corroboration of witnesses' testimony. Our four biblical Gospels contain a plethora of incidental details and undesigned coincidences that confirm their historical reliability. We will examine just one example of each type of internal evidence.

### *Incidental details: John 5:1–5.*

> Some time later, Jesus went up to Jerusalem for a feast of the Jews. Now there is in Jerusalem near the Sheep Gate a pool, which in Aramaic is called Bethesda and which is surrounded by five covered colonnades. Here a great number of disabled people used to lie—the blind, the lame, the paralyzed. One who was there had been an invalid for thirty-eight years. (John 5:1–5)

As the narrative proceeds, Jesus heals the man on the Sabbath, creating a ruckus among the Pharisees. But notice the details contained within John's account. How long has the man been an invalid? Precisely thirty-eight years—an incidental detail that adds nothing to the story but supports eyewitness knowledge of the event. It is interesting to note that Jewish literature frequently rounds off numbers for the sake of effect. The number forty, for example, contained significance: forty years was representative of a generation (e.g., the Israelites who wandered in the wilderness); forty days was representative of a long period of time (e.g., Jesus's temptation in the desert after his baptism). So it would be typically Jewish for John to round off the thirty-eight years to forty or "about forty years," particularly if John is making up the story. Instead, John tells us that the man had been an invalid for thirty-eight years. Why? It seems reasonable to suppose that it is because that is indeed the precise and accurate number.

There are additional incidental details in John 5. Where is the man healed? Not just "in Jerusalem," but at a particular pool near "the Sheep Gate," known in Aramaic as "Bethesda." Notice that

John provides not only the exact name of the gate and pool, but also the unusual architectural structure of five surrounding covered colonnades.

My wife, Vanessa, and I are very different. We both enjoy stories, particularly good mysteries. But she doesn't really care for the lengthy descriptive passages contained in many longer novels. She is interested in the story itself. On the other hand, I love passages that draw a verbal picture. Skilled authors can bring you to the place of their writing, drawing a picture of the views, smells, sights, and sounds of the story.

That is precisely what John is doing here. He is bringing the story to life, giving us details that allow us to picture it in our own minds. The picture admittedly does not carry as much power with us as it would have for John's original audience, who would have been familiar with the places John writes about. But here John effectively demonstrates his familiarity with exactly what happened and exactly where.

I should also mention, in passing, that for skeptics and critics, incidental details don't help. In situations like these, a critical scholar can happily claim, "John wasn't really there. He just adds all of these details, some of them (like the name of the pool and gate) recalled from his memory of Jerusalem, others (such as the length of his injury) purely imagined by him, to make us think that he was actually there." For such scholars, the level of detail is not confirmation of eyewitness standing, but rather evidence of deliberate deception.

Conveniently, however, the same scholars will cite the *lack* of such details as evidence that the Gospel writer wasn't present at the scene. In fact, in this very passage, someone could point to verse 1 and ask, "Why didn't John identify *which* feast? Obviously, because John wasn't there, this didn't really happen, and so he can't say when the feast was." So the lack of one detail is evidence that John wasn't there, and the presence of other details is evidence of John's deliberate deception. John just can't win! If incidental details are there, it "proves" that John is making them up and putting them in to make the reader think he was actually there. If the details are not there, it "proves" that John wasn't an eyewitness to what he relates. Nonetheless, it is reasonable to conclude that the presence of incidental details is confirmation of the reliability of Gospel narratives.

***Undesigned coincidences: The feeding of the five thousand.*** Timothy and Lydia McGrew have opened my eyes to the existence of "undesigned coincidences" in the Gospels that further strengthen the eyewitness claims and historical reliability of the Gospels. [20] An undesigned coincidence occurs when multiple accounts of the same event complement one another, such that one account raises a question that is then answered by another account.

For example, consider three accounts of our family's outdoor Thanksgiving dinner last year. My son recalls what four people were wearing: our niece in shorts and a T-shirt, our nephew in jeans and a heavy sweater, our aunt in light pants and an autumn jacket, and our uncle in sweats and a flannel shirt. Given those descriptions, two people stand out as somewhat being oddly dressed, our niece and nephew. Why would one be in such light clothing, the other in such heavy clothing, given the moderate clothing of the others?

Our daughter, however, tells the story of the dinner focusing not on what people wore, but on how people were feeling. She recounts that our nephew was afflicted with the flu during the holiday season and was suffering from chills throughout the day—thereby explaining his heavier-than-normal clothing.

---

[20]    The best contemporary account of undesigned coincidences is found in Lydia McGrew, *Hidden in Plain View: Undesigned Coincidences in the Gospels and Acts* (Chillicothe, OH: DeWard, 2017).

My wife, meanwhile, reminisces that our niece and her family visited from Calgary, Alberta, and were enjoying the substantially warmer Thanksgiving weather in our hometown of Shawnee, Oklahoma—thereby explaining our niece's lighter-than-normal clothing.

If you had only one of our three family accounts from Thanksgiving, you would not have the whole story; but putting together all three parallel accounts fleshes out the context. This is, admittedly, a rather simple and trivial undesigned coincidence. The Gospel accounts of the feeding of the 5,000, on the other hand, are significantly more complex and illuminating.

John 6:1–15 recounts Jesus's feeding 5,000 people, one of few miracles recorded in all four Gospels. Here are the relevant (for our purposes) portions of verses 1–5.

> Some time after this, Jesus crossed to the *far shore of the Sea of Galilee* . . . and a great crowd of people followed him because they saw the miraculous signs he had performed on the sick. Then Jesus went up on a mountainside and sat down with his disciples. *The Jewish Passover Feast was near.*
>
> When Jesus looked up and saw a great crowd coming toward him, he said *to Philip*, "Where shall we buy bread for these people to eat?" (John 6:1–5, emphasis mine)

Now, you might ask, what is so significant about that little part of the passage? Well, let me ask you a question in a roundabout way. If you were John, and you were going to make up a story about Jesus multiplying food to feed lots of people, what disciple or disciples would you put in the story? For most of us, it would be Peter, John,

197

and/or James, perhaps even Judas because of his later notoriety, or Thomas because of his later doubt. How many of us would put Philip in a made-up story? Probably none. Why does John write that Jesus asked *Philip*, "Where shall we buy bread for these people to eat?" The simple answer is that this is the way it happened, and John is just telling us the truth. John wouldn't have made that up.

But go deeper. Why Philip? Philip is an obscure disciple. He shows up very infrequently in the Gospels, particularly after his initial calling. Why does he show up here in John 6, the feeding of the 5,000? Why does Jesus direct his inquiry to Philip in particular?

In first-century Jewish culture, as well as most ancient (and contemporary) cultures, when visitors come to your home, it is your responsibility to feed them and give them shelter. Moreover, if relatives arrive in your hometown, it is your responsibility to do the same. It would be a grievous sin, bringing shame upon the family name, to refuse to have visiting relatives over for dinner. So in Genesis 28–29, when Jacob arrives on Laban's doorstep, there is no hesitation: "Come in for dinner and stay with us, young man." In Exod 2:16–25, Moses shows up at Jethro's well and there is no hesitation: "Come stay with us and dine with us." Similarly, in Mark 1:29–34, when Jesus and his disciples are in Peter's hometown of Capernaum, Peter (via his mother-in-law) is on the hook to provide food and shelter. Hospitality was culturally expected, especially hospitality toward visitors and particularly visiting relatives.

How does that help with Philip? Well, given just what we have in John 6, it doesn't. But if we broaden our perspective, it begins to make sense. Where does the feeding of the 5,000 take place? John does not tell us precisely; just that they are on "the far shore of the Sea of Galilee." If we go to Luke's narrative of the feeding of the 5,000, in Luke 9:10–17, however, we find some of our questions answered. The disciples have just come back from a short trip without Jesus, and we read, "When the apostles returned, they reported to Jesus what they had done. Then he took them with him and they withdrew by themselves to a town called Bethsaida" (v. 10).

Where is Jesus at the feeding of the 5,000? At Bethsaida. Why does Jesus ask Philip, "Where shall we get bread to feed these people?" Because Philip was from—you guessed it—the town of Bethsaida. We don't know that from John 6 or from Luke 9. Rather, we learn that in John 1:44 and 12:21. In John 12, some Greeks were coming to Jerusalem for a Jewish feast, and we are told, "They came to Philip, who was from Bethsaida in Galilee, with a request." The feeding of the 5,000 occurs around Bethsaida. Why does Jesus approach Philip? Because Jesus and the disciples are in Philip's hometown. Jesus is saying to Philip, "Look, we're in your backyard, your hometown. Our extended family has come for a visit. It's your responsibility to have them over, to feed them supper. Where are you going to get all the food?" *That's* why Jesus asks Philip. But note, again, that you cannot patch that together only from John 6. You need John 12 and Luke 9 to work out the whole picture. These types of undesigned coincidences support the claim that the Gospels individually contain eyewitness testimony and collectively provide a reliable historical record of what occurred.

But there's more! Look at the parallel passage in Mark 6:30–44. At the beginning of the passage, as in Luke 9, the disciples have returned from their trip, and in verses 30–31, "The apostles gathered around Jesus and reported to him all they had done and taught. Then, because so many people were coming and going that they did not even have a chance to eat, he said to them, 'Come with me. . . .'" Mark tells us it was crazy busy where they were. But he does not tell us *where* Jesus and the disciples were. We find that out from Luke—in Bethsaida. But neither Mark nor Luke tell us *why* it was so busy, with people coming and going. We get that from John 6:4:

"The Jewish Passover Feast was near." Coincidental details from Luke help us understand John; coincidental details from John help us understand Mark. On their own, these three accounts of the miraculous feeding are helpful and interesting; when you put them together, they provide us with the full story. That is important for two reasons.

First, the undesigned coincidences among the Gospel accounts enrich our understanding of the life and ministry of Jesus of Nazareth. The intertextual resonance among John 6, Luke 9, and Mark 6 give us a richer and more complete picture than any of the individual Gospels on their own.

Second, and more important for my purposes here, you simply can't make this stuff up. The three Gospels are independent eyewitness accounts of the same event, each one giving an account of the feeding, but from a different perspective. Mark, Luke, and John focus on diverse details, choosing different points of emphasis. Nonetheless, the accounts fit neatly with one another. There are no contradictions, and the details provided in one account answer questions raised by the others. These undesigned coincidences provide the ring of eyewitness authenticity to the Gospels.

Combining the effect of incidental details and undesigned coincidences provides strong support for the historical reliability of the Gospels.

### *External Evidence for the Gospels: Support of the Gospels' Historical Accuracy*

A fifth reason to trust the historical reliability of the Gospels is the evidential support provided by other ancient documents and archaeological discoveries.

If police are presented with a professed eyewitness of a crime, they like to find empirical, objective confirmation that the individual was, in fact, at the scene. This is not always possible, but sometimes it is. The same is true with the New Testament Gospels. It is sometimes possible to confirm, through objective evidence, that the Gospel writers had firsthand knowledge of what they wrote about.

Consider two quick examples. First, note the way the Gospel writers cite geographical details—names of towns, bodies of water, roads, and directions of travel. Unlike the noncanonical gospels, which rarely (if ever) mention place names, the biblical Gospels name more than twenty-five towns, including small villages. They correctly refer to bodies of water and roads, even by their appropriate shorthand terms (e.g., "the Sea" for the Sea of Galilee). The internal details provided by the Gospels is confirmed by external sources that verify the existence and relationship of the places mentioned by the Gospel writers.[21]

Second, the discipline of archaeology is able to verify numerous details contained in the Gospels. One fascinating example concerns a passage already discussed, the healing of a disabled man in John 5. For years, critical scholars rejected the eyewitness standing of John's account on the basis that the name of the gate was not empirically verified and the identification of five surrounding colonnades was structurally unlikely and, again, not verified through archaeological discoveries. There is a methodological problem with their argument: the absence of archaeological evidence for the Sheep Gate and five colonnades demonstrated only that, so far as our limited archaeological evidence demonstrated, we could not confirm these historical details. That does not *prove* that John was making things up or wrong or lying. Eventually, though, archaeological discoveries verified the identity and name of the Sheep Gate

---

[21] For more, see the helpful work, Williams, *Can We Trust the Gospels?*, 51–63.

by the Pool of Bethesda, as well as the presence of five porticoes or colonnades.[22]

## Conclusion

We have just raced through five lines of evidence and argumentation supporting the historical reliability of the New Testament, with particular focus on the Gospels. It seems to me that when we combine the eyewitness claims, early date of writing, historical church affirmation, internal evidence (in both incidental details and undesigned coincidences), and external evidence, we have a strong case that we can indeed trust the story! In the first half of the chapter, we saw good reasons to trust the text as well. In sum, there is good reason to take the New Testament accounts very seriously, indeed, as accurate historical records of the life, ministry, death, and resurrection of Jesus.[23]

The original authors were in a position to record an accurate historical account. Internal and external evidence support their accuracy. The historical church affirmed their accuracy. The wealth of

---

[22] See, e.g., James K. Hoffmeier, *The Archaeology of the Bible* (Oxford: Lion, 2008), 147; and Randall Price, *The Stones Cry Out: What Archaeology Reveals about the Truth of the Bible* (Eugene, OR: Harvest House, 1997), 317.

[23] Despite these good reasons to trust the historical reliability of the Gospels, some skeptics argue that the New Testament contains a myriad of errors and/or contradictions. The presence of such mistakes or contradictions demonstrates, they argue, that the Gospels cannot be trusted to convey accurate historical information about Jesus of Nazareth. We do not have time to pursue the accusation of errors and contradictions here. But if you would like to pursue the topic further, a couple of helpful resources are Walter Kaiser, Peter Davids, F. F. Bruce, and Manfred Brauch, *Hard Sayings of the Bible*, repr. ed. (Downers Grove, IL: IVP Academic, 2010); Steven B. Cowan and Terry L. Wilder, eds., *In Defense of the Bible: A Comprehensive Apologetic for the Authority of Scripture* (Nashville: B&H Academic, 2013); and Norman L. Geisler and Thomas Howe, *The Big Book of Bible Difficulties: Clear and Concise Answers from Genesis to Revelation* (Grand Rapids: Baker, 2008).

New Testament manuscripts establishes the trustworthiness of the text; we have access to what the original authors wrote.

Put together, we should read the New Testament to learn who Jesus was, what he did and said, and what that implies for us. In Chapter 8, we will turn to a consideration of the person of Jesus of Nazareth to see what we can learn from the Gospels.

## Recommended Resources for Further Exploration

Bauckham, Richard. *Jesus and the Eyewitnesses: The Gospels as Eyewitness Testimony*. 2nd ed. Grand Rapids: Eerdmans, 2017.

Blomberg, Craig L., and Robert Stewart. *The Historical Reliability of the New Testament: Countering the Challenges to Evangelical Christian Beliefs*. Nashville: B&H Academic, 2016.

Bock, Darrell L. *The Missing Gospels: Unearthing the Truth behind Alternative Christianities*. Nashville: Thomas Nelson, 2007.

Keener, Craig S. *Christobiography: Memory, History, and the Reliability of the Gospels*. Grand Rapids: Eerdmans, 2019.

Licona, Michael R. *Why Are There Differences in the Gospels? What We Can Learn from Ancient Biography*. Oxford: Oxford University Press, 2016.

McGrew, Lydia. *Hidden in Plain View: Undesigned Coincidences in the Gospels and Acts*. Chillicothe, OH: DeWard, 2017.

Williams, Peter J. *Can We Trust the Gospels?* Wheaton, IL: Crossway, 2018.

# CHAPTER 8

## *The Man*

### Who/What Is Jesus of Nazareth?

In the Gospel of John, we witness a fascinating exchange between Jesus and "the Jews" (the teachers of the law and the Pharisees).

> The Jews answered him, "Aren't we right in saying that you are a Samaritan and demon-possessed?"

> "I am not possessed by a demon," said Jesus, "but I honor my Father and you dishonor me. I am not seeking glory for myself; but there is one who seeks it, and he is the judge. I tell you the truth, if anyone keeps my word, he will never see death."

> At this the Jews exclaimed, "Now we know that you are demon-possessed! Abraham died and so did the prophets, yet you say that if anyone keeps your word, he will never taste death. Are you greater than our father Abraham? He died, and so did the prophets! Who do you think you are?"

Jesus replied, "If I glorify myself, my glory means nothing. My Father, whom you claim as your God, is the one who glorifies me. Though you do not know him, I know him. If I said I did not, I would be a liar like you, but I do know him and keep his word. Your father Abraham rejoiced at the thought of seeing my day; he saw it and was glad."

"You are not yet fifty years old," the Jews said to him, "and you have seen Abraham!"

"I tell you the truth," Jesus answered, "before Abraham was born, I am!" At this, they picked up stones to stone him, but Jesus hid himself, slipping away from the temple grounds. (John 8:48–59)

Why do the Jews try to stone Jesus at the end of that passage? Because Jesus is making two bold claims. First, he claims to be eternal (or at least super ancient): he says he was around before Abraham, some 2,000 years prior. Second, he claims to be God. I AM—Jesus invokes for and applies to himself the self-revealed name of Yahweh, the God of Israel.[1] You can hear the exasperation and disbelief in the voices of Jesus's Jewish opponents: Jesus, who do you think you are?!

---

[1]   In Exod 3:13, Moses effectively asks, "God, what is your name?" God answers, "I AM WHO I AM [Hebrew: *Yahweh*] . . . I AM [Yahweh] has sent me to you [the people of Israel]." That self-revealed Hebrew name of God, translated "Lord" in most English Bibles, comes into the Greek Old Testament (the Septuagint) as *ego eimi*, the emphatic (and grammatically unnecessary) form of "I [*ego*] am [*eimi*]." In the Gospel of John, Jesus uses this emphatic divine name, *ego eimi*, to refer to himself: "Before Abraham was born, *ego eimi*, I AM."

That is really the question we want to tackle in this chapter: Who did Jesus think he was? And what do his words and actions show about the claims he made for himself? Orthodox Christianity holds that Jesus of Nazareth was not just a great guy, not just a tremendous teacher, not just a religious leader; rather, Jesus was God in the flesh, the divine Son of God, the Messiah sent to redeem Israel (and all the world). Professing to be God is a pretty radical claim; holding someone else to be God is similarly far reaching.

Is there good reason to think that Jesus thought he was God in the flesh? Is there good reason to think that Jesus actually *was* God in the flesh?

American Wayne Bent (aka Michael Travesser, born 1941) founded The Lord Our Righteousness Church and claims to be the embodiment of God Almighty: the God-Man. Japanese Mitsuo Matayoshi (aka Iesu Matayoshi, 1944–2018) was convinced that he was both God and Christ (Savior). Jim Jones (1931–78) founded Peoples Temple and claimed to be the reincarnation of Jesus and the manifestation of Father Divine before organizing a mass suicide of his followers in Jonestown, Guyana. Brazilian Inri Cristo, founder of the Supreme Universal Order of the Holy Trinity, claims to be the reincarnation of Jesus of Nazareth.

These four men are interesting case studies. They have little in common, except for their mutual claim to some sort of divine status and their spectacular failure to demonstrate their divinity in their words and deeds.

Is Jesus just another crazy person with grandiose self-delusions? Are Jesus-followers (Christians) sadly deceived suckers who have been taken in by a myth? Matthew 16:13–16 contains a crucial exchange between Jesus and his disciples.

When Jesus came to the region of Caesarea Philippi, he
asked his disciples, "Who do people say the Son of Man
is?"

They replied, "Some say John the Baptist; others say Elijah; and still others, Jeremiah or one of the prophets."

"But what about you?" he asked. "Who do you say I am?"

Simon Peter answered, "You are the Christ, the Son of the
living God."

"Who do you say I am?" This is, again, our key question in
this chapter: who is Jesus? The truth, power, and appeal of Christianity depends entirely on the person and work of Jesus Christ.
Christianity is not primarily a belief system or a set of religious
doctrines and practices. At its core, Christianity is a commitment to
a particular historical figure, Jesus of Nazareth, son of Mary, who
is regarded as not merely human, but also divine. The person and
work of Jesus Christ sets Christianity entirely apart from every other
religion and philosophy. What we believe about Jesus is unique and
determinative.

The Nicene Creed represents a summary statement of what
Christians through the ages believe:

We believe . . . in one Lord Jesus Christ, the only-begotten
Son of God, Begotten of the Father before all ages, Light
of Light, true God of true God, begotten, not made, of
one substance with the Father, through whom all things
were made; who for us men and for our salvation came
down from the heavens, and was made flesh of the Holy

Spirit and the Virgin Mary, and became man, and was crucified for us under Pontius Pilate, and suffered and was buried, and rose again on the third day according to the Scriptures, and ascended into the heavens, and sitteth on the right hand of the Father, and cometh again with glory to judge the living and the dead, of whose kingdom there shall be no end.[2]

So what do Christians believe about Jesus that is so remarkable?

1. **Jesus is God incarnate.** Jesus is not just a prophet, not just a teacher, not just a good moral example. He is God in the flesh, dwelling among humankind.
2. **Jesus died for us and for our salvation.** Jesus was crucified and died, but his death was not a martyr's death. His death purchased our salvation, our eternal life.
3. **Jesus rose from the dead.** Jesus's death was not the end of his story. He rose from the dead and lives on in a glorified body.
4. **Jesus determines our eternal destiny.** Jesus will come back to judge the living and the dead. Where we go after we die is determined by our relationship to Jesus Christ.

That's a core set of Christian beliefs about Jesus—not exhaustive, but it expresses the heart of the Christian faith.[3] But many think these claims are not true.

---

[2]  The Nicene Creed, in *Documents of the Christian Church, new ed., ed.* Henry Bettenson and Chris Maunder (Peabody, MA: Hendrickson, 1999), 28.
[3]  My mentor and friend Gary Habermas likes to talk about the threefold core of Christian beliefs about Jesus: his deity, his atoning death, and his bodily resurrection.

The 2003 Dan Brown novel (and 2006 blockbuster movie), *The Da Vinci Code*, made some striking claims about Jesus of Nazareth. The novel's authoritative teacher, Sir Leigh Teabing, declares,

> Jesus Christ was a historical figure of staggering influence, perhaps the most enigmatic and inspirational leader the world has ever seen. . . . The Council of Nicaea . . . debated and voted upon . . . the *divinity* of Jesus. . . . Until *that* moment in history, Jesus was viewed by His followers as a mortal prophet . . . a great and powerful man, but a man nonetheless. A mortal.
>
> . . . Many scholars claim that the early Church literally *stole* Jesus from His original followers, hijacking His human message, shrouding it in an impenetrable cloak of divinity, and using it to expand their own power.
>
> The vast majority of educated Christians know the history of their faith. Jesus was indeed a great and powerful man. Constantine's underhanded political maneuvers don't diminish the majesty of Christ's life. Nobody is saying Christ was a fraud, or denying that He walked the earth and inspired millions to better lives . . . [but] Constantine upgraded Jesus' status almost four centuries *after* Jesus' death.[4]

Although most people are smart enough not to take their theological education from a novel or a summer movie, the views espoused in *The Da Vinci Code* have found a wide following among

---

[4]    Dan Brown, *The Da Vinci Code* (New York: Doubleday, 2003), 231–34.

North Americans, even many Christians. The popular belief is that Jesus was a great man, a prophet, a revolutionary world-changer, but *not* God in the flesh. Jesus was a lot of wonderful things and made a huge difference, but he is most certainly not who the Christian church historically has claimed him to be.

*The Da Vinci Code* raises the question, is there any reason to accept traditional Christian beliefs about Jesus? I hope to show that there is, in fact, good reason to accept two central claims: (1) Jesus thought of himself as being a God-man, God in the flesh, and (2) his self-understanding was accurate. We will look at two sets of data in pursuit of my conclusions: (1) titles or designations applied to Jesus by himself and by others that point to a divine self-understanding and (2) things that Jesus does that demonstrate divine status.

As I walk through the two sets of data in pursuit of the two central claims, we will be relying on the New Testament Gospels. That might seem unfair or prejudicial to some: How can I use the Bible to support my claim that Christianity's central claims (about Jesus of Nazareth) are true?

In response, I suggest you keep three things in mind. First, this is not step 1 of eating an elephant. In Chapter 7, I presented several reasons to trust the textual integrity and historical reliability of the New Testament, particularly the Gospels. If successful, I showed that we can indeed "trust the story" contained in the Gospels.

Second, the majority of Gospel passages I use to build my case in this chapter are accepted as authentic (historical) by virtually all scholars. That is, even those who do not believe Christianity is true nonetheless accept that most of what I present here provides an accurate historical picture of what Jesus (and others) said and did.

Third, I will not be using the New Testament Gospels with any sort of understanding or expectation that they are divinely inspired texts. Rather, I will be treating them as historical documents that tell us about what was said and done by specific people at a particular point in time. What we will see, I hope, is that these historically reliable narratives of Jesus's life and times provide strong reason to conclude that he was, in fact, God in the flesh.

## Jesus's Titles

Let us look first at how Jesus was understood and referred to, by himself and by others. What terms and titles did he use for himself? How did other people refer to him? There are three titles commonly used of Jesus in the Gospels.

### *Christ*

The first title used of Jesus, and the one most familiar to us, is the Greek *Christ* (*Christos*) derived from the Hebrew *Messiah* (*maschiach*). The title Messiah or Christ is not an explicitly divine title; rather, it is the acknowledgment of a divine anointing. In the Old Testament, King David (among others) was referred to as Messiah, the anointed of the Lord.

As Jewish history progressed, however, *Messiah* became a more technical designation for the anointed of the Lord who was expected to come to redeem or rescue Israel from oppression and bondage. During and after Jesus's life, Christ quickly became the most popular title for Jesus, such that from Paul's New Testament letters through to today's Christianity, Christ effectively serves as a surname for Jesus. This title for Jesus is affirmed throughout the Gospels. We will look at just three examples.

First, in Matt 16:16, the disciple Peter professes that Jesus is "the Christ, the Son of the living God." Jesus responds by affirming Peter's response: "Blessed are you, Simon son of Jonah, for this was not revealed to you by man, but by my Father in heaven." In other words, "Yes, Peter, you get it. I *am* the Messiah, the Christ."

Second, in Luke 7, John the Baptist begins to wonder whether Jesus is who John had thought him to be (namely, the Messiah). So John sends his own disciples to Jesus to ask, "Are you the one who was to come, or should we expect someone else?" (v. 20) In Luke 7:21–23, we find Jesus's reply:

> At that very time Jesus cured many who had diseases, sicknesses and evil spirits, and gave sight to many who were blind. So he replied to the messengers, "Go back and report to John what you have seen and heard: The blind receive sight, the lame walk, those who have leprosy are cured, the deaf hear, the dead are raised, and the good news is preached to the poor. Blessed is the man who does not fall away on account of me."

Jesus's reply, calling attention to the deeds he has been performing, hearkens back to Isa 35:5–6[5] and Isa 61:1,[6] which first-century Jews regarded as messianic promises. The words from Isaiah's messianic prophecies are echoed in the words Jesus uses to reply to John's disciples. "Yes, I am the Messiah. See how my ministry fulfills what was promised through the prophet Isaiah?" Jesus doesn't have to come right out and say it; the allusions to Isaiah are sufficient implicit affirmation of his messianic identity.

---

[5]   Isaiah 35:5–6 reads, "Then will the eyes of the blind be opened and the ears of the deaf unstopped. Then will the lame leap like a deer, and the mute tongue shout for joy. Water will gush forth in the wilderness and streams in the desert."

[6]   Isaiah 61:1 reads, "The Spirit of the Sovereign LORD is on me, because the LORD has anointed me to proclaim good news to the poor. He has sent me to bind up the brokenhearted, to proclaim freedom for the captives and release from darkness for the prisoners."

Third, Jesus's messianic self-understanding is confirmed by his crucifixion. When the Roman governor Pontius Pilate assented to Jesus's execution, he had to write the charges against Jesus on a placard at the cross. What were the official charges? Mark 15:26 reads, "The written notice of the charge against him read: THE KING OF THE JEWS." This, "the King of the Jews," was a title used by Jews for the expected Messiah. As J. D. G. Dunn points out, Jesus was executed "on the charge of being a messianic pretender."[7] That is, Jesus was executed because he claimed to be the Messiah, the coming redeemer of Israel, bringing a charge of treason, punishable by death. Note that it is not just Jesus who thinks that Jesus is the Messiah. The Romans, who crucify Jesus, also identify him as the one claiming to be the Messiah of Israel.

### Son of God

The second title used of Jesus in the Gospels is "Son of God." Today Son of God is understood as being an explicit claim to Godhood, but this was not the case in the first century. Claiming to be the Son of God did not automatically mean that Jesus was claiming to be God in the flesh. However, the term does claim for Jesus a unique intimate relationship and connection with God. Let us look, once again, at three representative passages.

First, in Matt 11:25–27, Jesus explicitly claims to be the Son.

> At that time Jesus said, "I praise you, Father, Lord of heaven and earth, because you have hidden these things from the wise and learned, and revealed them to little children. Yes, Father, for this was your good pleasure.

---

[7] James D. G. Dunn, *Jesus Remembered: Christianity in the Making*, vol. 1 (Grand Rapids: Eerdmans, 2003), 86.

All things have been committed to me by my Father. No
one knows the Son except the Father, and no one knows
the Father except the Son and those to whom the Son
chooses to reveal him.

These are strong words, in which Jesus claims a unique father-
son relationship with the God of Israel.

Second, in Mark 12:1–12, the parable of the wicked tenants,
Jesus implicitly identifies himself as the Son of the Creator, Yahweh, the God of Israel. Jesus tells the story of a man who planted a
vineyard (Israel was often pictured as God's vineyard, intended to
flourish and be fruitful) and then rented it out to some tenants (the
Israelites). The tenants, however, were wicked and rejected the servants (the prophets) that the vineyard owner would send to collect
his share of the crops (the fruit God expected of Israel, particularly
the blessing of the nations). Finally, Mark 12:6 recounts, "He had
one left to send, a son, whom he loved. He sent him last of all, saying, 'They will respect my son.'" Instead, the tenants beat and killed
the son. Jesus concludes the parable, in verses 9–10: "What then
will the owner of the vineyard do? He will come and kill those tenants and give the vineyard to others. Haven't you read this scripture:
'The stone the builders rejected has become the capstone; the Lord
has done this, and it is marvelous in our eyes'?"

Jesus is identifying himself as the son of the vineyard owner.
The tenants (the Jewish leaders) are going to beat and kill him. The
owner (God) will respond by killing those tenants (the Jewish leaders, foreshadowing the devastation of Jerusalem and the destruction
of the temple in AD 70) and giving the vineyard to others (foreshadowing the mission to the Gentiles). How do the Jewish leaders
respond to this parable? They clearly understand Jesus, as shown in

verse 12: "Then they looked for a way to arrest him because they knew he had spoken the parable against them."

Third, Jesus makes intimate claims to sonship in his "Abba" prayers: "Going a little farther, Jesus fell to the ground and prayed that if possible the hour might pass from him. '*Abba*, Father,' he said, 'everything is possible for you. Take this cup from me. Yet not what I will, but what you will'" (Mark 14:35–36).

In his prayers, Jesus regularly refers to God as Father. Such familial intimacy with God was unexpected in Judaism. God was Lord, Yahweh, sovereign of the universe. A self-respecting Jew would find it quite presumptuous to call God "Father." They would refer to Abraham as Father—or Jacob or even Moses. But to call God "Father" was to demonstrate spiritual arrogance and pride. Jesus, however, was comfortable praying to his Father in heaven and even encouraged his followers to do the same.[8] Both implicitly and explicitly, then, Jesus identifies himself as the Son of God, one standing in a unique, intimate relationship to Yahweh, the God of Israel.

### Son of Man

Although Messiah or Christ is the most popular title for Jesus today, and while Son of God carries (to our ears) the strongest claims to deity, I think the most important Gospel term used for Jesus is Son of Man. First, it was Jesus's favorite self-designation. For example, in Matt 16:13, in the passage leading to Peter's profession of Jesus as "the Christ, the Son of the living God," Jesus asks his disciples, "Who do people say the Son of Man is?" Jesus uses the term about

---

8    Thus, the beginning of the Lord's Prayer in Matthew 6:9: "This, then, is how you should pray: 'Our Father in heaven, hallowed be your name.'"

seventy-eight times[9] in the Gospels with reference to himself. It is interesting as well that although Son of Man is Jesus's favorite self-designation, it is only used *one time* by someone else—Stephen in Acts 7:56 as he is about to be condemned to death by the Jewish leaders in Jerusalem. In other words, Son of Man is what Jesus, and only Jesus, used regularly to describe or identify himself.

Second, Son of Man carried very strong divine connotations in first-century Palestine. Jesus's self-designation of "the Son of Man" is distinct from the generic "son of man" (without the definite article) in Ezekiel. The Son of Man (with definite article) is, to my knowledge, unknown in Aramaic (the common language of most first-century Jews) and occurs only once in first-century Hebrew (DSS 1QS 10.20). With the attached definite article (*the* Son of Man), which Jesus uses consistently throughout the Gospels, reference is given explicitly to Daniel 7.

Daniel 7:13–14 recounts a heavenly vision granted to the prophet Daniel.

> In my vision at night I looked, and there before me was
> one like a son of man, coming with the clouds of heaven.
> He approached the Ancient of Days and was led into his
> presence. He was given authority, glory and sovereign
> power; all peoples, nations and men of every language
> worshiped him. His dominion is an everlasting dominion
> that will not pass away, and his kingdom is one that will
> never be destroyed.

Daniel's Son of Man is a human-looking figure but is endowed with divine attributes. Who, according to Hebrew theology, dwelt

---

9   Give or take a few; this is based on my count, and it's entirely possible that I missed (or double-counted) a few.

among the clouds of heaven? Who was the Ancient of Days? Who alone possessed glory and sovereign power? Who alone was rightly to be worshiped by "men of every language"? Who alone has an everlasting dominion? Who alone heads a kingdom that will never be destroyed? The Lord God, the God of Israel. And yet in Daniel's night vision, this obscure Son of Man figure appears coming on the clouds of heaven (the understood dwelling place of God), approaches God (who is unapproachable by sinful humanity), and is given authority, glory, power, and dominion (which belong solely to the Lord God). Finally, this Son of Man is worshiped by all tribes and nations—a treatment only appropriate for God. So the title that Jesus chooses to use of himself most frequently is this somewhat obscure, but very pregnant term dripping with divine connotations.

### Mark 14:60–64
During Jesus's trial with the Jewish Sanhedrin, we see this fascinating and crucial exchange.

> Then the high priest stood up before them and asked Jesus, "Are you not going to answer? What is this testimony that these men are bringing against you?" But Jesus remained silent and gave no answer.

> Again the high priest asked him, "Are you the Christ, the Son of the Blessed One?"

> "I am," said Jesus. "And you will see the Son of Man sitting at the right hand of the Mighty One and coming on the clouds of heaven."

The high priest tore his clothes. "Why do we need any more witnesses?" he asked. "You have heard the blasphemy. What do you think?" They all condemned him as worthy of death. (Mark 14:60–64)

In this central confrontation, Jesus conflates all three titles. "Are you the Christ, the Messiah, the long-expected anointed one of God?" "Yes, I am." "Are you the Son of the Blessed One, the Son of God?" "Yes, I am. Not only that, but I am also the Son of Man." For good measure, Jesus adds that he will be "sitting at the right hand of the Mighty One and coming on the clouds of heaven." I have to think that in first-century Judaism, it does not get any clearer than that. Jesus answers the high priest's questions with an emphatic declaration of who he thinks he is: "I am God!" The high priest's response is, thus, entirely appropriate. If Jesus is *not in fact God*, then he has uttered blasphemy and deserves death under Jewish law.

Did Jesus understand himself to be divine, to be God incarnate? The titles that are used of Jesus, and particularly the way that Jesus talks about his own identity, suggest that, yes, Jesus understood himself to be the unique incarnation of almighty God. The attempts of skeptical scholars (and *The Da Vinci Code*) to argue otherwise fail to account for passages such as Mark 14. Jesus was crucified for being a blasphemer, a messianic pretender. Jesus claimed to be the Messiah, the Son of God, and the divine Son of Man.

But we do not just have Jesus's self-understanding and self-designations to go on. Jesus also assumed divine authority and status through his works, his actions.

219

## Jesus's Actions

With Jesus's titles and self-designations, I believe we have a clear claim to divine status and identity. But with Jesus's actions, we have further claims to divine identity. Furthermore, with *some of* his deeds, we have not only a claim to divine status, but also an ability to *test* his claims. Although examples could be multiplied, I want to look at four areas where Jesus claims to possess authority that belongs properly to God alone; in two of these areas, he then backs up his claims with actions that demonstrate his divine authority.

### *Authority to Forgive Sin*

First, Jesus takes upon himself the right to forgive sin. My favorite example of this claim comes from the powerful and entertaining story in Mark 2:1–12.

> A few days later, when Jesus again entered Capernaum, the people heard that he had come home. So many gathered that there was no room left, not even outside the door, and he preached the word to them. Some men came, bringing to him a paralytic, carried by four of them. Since they could not get him to Jesus because of the crowd, they made an opening in the roof above Jesus and, after digging through it, lowered the mat the paralyzed man was lying on. When Jesus saw their faith, he said to the paralytic, "Son, your sins are forgiven."
>
> Now some teachers of the law were sitting there, thinking to themselves, "Why does this fellow talk like that? He's blaspheming! Who can forgive sins but God alone?" (Mark 2:1–7)

Who has the right to forgive sins? According to Jewish law and theology, only God has the ability and authority to forgive sin; according to the teachers of the law, God forgives sin only through the sacrificial system. The teachers of the law are effectively asking, "Who does this Jesus fellow think he is?!" Jesus is claiming for himself the divine authority to bypass the temple system altogether and forgive sins himself, in his own name and by his own word. The passage continues:

> Immediately Jesus knew in his spirit that this was what
> they were thinking in their hearts, and he said to them,
> "Why are you thinking these things? Which is easier: to
> say to the paralytic, 'Your sins are forgiven,' or to say,
> 'Get up, take your mat and walk'? But that you may know
> that the Son of Man has authority on earth to forgive
> sins . . ." He said to the paralytic, "I tell you, get up, take
> your mat and go home." He got up, took his mat and
> walked out in full view of them all. This amazed every-
> one and they praised God, saying, "We have never seen
> anything like this!" (Mark 2:8–12)

Jesus claimed divine authority for himself and then acted on it. I love the cheekiness of his question: "Which is easier: to say to the paralytic, 'Your sins are forgiven,' or to say, 'Get up, take your mat and walk'?" I've actually tested Jesus's question here: it is easy to say either phrase! But Jesus's point, the thrust behind the question, is that it is "easier" to say, "Your sins are forgiven," because *nobody can check up on the claim*! That is, there is no way (right here, right now) for you or me to figure out whether what Jesus declared ("your sins are forgiven") has actually happened. If there is such a thing as sin and such a thing as forgiveness, then forgiveness

221

for sin occurring would seem to be the kind of thing that only God could know.

But the command "Get up, take your mat and walk"—now *there's* a claim that can be checked! Jesus tells the man who cannot walk to get up and walk. The thing that Jesus declares (effectively, the man's physical healing) either happens or it does not happen: and all the assembled witnesses will see Jesus's words either being fulfilled or not.

Jesus then ties the man's healing to his own authority as (did you note his self-designation?) the Son of Man to forgive sins. Jesus is claiming divine authority to forgive sins and vindicating that claim by demonstrating his divine *approval* through physical healing. The implicit question he asks is, would God heal through a blasphemer? If Jesus is falsely claiming to be God in the flesh, would almighty God allow divine healings to occur by his (Jesus's) word? The answer to the rhetorical question is no! So Jesus is claiming that his divine claim to forgive sin is proven true by the physical healing of the paralytic.

### Authority to Determine People's Eternal Destiny
Jesus claims authority to forgive sin, but even more astounding, he claims the authority and right to determine people's eternal destiny. Let's consider two illustrative passages.

> [Jesus said,] "I tell you, whoever acknowledges me
> before men, the Son of Man will also acknowledge him
> before the angels of God. But he who disowns me before
> men will be disowned before the angels of God." (Luke
> 12:8–9)

222

Jesus claims in Luke 12 that he, the Son of Man, will have the authority to determine who is able to stand (and survive) in the presence of almighty God after their death. The person who follows Jesus faithfully in this life will be judged worthy after death to stand before God; the person who rejects Jesus in this life will be rejected by God in the afterlife.

> Then came the Feast of Dedication at Jerusalem. It was winter, and Jesus was in the temple area walking in Solomon's Colonnade. The Jews gathered around him, saying, "How long will you keep us in suspense? If you are the Christ, tell us plainly."

> Jesus answered, "I did tell you, but you do not believe. The miracles I do in my Father's name speak for me, but you do not believe because you are not my sheep. My sheep listen to my voice; I know them, and they follow me. I give them eternal life, and they shall never perish; no one can snatch them out of my hand." (John 10:24–28)

A lot is packed into this brief passage. Jesus's audience is curious about his identity; they want to know if he is the long-awaited Messiah. Jesus professes to have answered their question as to his identity clearly, through both his words and his deeds. For our purposes right now, his final two sentences pack the punch. "My sheep listen to my voice; I know them, and they follow me." As in Luke 12, the focus here is on being a faithful follower of Jesus—hearing and heeding his voice.

Then comes the kicker: "I give them eternal life, and they shall never perish." For a first-century Jew who affirms resurrection and life after death, who is the one who both promises and delivers that eternal life? The clear answer, again, is Yahweh—the Lord, the God of Israel. But Jesus declares that it is he himself who gives his followers eternal life. This is a clear claim to possession of divine authority to determine people's eternal destiny.[10]

### Authority to Teach Divine Truth in His Own Name

In another astounding claim, at least to the Jews of the first century, Jesus professes the authority to teach divine truth in his own name. The best demonstration of this is found in the Sermon on the Mount, Matthew chapters 5–7. In Matt 5:17, Jesus insists, "Do not think that I have come to abolish the Law or the Prophets; I have not come to abolish them, but to fulfill them." In other words, Jesus claims to be the fulfillment of the Old Testament.

Then, beginning in 5:21, we find a series of six hard teachings. Each time, Jesus begins, "You have heard that it was said," and continues by claiming, "But I tell you." Jesus takes either an Old Testament law or a rabbinical interpretation of an Old Testament law and turns it upside down. He deepens the teachings and challenges the interpretations of the Pharisees. And he does it on his own authority! Thus, at the end of the Sermon on the Mount, we read, "When Jesus had finished saying these things, the crowds were amazed at his teaching, because he taught as one who had authority, and not as their teachers of the law" (Matt 7:28–29).

Jesus takes upon himself the teaching and guiding authority of God Almighty. In the same way, Jesus uses the formula "Amen,

---

[10]  I could also point to numerous verses that tie people's eternal judgment directly to Jesus. For example, John 3:16, one of the best-known verses in the New Testament: "For God so loved the world that he gave his one and only Son, that whoever believes in him shall not perish but have eternal life." John 3:16 does not explicitly state that Jesus directly determines who will receive eternal life (Luke 12 and John 10 both do state that explicitly), but it nonetheless does state that one's eternity is determined based on one's faith in Jesus.

amen," "I tell you the truth" (NIV) or "Truly, truly I say to you" (NAS) to introduce his divine teaching authority. This formula is used twenty-five times in John's Gospel and shows that Jesus is not merely speaking *for* God, but is speaking *as* God. William Lane Craig notes:

> Jesus thus equated his own authority with that of the
> divinely given Torah . . . But it's not just that Jesus placed
> his personal authority on a par with that of the divine Law.
> More than that, he adjusted the Law on his own authority.[11]

A "good Jewish rabbi" would teach in accordance with a long line of Jewish rabbinic tradition. So a Jewish scholar might argue, for example, "The rabbi Gamaliel said that the rabbi Hezekiah said, that the rabbi Ananias said, that the rabbi Joshua said, that the prophets have said. . . ." In such a fashion, the tradition and authority of their forefathers would come to bear in the present teaching. Jesus goes around all such claims to traditional authority and instead takes upon himself the teaching and guiding authority of God Almighty. Thus, as Ben Witherington says,

> It is insufficient to compare it to "thus says the Lord". . . .
> Jesus is not merely speaking for Yahweh, but for himself
> and on his own authority. . . . This strongly suggests that
> he considered himself to be a person of authority above
> and beyond what prophets claimed to be. He could attest
> to his own truthfulness and speak on his own behalf, and
> yet his words were to be taken as having the same or
> greater authority than the divine words of the prophets.

---

[11]   Craig, *Reasonable Faith*, 320 (see chap. 4, n. 4).

> Here was someone who thought he possessed not only
> divine inspiration . . . but also divine authority and the
> power of direct divine utterance.[12]

Note that conclusion: "Here was someone who thought he possessed divine authority and the power of direct divine utterance." Once again, if Jesus was *not* in fact divine, if he was not God in the flesh, then this sort of self-understanding would be the height of blasphemous self-delusion. The question then is, who really *was* Jesus? Was he in fact divine?

### Authority to Heal and Exorcise

Throughout the Gospels, we also see Jesus claiming authority over sickness, disease, and afflictions caused by evil spirits. Once again, first-century Jews would have understood that only God has the ability and authority to directly heal the body and exorcise demons; hence, Jesus is presuming divine authority to perform miraculous healings and exorcisms. Let's look briefly at six representative examples.

> *Healing leprosy.* While Jesus was in one of the towns,
> a man came along who was covered with leprosy. When
> he saw Jesus, he fell with his face to the ground and
> begged him, "Lord, if you are willing, you can make me
> clean."

---

[12]   Ben Witherington III, *The Christology of Jesus* (Minneapolis: Fortress, 1991), 188; cited in Craig, *Reasonable Faith*, 321 (see chap. 4, n. 4).

Jesus reached out his hand and touched the man. "I am willing," he said. "Be clean!" And immediately the leprosy left him. (Luke 5:12–13)

Leprosy was a name for a family of skin diseases, most of them contagious and all necessitating isolation from the rest of the community (including one's own family). In the first century, leprosy could not be cured through medical means (though thankfully we do have such means today). So lepers could only be healed, it was understood, by a direct act of God. Here in Luke 5, Jesus declares the man clean by his own word ("Be clean"), implicitly claiming divine authority. Furthermore, the man's immediate healing is a demonstration that Jesus truly possesses the divine authority that he professes. The words are shown true by the results.

***Curing blindness.*** As he went along, he saw a man blind from birth. His disciples asked him, "Rabbi, who sinned, this man or his parents, that he was born blind?"

"Neither this man nor his parents sinned," said Jesus, "but this happened so that the works of God might be displayed in his life. . . ."

Having said this, he spit on the ground, made some mud with the saliva, and put it on the man's eyes. "Go," he told him, "wash in the Pool of Siloam" (this word means Sent). So the man went and washed, and came home seeing. (John 9:1–3, 6–7)

Here is a man born blind, a condition that again was far beyond the powers of ancient medicine to rectify. Some enterprising modern skeptics suggest that perhaps Jesus was just a supersmart doctor who carried around powerful healing remedies. When faced with illnesses that were beyond the ability of his contemporaries to heal, Jesus would break out his secret stash of prescription meds to restore the person to health. The claim is pretty outrageous and entirely unevidenced. Furthermore, if the claim were true, it would make Jesus out to be not only the smartest and most advanced ancient scientist or doctor, but also the most evil! After all, Jesus would have had at hand the remedy to all sorts of illnesses and diseases, but he was refusing to share those remedies with anybody else.

But, to return to the story, the healing of the blind man in John 9 affirms Jesus's power of divine healing.

***Casting out the impure spirit.*** Mark 9:14–29 depicts a lengthy scene of Jesus delivering a boy from the torment of an unclean spirit or demon. We will pick up the story in verse 20:

> When the spirit saw Jesus, it immediately threw the boy into a convulsion. He fell to the ground and rolled around, foaming at the mouth.

> Jesus asked the boy's father, "How long has he been like this?"

> "From childhood," he answered. "It has often thrown him into fire or water to kill him. But if you can do anything, take pity on us and help us."

> "'If you can?'" said Jesus. "Everything is possible for one who believes."

Immediately the boy's father exclaimed, "I do believe; help me overcome my unbelief!"

When Jesus saw that a crowd was running to the scene, he rebuked the evil spirit. "You deaf and mute spirit," he said, "I command you, come out of him and never enter him again."

The spirit shrieked, convulsed him violently and came out. The boy looked so much like a corpse that many said, "He's dead." But Jesus took him by the hand and lifted him to his feet, and he stood up. (Mark 9:20–27)

In verse 23, Jesus delivers a mild rebuke to the boy's father, who seems to be subtly questioning whether even Jesus, a renowned healer and exorcist, can do anything to help his afflicted child. Jesus then demonstrates his divine authority over evil spirits by casting out the evil spirit with a simple command issued in his own name. Once again, his exalted claim is vindicated by the outcome.

***Long-distance healing.*** Once more he visited Cana in Galilee, where he had turned the water into wine. And there was a certain royal official whose son lay sick at Capernaum. When this man heard that Jesus had arrived in Galilee from Judea, he went to him and begged him to come and heal his son, who was close to death.

"Unless you people see miraculous signs and wonders," Jesus told him, "you will never believe."

The royal official said, "Sir, come down before my child dies."

Jesus replied, "You may go. Your son will live."

The man took Jesus at his word and departed. While he was still on the way, his servants met him with the news that his boy was living. When he inquired as to the time when his son got better, they said to him, "The fever left him yesterday at the seventh hour."

Then the father realized that this was the exact time at which Jesus had said to him, "Your son will live." So he and his whole household believed. (John 4:46–53)

When Jesus heals people in the Gospels, he typically includes a compassionate physical touch, often making himself ritually unclean by coming into direct contact with the sick person. But here in John 4 (and in similar or parallel passages in Luke 7:1–10 and Matt 8:5–13), Jesus makes it clear that he does not need to touch someone to heal them. In fact, he need not even be in the person's physical proximity. He can also heal a person with a word at a distance.

*Making many well.* As soon as they left the synagogue, they went with James and John to the home of Simon and Andrew. Simon's mother-in-law was in bed with a fever, and they told Jesus about her. So he went to her, took her hand and helped her up. The fever left her and she began to wait on them.

That evening after sunset the people brought to Jesus all
the sick and demon-possessed. The whole town gathered at the door, and Jesus healed many who had various
diseases. He also drove out many demons, but he would
not let the demons speak because they knew who he was.
(Mark 1:29–34)

In Mark 1, Jesus begins by healing their hostess of a fever and then
proceeds to demonstrate his compassion by healing a variety of "sick"
and "demon-possessed" people from the town. None of the illnesses
is mentioned by name, except the fever that had struck Peter's mother-in-law. Mark's point here is broader: Jesus has authority to heal a
variety of sicknesses in his own name.

***Raising the dead.*** When I was young, my mother claimed that
I was loud enough to raise the dead. I don't think she was under
the impression that I had the ability to resurrect our deceased loved
ones; she was just trying to get me to produce less of a ruckus. Jesus,
however, both claims and demonstrates the authority to raise those
who are physically dead.

The Gospels present us with three occasions on which Jesus
raises the dead. The most famous is the raising of Lazarus in John
11:1–44. We will look at the final seven verses of the passage.

Jesus, once more deeply moved, came to the tomb. It was
a cave with a stone laid across the entrance. "Take away
the stone," he said.

"But, Lord," said Martha, the sister of the dead man, "by
this time there is a bad odor, for he has been there four
days."

231

Then Jesus said, "Did I not tell you that if you believed, you would see the glory of God?"

So they took away the stone. Then Jesus looked up and said, "Father, I thank you that you have heard me. I knew that you always hear me, but I said this for the benefit of the people standing here, that they may believe that you sent me."

When he had said this, Jesus called in a loud voice, "Lazarus, come out!" The dead man came out, his hands and feet wrapped with strips of linen, and a cloth around his face.

Jesus said to them, "Take off the grave clothes and let him go." (John 11:38–44)

Lazarus has been dead for three full days by the time Jesus comes on the scene in Bethany. Yet Jesus affirms that he is "the resurrection and the life" and that "whoever lives and believes in me will never die" (John 11:25–26). Along with his earlier claim to have the authority to determine our eternal fate, Jesus now claims and demonstrates his power over death itself![13]

---

[13] A second prominent raising occurs in Mark 5:21–24, 35–42. Jesus is approached by a synagogue leader, Jairus, whose daughter is close to the point of death. After a brief interruption, Jesus and Jairus approach his house. Then we read, "Some people came from the house of Jairus, the synagogue leader. 'Your daughter is dead,' they said. 'Why bother the teacher anymore?' Ignoring what they said, Jesus told the synagogue leader, 'Don't be afraid; just believe.' He did not let anyone follow him except Peter, James, and John the brother of James. When they came to the home of the synagogue leader, Jesus saw a commotion, with people crying and wailing loudly. He went in and said to them, 'Why all this commotion and wailing? The child is not dead but asleep.' But they laughed at him. After he put them all out, he took the

In summary, Jesus shows his authority and ability to heal leprosy, blindness, demon possession, distant sickness, various illnesses (including fever), and even death.

### Jesus's Cumulative Authority

I suspect that it is wrong to do so, but I have a favorite book in the Bible. The Gospel of Matthew has always been my favorite! Earlier in this chapter, I noted that Jesus claims the authority to teach divine truth in his own name. I think that the Sermon on the Mount, Matthew 5–7, is the best example of Jesus's claiming to reveal divine truth. In Matthew 5–7, then, Jesus seems to be claiming this unique divine authority for himself. Strikingly, but mathematically not surprisingly, Matthew 5–7 is followed immediately by Matthew 8–9, which contains a beautiful cumulative description of the all-encompassing authority of Jesus.

In Matthew 8–9, Jesus demonstrates his authority over many things:

1. Leprosy (disease): in 8:1–4, Jesus heals a leprous man with a compassionate touch and a word.
2. Distance (sickness): in 8:5–13, Jesus heals the centurion's paralyzed servant without coming to his house.
3. Multiple illnesses: in 8:14–17, Jesus heals Peter's mother-in-law of a fever and heals many others as well.

---

child's father and mother and the disciples who were with him, and went in where the child was. He took her by the hand and said to her, 'Talitha koum!' (which means 'Little girl, I say to you, get up!'). Immediately the girl stood up and began to walk around (she was twelve years old). At this they were completely astonished" (Mark 5:35–42).

4. Nature (storms): in 8:23–27, Jesus awakens to a furious storm on the lake and calms the winds and the waves with a word.

5. Demons (evil spirits): in 8:28–34, Jesus casts demons out of two demon-possessed men.

6. Sin (and physical paralysis): in 9:1–8, Jesus announces forgiveness of sin for the paralyzed man and then heals his broken body.

7. Death (and chronic bleeding): in 9:18–26, Jesus raises the dead daughter of a synagogue ruler back to life; in the middle of the passage, he also heals a woman stricken with chronic bleeding.

8. Blindness and muteness: in 9:27–34, Jesus cures a man of blindness and enables a mute man to speak.

Note the beauty of Matthew's structure. He spends three chapters (5–7) showing us Jesus's words and how he claims divine standing and teaches divine truth. He then immediately spends two chapters (8–9) showing us Jesus's actions and how he confirms his divine authority and identity with powerful deeds.

## Conclusion: Liar, Lunatic, or Lord?

When you put together what Jesus says about himself and what he does, you are left with the unmistakable impression that he thought he possessed divine authority and that his actions backed up his claims. Years ago, these facts led C. S. Lewis to pose his famous trilemma about the person of Jesus Christ.

A man who was merely a man and said the sort of things Jesus said would not be a great moral teacher. He would

either be a lunatic—on a level with the man who says he
is a poached egg—or else he would be the Devil of Hell.
You must make your choice. Either this man was, and is,
the Son of God, or else a madman or something worse.
You can shut Him up for a fool, you can spit at Him and
kill Him as a demon; or you can fall at His feet and call
Him Lord and God. But let us not come with any patron-
izing nonsense about His being a great human teacher. He
has not left that open to us. He did not intend to.[14]

We began this chapter asking, who is Jesus? Christianity claims
that Jesus is God in the flesh, and I have tried to provide reasons
to believe that Jesus indeed both claimed and demonstrated that he
possessed divine authority and identity.

In an interview with Michka Assayas, Bono, lead singer of the
band U2, was asked about his Christian faith: "Christ has his rank
among the world's great thinkers. But Son of God, isn't that farfetched?" Bono had this to say in response:

Look, the secular response to the Christ story always
goes like this: He was a great prophet, obviously a very
interesting guy, had a lot to say along the lines of other
great prophets, be they Elijah, Muhammad, Buddha, or
Confucius. But actually Christ doesn't allow you that.
He doesn't let you off that hook. Christ says, No. I'm not
saying I'm a teacher, don't call me teacher. I'm not saying
I'm a prophet. I'm saying: "I'm the Messiah." I'm saying:
"I am God incarnate" . . . . So what you're left with is
either Christ was who He said He was—the Messiah—or

---

[14]    Lewis, *Mere Christianity*, 52 (see chap. 5, n. 12).

a complete nutcase. . . . The idea that the entire course of
civilization for over half of the globe could have its fate
changed and turned upside-down by a nutcase, for me
that's farfetched.[15]

This is who the historical record in the Gospels presents to us
clearly and consistently: Jesus the Messiah, the Son of God, the Son
of Man. Jesus, who has the authority to forgive sin, who will determine our eternal destinies, who has the authority to teach divine
truths in his own name, who has the ability to heal sickness in his
own name.

The Jesus presented by the historical record is a Jesus who talks
and acts like one who believes he is, and is in fact, God in the flesh.
Jesus shows himself to be the Christ, the divine Son of God. We
have seen good reason for thinking that Jesus is the God-man whom
Christianity claims.

But perhaps a skeptic could argue that there is a fourth option:
instead of liar, lunatic, or Lord, maybe Jesus is a legend. This is the
approach of the *Da Vinci Code* and the Jesus Seminar. The original
Jesus was just a man, but the church deified him, miracle-ized him,
and even raised him from the dead.

Why is that *not* a serious historical option? Remember what
was shown in Chapter 7.

First, textual integrity: we can have confidence that the text we
have in our New Testament today is an accurate reflection of the
New Testament written by the original authors.

Second, historical reliability: we can have confidence that the
original authors were in the right time and place to record accurately
what Jesus said and did, and that they sought to do just that.

---

15    Michka Assayas, *Bono on Bono* (New York: Riverhead, 2005), 239.

When you combine textual integrity with historical reliability with the titles and actions of Jesus of Nazareth, you really are left with Lewis's trilemma: What are you going to do with this Jesus? Shut him up for a fool? Spit at him and kill him as a demon? Or fall at his feet and call him Lord and God?

## Recommended Resources for Further Exploration

Bowman, Robert M., Jr., and J. Ed Komoszewski. *Putting Jesus in His Place: The Case for the Deity of Christ.* Grand Rapids: Kregel, 2007.

Evans, C. Stephen. *The Historical Christ and the Jesus of Faith: The Incarnational Narrative as History.* Oxford: Oxford University Press, 1996.

Hurtado, Larry W. *How on Earth Did Jesus Become God? Historical Questions about Earliest Devotion to Jesus.* Grand Rapids: Eerdmans, 2005.

Pitre, Brant. *The Case for Jesus: The Biblical and Historical Evidence for Christ.* New York: Image, 2016.

Witherington, Ben, III. *The Christology of Jesus.* Minneapolis: Fortress, 1991.

# CHAPTER 9

## *The Fulcrum*

### Did Jesus Rise from the Dead?

The historic Christian faith, from its earliest recorded days, has been centered on the person and work of Jesus of Nazareth and has always included three fundamental beliefs about Jesus at its core: his deity, atoning death, and resurrection. In Chapter 8, we looked at reasons to believe that Jesus claimed to have the identity and authority of God, and backed up that claim with actions demonstrating his divine identity and authority. That claim is significant within Christianity, but it is not the most important.

Rather, the fulcrum of Christianity—that upon which the rest of the faith hinges—is the events of Easter weekend: Jesus's crucifixion on Good Friday and his resurrection on Easter Sunday. Christians believe Jesus died on a criminal's cross in Jerusalem but that his death was not just an ordinary execution. Rather, Christianity teaches that on the cross Jesus bore our sins and punishment: he suffered and died, as the New Testament puts it, "for our sins."

In this chapter, I will look at the Christian belief in Jesus's resurrection—the belief that on the third day Jesus was raised from the dead in a physical, bodily resurrection. I will first briefly consider why it matters whether Jesus was raised from the dead. Then we will examine the crucial question: are there good reasons to believe that Jesus actually was raised from the dead? I will present seven lines of evidence that together point to the conclusion that Jesus was in fact raised from the dead as Christians claim.

## Does the Resurrection Matter?

There are many things that individual Christians (and even Christians as a broad community) believe are relatively unimportant in the big scheme of things. For example, I believe that peanut butter is a delicious snack, that the earth revolves around the sun, and that the author of the New Testament Epistle of James is the half brother of Jesus of Nazareth. Those beliefs all play a role in my comprehensive worldview, but they could easily be adjusted or rejected without sacrificing my core Christian worldview. The same cannot be said for my belief in the resurrection of Jesus.

I call 1 Corinthians 15 the resurrection chapter. It has the longest sustained teaching and reflection on the resurrection of Jesus, and the first half of the chapter helps illuminate why the resurrection lies at the very center of the Christian faith.

> Now, brothers, I want to remind you of the gospel I
> preached to you, which you received and on which you
> have taken your stand. By this gospel you are saved, if
> you hold firmly to the word I preached to you. Otherwise,
> you have believed in vain.
>
> For what I received I passed on to you as of first impor-
> tance. (1 Cor 15:1–3)

I stop here for a moment to make sure we see what's going on. Paul is not reciting his own personal understanding of Christianity. Rather, the passage that follows, through to verse 8, is an ancient creed that far predates Paul's usage of it. Paul emphasizes this fact— what he *received* from others, he is now passing on to the Corinthian Christians. This is not Paul's statement of faith; the creed comes from the very early church, originating within five years of Jesus's death and resurrection.

> For what I received I passed on to you as of first impor-
> tance: that Christ died for our sins according to the
> Scriptures, that he was buried, that he was raised on the
> third day according to the Scriptures, and that he appeared
> to Peter, and then to the Twelve. After that, he appeared
> to more than five hundred of the brothers at the same
> time, most of whom are still living, though some have
> fallen asleep. Then he appeared to James, then to all the
> apostles, and last of all he appeared to me also, as to one
> abnormally born. (1 Cor 15:3–8)

This creedal passage emphasizes the central elements of early Christian belief. Note that the two focal points are Jesus's sacrificial death ("died for our sins") and Jesus's resurrection ("was raised"). The remaining elements of the creed recite appearances of the risen Jesus to various individuals and groups—effectively pieces of evidence to support resurrection faith. Paul then goes on to emphasize the importance of the resurrection.

> But if it is preached that Christ has been raised from the
> dead, how can some of you say that there is no resurrec-
> tion of the dead? If there is no resurrection of the dead,

then not even Christ has been raised. And if Christ has not been raised, our preaching is useless and so is your faith. More than that, we are then found to be false witnesses about God, for we have testified about God that he raised Christ from the dead. But he did not raise him if in fact the dead are not raised. For if the dead are not raised, then Christ has not been raised either. And if Christ has not been raised, your faith is futile, you are still in your sins. Then those also who have fallen asleep in Christ are lost. If only for this life we have hope in Christ, we are to be pitied more than all men. (1 Cor 15:12–19)

Paul teaches that the resurrection of Jesus Christ makes all the difference in the world, and he gives two primary reasons for it. First, Jesus's resurrection is the assurance of our own future resurrection to eternal life. If Jesus is not raised from the dead, then we have no hope for eternity either. If Jesus's death is "for our sins," and death is the final word for Jesus, then the sins of humanity will result in death being the final word for us as well. Hence the conclusion, "If only for this life we have hope in Christ, we are to be pitied more than all men." From a non-Christian perspective, Christians are laughably naive and foolish; they put their hope in pie in the sky by and by, when, in reality, after they die they will rot in the grave and be eaten by worms. If Jesus was not raised from the dead, then that is what really happens, and indeed we are to be pitied more than all men.

Second, if Jesus is not raised from the dead, then Christianity is exposed as a fraudulent, deceptive religion. After all, Paul says, "We have testified about God that he raised Christ from the dead" (1 Cor 15:15). If this did not happen, then Paul is a false witness, as are all the other apostles. Paul goes on, however, to insist:

But Christ has indeed been raised from the dead, the
firstfruits of those who have fallen asleep. For since death
came through a man, the resurrection of the dead comes
also through a man. For as in Adam all die, so in Christ all
will be made alive. (1 Cor 15:20–22)

Earlier, in verse 8, Paul insists that he *knows* that Christ has
been raised from the dead, because the resurrected Jesus Christ
appeared to Paul himself. Paul knows that Jesus is risen.

So this is the twofold Christian *claim*: that Jesus has been risen
from the dead, and that his resurrection makes all the difference in
the world. But the question remains: Is it true? Did Jesus really rise
from the dead? Are there good reasons to believe in the resurrection
as a historical occurrence?

## Did the Resurrection Happen?

I argue that there is strong historical evidence that supports the conclusion that God raised Jesus from the dead. I will present seven
pieces or lines of evidence that help establish the resurrection.
Before diving into that historical evidence, I need to respond to two
potential objections and make two preliminary points.

First, two potential objections. On the one hand, someone
might object to the very possibility of something like a resurrection
from the dead. After all, wouldn't Jesus's resurrection be a miracle? And aren't miracles impossible? This objection would render
evidence for Jesus's resurrection effectively irrelevant: it doesn't
matter how good or strong the evidence is if the supposed event
is an impossibility. In response, please note that an objection like
this is basically an excuse for narrow-mindedness. The person who
protests that miracles are impossible, and therefore any evidence for

the resurrection is irrelevant, has a close relative in the person who protests that biological evolution is impossible and therefore any evidence for evolution is irrelevant. Furthermore, even if we were to agree that miracles such as resurrection are impossible *given the ordinary working of the laws of nature*, it should be straightforward to recognize that if God exists, the ordinary working of the laws of nature do not exhaust the possibilities. In other words, if God exists (as I argued in chaps. 4–6), then miracles such as the resurrection are distinct possibilities.

On the other hand, someone might object to the way that I'm about to argue for the resurrection. Much of the historical evidence I will cite comes from passages in the New Testament (such as 1 Corinthians 15, which I have already quoted). Isn't that begging the question or assuming what I'm trying to prove? Isn't it unfair to use the Christian Bible to support the truth of Christian beliefs? In response, refer back to Chapter 7, where I argued that there are good reasons to conclude that the New Testament (in general and the Gospels in particular) is historically reliable in its broad and specific claims. The historical reliability of the New Testament does not automatically prove that Christianity is true, but it does mean that we can take historical claims made by New Testament authors very seriously.

Second, two preliminary points. On the one hand, I am not going to go in-depth into any of the evidence I will present. There is simply not enough time and space. I teach a semester-long course at Oklahoma Baptist University called Historiography, Miracles and the Resurrection, and even in that class we do not exhaust the materials![1]

---

[1]    Indeed, we do not even come close to exhausting the material. I assign three very large treatments of evidence related to Jesus's resurrection: Michael R. Licona, *The Resurrection of Jesus: A New Historiographical Approach* (Downers Grove, IL:

On the other hand, the argument that follows is adopted from Gary Habermas's "minimal facts" approach to the resurrection.[2] The minimal facts approach uses only facts and sources that are accepted by virtually all scholars who study this material. Thus, each of the historical and evidential lines of support for the resurrection that I mention here has extremely broad, nearly universal support among scholars. That is, more than 95 percent of all scholars who study in this area (ancient history and biblical studies) grant the truth of each piece of evidence that I present (with one exception, which I will note). This scholarly consensus includes non-Christian scholars who reject the truth of the resurrection. In other words, the level of support for these lines of evidence is astounding.

With those preliminary points in mind, let us consider seven pieces of evidence that together build a very strong historical case for the resurrection of Jesus of Nazareth.

## Jesus's Crucifixion and Death

First, Jesus was crucified by the Roman authorities at the instigation of the Jewish leadership in Jerusalem, and he died an agonizing death on a cross. Quite clearly, Jesus cannot be raised from the dead if he does not die in the first place; to argue for the resurrection, we

---

IVP Academic, 2010); N. T. Wright, *The Resurrection of the Son of God,* Christian Origins and the Question of God, vol. 3 (Minneapolis: Fortress, 2003); and Craig S. Keener, *Miracles: The Credibility of the New Testament Accounts*, 2 vols. (Grand Rapids: Baker Academic, 2011). Even the 2,500 combined pages of those magisterial works do not cover all the necessary contours of the conversation! There is always much more to say.

[2]   See, e.g., Gary R. Habermas, Th*e Risen Jesus and Future Hope* (Lanham, MD: Rowman & Littlefield, 2003); Gary R. Habermas and Michael R. Licona, *The Case for the Resurrection of Jesus* (Grand Rapids: Kregel, 2004). The broad contours of the following argument, along with many of the specific details, rely on Habermas and Licona's minimal facts presentation.

first need to have a dead man! The New Testament Gospels all record the death of Jesus Christ; other New Testament writings argue both for and from Jesus's death. Furthermore, Jesus's death is attested by numerous other ancient sources; the Jewish historian Josephus, the Roman historian Tacitus, the Greek satirist Lucian, and the Jewish Talmud all reference Jesus's death by crucifixion. With the exception of many Islamic scholars, and a couple of scholars who deny that Jesus of Nazareth even existed, every ancient historian accepts the general historical reliability of the Gospel accounts of Jesus's death. The first plank in a historical argument for the resurrection, then, is Jesus's crucifixion and death.

### Jesus's Burial

Presently we will discuss the empty tomb. Well, for a tomb to be found empty, it has to have been previously occupied. And so the second historical plank in our argument for the resurrection is that Jesus was buried in a tomb. If he is never buried, there is no tomb to be discovered empty. If he is buried, there is a tomb to check up on. For the burial of Jesus, we are dependent on the New Testament Gospels and 1 Corinthians (along with later Christian writings in the first and second centuries). But again, with respect to the burial of Jesus, scholars are almost unanimously agreed that there is no reason to doubt that it really happened.

### The Discovery of the Empty Tomb

Given the death and burial of Jesus, the other physical prerequisite to the resurrection is the discovery of the empty tomb. Of the seven planks in my argument, the empty tomb is the only one that does not qualify as a minimal fact. That is, there is not nearly unanimous agreement among biblical scholars and ancient historians on this fact. Nonetheless, more than two-thirds of critical scholars accept that the tomb Jesus was buried in on Good Friday was found empty on Easter Sunday. Although not nearly unanimous, this level of scholarly support is surprising given the importance of the empty tomb in arguments for the resurrection. Why ought we to believe that the tomb was, in fact, found empty on Easter Sunday?

On the one hand, the books of the New Testament all either explicitly state or implicitly presume that Jesus's tomb was found empty. Each Gospel has an account of the tomb being found empty.[3] But there are other reasons as well.

First, you have the reality that Jesus was crucified and buried in Jerusalem. If Christians began proclaiming the resurrection, and Jesus's tomb was *not* empty, then Christianity's opponents would have capitalized on that fact. As Habermas and Licona write,

> It would have been impossible for Christianity to get
> off the ground in Jerusalem if the body had still been in
> the tomb. [Jesus's] enemies in the Jewish leadership and
> Roman government would only have had to exhume the
> corpse and publicly display it for the hoax [of the resur-
> rection] to be shattered. Not only are Jewish, Roman, and
> all other writings absent of such an account, but there is
> a total silence from Christianity's critics who would have
> jumped at evidence of this sort.[4]

In other words, as soon as the disciples began preaching that Jesus was raised from the dead, their opponents would have leaped at any opportunity to produce Jesus's corpse, to debunk the resurrection claims. But they did not because they could not.

---

3  See Matt 28:1–15; Mark 16:1–8; Luke 24:1–12; John 20:1–18.
4  Habermas and Licona, *Case for the Resurrection*, 70.

Instead, opponents of Christianity acknowledged that the tomb was found empty and then accused the disciples of having stolen Jesus's body.

> While the women were on their way, some of the guards went into the city and reported to the chief priests everything that had happened. When the chief priests had met with the elders and devised a plan, they gave the soldiers a large sum of money, telling them, "You are to say, 'His disciples came during the night and stole him away while we were asleep.' If this report gets to the governor, we will satisfy him and keep you out of trouble." So the soldiers took the money and did as they were instructed. And this story has been widely circulated among the Jews to this very day. (Matt 28:11–15)

The second-century Christian writer Justin Martyr writes, in *Dialogue with Trypho*, that the Jews were still circulating the same rumor in AD 150 (more than a hundred years later)—that the disciples had stolen Jesus's body. In other words, even the enemies of Christianity acknowledged that Jesus's tomb was empty. They did not argue that Jesus hadn't been buried at all or that Jesus's body was still in a tomb somewhere. They admitted that the tomb was empty and accused the disciples of stealing the body.

### The Disciples Claim to Have Experiences of a Resurrected Jesus
The first three planks that support belief in Jesus's resurrection are physical pieces of evidence: Jesus's death, Jesus's burial, and the empty tomb. With our fourth plank, we transition to evidence that is more personal in nature: Jesus's disciples claim to have seen Jesus

after his crucifixion, death, and burial. He was no longer dead but alive and walking about in a resurrected body.

The ancient creed in 1 Corinthians 15 (which the ultraskeptical John Dominic Crossan argues originated less than two years after Jesus's death) narrates numerous experiences of the risen Jesus. The resurrection appearances of Jesus are not all at the same time or in the same place. Rather, they occur over the course of about forty days, in Jerusalem and Galilee. Some of the resurrection appearances are recorded elsewhere in the New Testament: Matt 28:8–10 (the female disciples); 28:16–20 (a large group, perhaps the five hundred mentioned in 1 Cor 15:6); Luke 24:13–32 (two disciples on the road to Emmaus); 24:34 (Peter); 24:36–49 (all the disciples); John 20:19–23 (ten disciples); 20:24–29 (doubting Thomas); 21:1–14 (the fishing disciples); Acts 9:3–9 (Saul/Paul). Other resurrection appearances are unique to 1 Corinthians 15; for example, the appearance to James, which we are told happened but is nowhere else described.

Four noteworthy features surround the disciples' encounters with the risen Jesus.

First, he appears not only to isolated individuals, but also to groups and even to at least one large group of about five hundred. That means that these are not delusions or personal visions experienced by singular individuals. It is fashionable to suggest that the disciples truly *believed* that they encountered the risen Jesus, but that their belief was constructed on the basis of subjective visionary experiences or grief hallucinations. But visions, delusions, and hallucinations are both personal and private and are neither shared nor shareable. The fact that appearances of the risen Jesus are experienced by both individuals and groups means that the appearances cannot be explained by hallucination or vision.

Second, the risen Jesus appears not just to his close friends and followers, but also to his half brother, the skeptic James, who did not believe in Jesus's identity as Messiah prior to his crucifixion and death. In Mark 3:21, Jesus's family members (presumably including James) conclude that Jesus is "out of his mind," and seek to "take charge of him." In John 7:5, we are explicitly told that Jesus's own brothers "did not believe in him."

But, according to 1 Cor 15:7, Jesus appears to the skeptical James after his crucifixion, death, and resurrection, and James subsequently becomes not just a follower (see Acts 1:14) but a key leader of the church in Jerusalem (see Acts 15:13). Why is James's experience important? It establishes that the resurrection appearances cannot be explained as a form of wish fulfillment. James thought his half brother Jesus was crazy; Jesus's death by crucifixion would have solidified that belief. Jesus's disciples may have had reason to hope or claim that Jesus had been raised from the dead in vindication of his claims and his ministry; James had no such reason.

Third, Jesus appears to Saul (we know him as Paul), an ardent persecutor of the Christian church. In Acts 7:54–8:1, Paul (Saul) appears on the scene, giving approval to the lynching of Stephen, who has just delivered a stirring sermon proclaiming Jesus as Messiah and risen Lord. Paul was convinced that Jesus died, justly, as a false prophet cursed by God. Subsequent to seeing the risen Jesus (an experience described in Acts 9, and recounted again in Acts 22 and Acts 26), Paul becomes a follower of Jesus and later emerges as a key church leader, especially in the evangelistic missionary movement throughout the Roman Empire. Like the appearance proclaimed for James, the appearance to Paul shows that it is not just followers who are positively inclined toward Jesus in the first place who have experiences that they interpret as Jesus raised from the dead.

Fourth, the appearances of the risen Jesus are unapologetically physical in nature. The risen Jesus the disciples encounter is no mere ghost or ephemeral spirit; he appears in a flesh-and-blood resurrected body. Thus, in John 20:24–28, we see Jesus invite Thomas to touch the nail holes with his fingers, to touch the wound in his side with his hand. Jesus says, "Stop doubting and believe." We are not told whether Thomas actually touches Jesus, but Thomas's response is clear and convinced: he calls Jesus "My Lord and my God!"

In Luke 24:39, we see Jesus insisting, "Look at my hands and my feet. It is I myself! Touch me and see; a ghost does not have flesh and bones, as you see I have." The resurrection appearances of Jesus to the disciples are explicitly physical, bodily appearances. It is sometimes fashionable today to claim that the early Christians believed that Jesus was "exalted" after his death or "ascended" to heaven in spiritual form. But the New Testament accounts do not leave us the option of concluding that the resurrection appearances are ghostly or immaterial or metaphorical or anything other than literal, physical, bodily appearances. The Gospels all make it exceedingly clear: what the disciples claim to see is the risen *bodily* Jesus.

It is also interesting that although the risen Jesus is *bodily* in nature, his resurrected body is of a somewhat different sort, what N. T. Wright calls a *transphysical* body.[5] Thus, in Luke 24, the disciples are gathered; Jesus has appeared to Mary, to Peter, and to the two disciples traveling on the road to Emmaus. Everybody is startled at what has been happening. Then Jesus makes his grand appearance:

> While they were still talking about this, Jesus himself
> stood among them and said to them, "Peace be with you."

---

[5]   Wright, *Resurrection of the Son of God*, 711.

251

They were startled and frightened, thinking they saw a ghost. He said to them, "Why are you troubled, and why do doubts rise in your minds? Look at my hands and my feet. It is I myself! Touch me and see; a ghost does not have flesh and bones, as you see I have."

When he had said this, he showed them his hands and feet. And while they still did not believe it because of joy and amazement, he asked them, "Do you have anything here to eat?" They gave him a piece of broiled fish, and he took it and ate it in their presence.

He said to them, "This is what I told you while I was still with you: Everything must be fulfilled that is written about me in the Law of Moses, the Prophets and the Psalms." (Luke 24:36–44)

The risen Jesus appears among the disciples from, it seems, out of nowhere. He has apparently passed through the walls of the house the disciples are gathered in. Nonetheless, Jesus is still a bodily presence; after all, he eats some broiled fish.

At this point, all we have are professed resurrection appearances, the disciples *claiming* to have seen the risen Jesus. How do we know that they are telling the truth? For that, we need to move to the fifth plank in an argument for the resurrection.

### The Disciples Are Transformed

A popular argument against believing that the resurrection of Jesus happened claims that the disciples made up the story of the resurrection. Perhaps the disciples stole the body and invented the resurrection; or, when the tomb was inexplicably found empty, they made up stories of having seen the risen Lord Jesus. But the radical transformation of Jesus's disciples in the days following his arrest and crucifixion make that suggestion highly unlikely.

What was the state of Jesus's disciples after he was arrested, tried, crucified, died, and buried? First, the disciples all desert Jesus and flee when he is arrested:

> Then the men stepped forward, seized Jesus and arrested him. With that, one of Jesus' companions reached for his sword, drew it out and struck the servant of the high priest, cutting off his ear. . . .

> At that time Jesus said to the crowd, "Am I leading a rebellion, that you have come out with swords and clubs to capture me? . . . But this has all taken place that the writings and the prophets might be fulfilled." Then all the disciples deserted him and fled. (Matt 26:50–51, 55–56)

Shortly thereafter, Peter, the boldest and most outspoken of Jesus's disciples, denies even knowing Jesus, calling down curses upon himself to emphasize his denial (Matt 26:69–75). Then Judas is overcome with grief and sorrow and commits suicide (Matt 27:1–10).

With the sole exception of John, the disciples are nowhere to be found at the scene of the crucifixion (John 19:25–27). They have all run away and are cowering in fear. John 20:19 presents the disciples on Easter Sunday as gathering together in an upper room "with the doors locked for fear of the Jews." Simply put, the disciples were a disillusioned, despondent, and fearful group. Shortly thereafter, however, they are radically transformed: from fearful, cowering individuals who denied and abandoned Jesus at his arrest and execution, into bold proclaimers of the gospel of the risen Lord. The disciples thereafter steadfastly follow and proclaim the risen Jesus in the face of imprisonment and even martyrdom.

From fleeing in terror during the trial of Jesus, the disciples are transformed into men who fearlessly preach that Jesus has been raised from the dead. In Acts 4:5–18, Peter and John are ordered to stop preaching in Jesus's name. They refuse: "But Peter and John replied, 'Judge for yourselves whether it is right in God's sight to obey you rather than God. For we cannot help speaking about what we have seen and heard'" (vv. 19–20).

The leaders are startled by Peter and John's *courage*, a courage that was noticeably lacking at the crucifixion. What causes that transformation? The simplest explanation is that they had an authentic experience wherein they saw Jesus, risen from the dead, and that this encounter empowered and changed their lives.

The martyrdom of Stephen in Acts 7 does not reduce the disciples' resolve; nor do the martyrdom of Peter, Paul, James, and other early Christians. Indeed, Stephen's martyrdom scatters the early Christians, but everywhere they go, they continue to preach the gospel of Jesus crucified and risen. If the disciples made up the story of the resurrection appearances, don't you think they would have given up the story at some point along the road rather than going to their death for it?

At this point, a skeptic might point out that people die for causes all the time, and often the causes they die for are lies. For example, German troops under Adolf Hitler were willing to go to their death to defend German sovereignty against the threats of foreign nations, oblivious to the reality that theirs was a war of aggression, not defense. Muslim suicide bombers may detonate themselves in crowded marketplaces under the mistaken belief that this act will guarantee their entrance to paradise. In short, people are quite regularly willing to die for causes to demonstrate their passionate commitment to the cause. What makes early Christian disciples any different from contemporary Muslim suicide bombers?

People will die for a lie they believe to be true; but people do not willingly die for something they know to be a lie. So, on the one hand, Muslim mujahideen will die for Islam, believing that Islam is the true religion, the straight path, and that dying for Allah will grant them immediate entrance into paradise. They are, from my viewpoint, dying for a lie. But the key is that they are convinced that they are dying for the truth. If they *knew* that their suicide would not grant them salvation, would they be willing to die for their faith?

Let's take a more recent example from history to explore that question: the Watergate conspiracy in the 1970s. The events surrounding the Watergate scandal are informative. Charles Colson and other confidants were involved in a conspiracy to protect President Richard Nixon from prosecution. But with the mere threat of imprisonment hanging over them, Nixon's closest advisers and friends quickly turned state's evidence and admitted to the conspiracy. People were not willing to suffer (let alone suffer death) for something they knew to be a lie.

So people will die for a lie they believe to be the truth, but they will not die for a lie they know to be a lie. Here's the kicker. The disciples *knew* whether Jesus had been raised from the dead. After all, they claimed to be the witnesses to the fact! Peter puts it succinctly and plainly: "God has raised this Jesus to life, and we are all witnesses of the fact" (Acts 2:32). The disciples did not die for something they mistakenly thought was true; they did not die for something they knew to be a lie. Rather, they died for their absolute conviction, their personal experiential knowledge, that Jesus was raised from the dead. They died for a belief they *knew* to be either true or false. Either the disciples had seen the risen Jesus or they had not. If they had not, it is inconceivable that they would have willingly suffered and died for what they knew to be a false claim. The more reasonable conclusion is that they in fact died for something—the resurrection of Jesus Christ—that they *knew* to be true.

### The Birth of the Church in Jerusalem

A sixth plank in my historical argument for the resurrection of Jesus is the public preaching of the gospel and the birth of the Christian church. Jesus of Nazareth was arrested, tried, and crucified in Jerusalem, the center of the Jewish religion and the Israelite people. Where was the Christian church born? In Jerusalem. Within months of Jesus's death, the disciples began preaching publicly, and their preaching centered on the resurrection of Jesus from the dead.

> [Peter said to the Israelites,] "Listen to this: Jesus of Nazareth was a man accredited by God to you by miracles, wonders and signs, which God did among you through him, as you yourselves know. . . . You, with the help of wicked men, put him to death by nailing him to the cross. But God raised him from the dead, freeing him from the agony of death, because it was impossible for death to keep its hold on him. "David said about him, 'I saw the Lord always before me. . . . My body also will rest in hope, because you will not abandon me to the grave, nor will you let your Holy One see decay. . . .'
>
> Brothers, I can tell you confidently that the patriarch David died and was buried, and his tomb is here to this day. But he was a prophet. . . . He spoke of the resurrection of the Christ, that he was not abandoned to the grave, nor did his body see decay. God has raised this Jesus to

life, and we are all witnesses of the fact. Exalted to the
right hand of God, he has received from the Father the
promised Holy Spirit. . . .

Therefore, let all Israel be assured of this: God has made
this Jesus, whom you crucified, both Lord and Christ."
(Acts 2:22–36)

One of the central tenets of the early preaching of the Christian
church was the resurrection of the Lord Jesus Christ. And this message was preached by Peter in Jerusalem, the very city where Jesus
had so recently been put to death. Again, all of the historical sources
that we have relate the early and public preaching of the gospel; they
all indicate that the church began in Jerusalem, and that the resurrection was a core element of that preaching.

If the resurrection never happened, if Jesus's body was still lin-
gering in some tomb, or if it had been buried in a common grave for
criminals, Jerusalem is the last place that the Christian church could
have sprouted. It would have begun in some backwater like Galilee,
where no one could have checked up on the facts concerning Jesus's
burial and tomb. In Jerusalem there was so much publicity and
awareness that it was not possible to fool the authorities or the people. But the church not only began in Jerusalem; it expanded exponentially. There was rapid growth, not even stalled by the breakout
of persecution as recorded in Acts 7–9.

### The Early Christian Worldview

A seventh and final plank pointing to the resurrection is the mutation of the first-century Jewish worldview among Jesus's original
followers. The earliest Jesus followers were predominantly Jewish.
The key apostles—Peter, James, John, Paul—were all devout Jews.

But as they wrestled with the significance of the life, teaching, ministry, and death of Jesus, they were eventually led to recast core features of Judaism. Two changes in particular are worth mentioning.

First, Jews were emphatically, unapologetically, and unswervingly monotheistic in the midst of a polytheistic, idolatrous, and pagan Roman Empire. Jewish monotheism was one of the distinguishing features that set Jews apart from their Gentile neighbors. Yet early Christians immediately acknowledged and even worshiped Jesus as Lord and God. These Christians continued to identify as Jewish but held Jesus to be coequal to the Lord God. If Jesus had remained dead after his crucifixion, it is exceedingly difficult to conceive of his followers thinking of him as divine, regardless of his teachings and miracles.

Second, early Christians began gathering to sing hymns to Christ and share commemorative meals together. These meetings did not occur on Saturday, the Jewish Sabbath, but rather on Sunday, the day of Jesus's supposed resurrection. By the time the book of Revelation was written, Sunday had already become known as "the Lord's Day" (Rev 1:10). The sharing of a commemorative meal itself points toward the death and resurrection of Jesus. But the Christian gathering on Sunday indicates a special significance of that day of the week. What could have been so significant that it justified changing the day of worship (or adding a second day of worship) for the Jewish-Christian community? The resurrection of Jesus on the third day (Friday–Saturday–Sunday) would be an event of sufficient importance to merit gathering for worship. Given the centrality of the resurrection in Christian preaching, the move to worshiping on "resurrection day" makes eminent sense.

## Conclusion

Let's quickly put these seven planks together. First, Jesus dies by crucifixion in Jerusalem. Second, he is buried in a tomb by Joseph of Arimathea. Third, his tomb is found empty on the third day. Fourth, the disciples (including James and Paul) claim to have experiences of encountering the risen Jesus. Fifth, the disciples are transformed from fearful cowards into bold and fearless proclaimers, suffering and even dying for the message that Jesus died for our sins and rose again on the third day. Sixth, the gospel message is preached within months of the death and resurrection of Jesus, in the very city and place where these events happened. Seventh, the first-century Jewish worldview is changed to accommodate belief in Jesus's divinity and worship on resurrection day. When you put these seven planks together, they build a strong and persuasive bridge to the conclusion that orthodox Christians have universally believed for nearly 2,000 years. Jesus of Nazareth, the incarnate Son of God, who died on the cross to atone for sins, was raised from the dead on the third day by God the Father.

If my arguments in part 3 of this book have been somewhat successful, there is good reason to think that the New Testament (especially the Gospels) is historically reliable, that Jesus claimed and demonstrated divine identity and authority, and that Jesus was raised from the dead after his crucifixion. So when asked, *Why believe that Christianity is true*? the answer is that there is strong evidence supporting that belief!

### Recommended Resources for Further Exploration

Craig, William Lane. *The Son Rises: The Historical Evidence for the Resurrection of Jesus*. Eugene, OR: Wipf & Stock, 2001.

Habermas, Gary R., and Michael R. Licona. *The Case for the Resurrection of Jesus.* Grand Rapids: Kregel, 2004.

Licona, Michael R. *The Resurrection of Jesus: A New Historiographical Approach.* Downers Grove, IL: IVP Academic, 2010.

Strobel, Lee. *The Case for Easter: A Journalist Investigates Evidence for the Resurrection.* Grand Rapids: Zondervan, 2018.

Wright, N. T. *The Resurrection of the Son of God.* Christian Origins and the Question of God. Vol. 3. Minneapolis: Fortress, 2003.

# PART 4

# WHAT ABOUT . . .?

*We're calling for an end to a specific kind of religious
faith: Christianity. I honestly think that with this book . . .
Christianity has been debunked. The jury has returned its
verdict. The gavel has come down. The case is now closed.*[1]

John Loftus

In the previous six chapters, I have presented reasons and evidence to believe that God exists (chaps. 4–6) and that Christianity is true (chaps. 7–9). There is much more to say about all of the issues addressed in those chapters, but I have sought to show that there is a strong cumulative case that can be constructed, pointing toward the conclusion that Christianity is reasonable to believe.

But it is clear that not everyone finds the reasons to believe convincing. Although there are numerous intelligent, thoughtful, and articulate Christians (e.g., Alvin Plantinga, Richard Swinburne, Alister McGrath, William Lane Craig, Peter Williams, Peter Kreeft, J. P. Moreland), there are also numerous intelligent, thoughtful, and articulate atheists (e.g., Graham Oppy, Daniel Dennett, Thomas

---

[1]  John W. Loftus, ed., *The End of Christianity* (Amherst, NY: Prometheus, 2011), 9.

Nagel, Evan Fales, Bart Ehrman, John Searle), along with intelligent, thoughtful, and articulate individuals who profess other religious worldviews.

Thoughtful non-Christians frequently interact with the arguments I presented in chapters 4–9, explaining why they find the reasons and evidence unpersuasive. But some go further and propose positive reasons that push them away from Christian faith. That is, many non-Christians set forth reasons to *disbelieve* in the God of Christianity.[2] For our purposes, I will call these "objections" to the Christian faith.

Entire books have been written in response to such objections.[3] I am offering neither a comprehensive presentation of objections to Christianity nor a comprehensive response to such objections. But it is worthwhile to at least outline some of the most common objections and indicate possible responses. In Chapter 10, I will address (1) the question of evil and suffering, (2) the hypocrisy of Christians, (3) historic and contemporary evils perpetrated in the name of Christianity, (4) the conflict between science and faith, and (5) Christianity's arrogant claim of exclusive truth.

---

[2]    See, e.g., Bart D. Ehrman, *God's Problem: How the Bible Fails to Answer Our Most Important Question—Why We Suffer* (New York: HarperOne, 2009); Loftus, *The End of Christianity*; Dawkins, *God Delusion* (see chap. 4, n. 1).

[3]    See, e.g., Alister McGrath and Joanna Collicutt McGrath, *The Dawkins Delusion? Atheist Fundamentalism and the Denial of the Divine* (Downers Grove, IL: InterVarsity, 2007). Two of my favorite responses are by the Canadian philosopher Paul Chamberlain: *Why People Don't Believe: Confronting Seven Challenges to Christian Faith* (Grand Rapids: Baker, 2011); and *Why People Stop Believing* (Eugene, OR: Cascade, 2018).

# CHAPTER 10

# *Cross-Examined*

## Answering Common Objections

In this chapter, I will address five of the most common reasons people cite not to believe in the God of Christianity: evil, hypocrisy, church-sponsored evil, science, and exclusivism. I will deal in some depth with the question of evil and suffering, which is historically the most significant intellectual and experiential objection to Christianity. The final four issues will be dealt with more briefly, not because they are unimportant, but because there is not enough space to say more about them!

## The Question of Evil and Suffering

If God is good, why is there so much evil and suffering in the world?

Villages get buried by mudslides. Towns are wiped out by volcanic eruptions. Tsunamis devastate an island's coastline. Forest fires decimate the landscape and eradicate animal populations. When the forces of nature wreak havoc and cause suffering, we ask, why?

Violent intruders beat an elderly couple before pillaging their home. Drug gangs take over a city neighborhood, causing youth and parents to live in constant fear. Mass murderers open fire on a crowded arena, killing dozens before taking their own lives. Parents physically and emotionally abuse their young children. Teachers and priests sexually assault youth under their authority. Authoritarian regimes wage genocidal war on minority populations. When humans perpetrate unspeakable evil upon one another, we ask, why?

The historical "problem of evil" asks the basic question, if God is powerful and loving, why do bad things happen to good people? The problem is raised in two very different ways.

On the one hand, those who *believe* in God wrestle intellectually and existentially with the evil and suffering they experience and witness. The biblical books of Job and Habakkuk, for example, graphically display the title characters' plaintive cries to the Lord God, praying for justice and relief from suffering. Christians through the centuries have frequently struggled to reconcile their beliefs about God with the ugly facts of earthly evil. From this vantage point, evil and suffering create *tension within* a Christian worldview but not a reason to reject God.

On the other hand, those who *do not believe* in God cite the world's evil and suffering as a primary intellectual and personal reason to reject Christian faith. Bart Ehrman's bestselling book, *God's Problem*, narrates Ehrman's turning away from Christianity based primarily on the prevalence of evil and suffering in the world. According to Ehrman, if the God of the Bible existed, we would not see the type and amount of suffering we see in the world. From this vantage point, evil and suffering create sufficient reason to reject the Christian worldview altogether. I will be considering this side of the problem of evil: evil and suffering as a reason to reject belief in God.

There are three versions of the problem of evil: logical, evidential, and existential. We will consider them each in turn.

## *The Logical Problem of Evil*

The *logical* version of the problem of evil makes the strongest claim: the presence of evil and suffering in the world entails the absolute impossibility of the existence of God. Generally, this argument suggests there is a logical inconsistency in the Christian conception of God. If the Christian God existed, possessing the characteristics that Christians think he has, then there should be no evil in the world. But since evil clearly exists, God therefore must not exist. Here is the logical presentation:

1. If God exists, then God is omnipotent (all-powerful), omniscient (all-knowing), and omnibenevolent (all-loving/ all-good).
2. If God is omnipotent, then God has the power (ability) to prevent (or eliminate) evil.
3. If God is omniscient, then God knows how to prevent (or eliminate) evil.
4. If God is omnibenevolent, then God desires to prevent (or eliminate) evil.
5. Therefore (from 1–4), if God exists, then there would be no evil (because God possesses the power, knowledge, and desire to prevent/eliminate evil).
6. There is evil in the world (i.e., it is false that there is no evil in the world).
7. Thus, God does not exist.[1]

Premise 1 is a straightforward articulation of orthodox Christian belief about the nature of God. Premise 5 seems to clearly

---

[1] This version of the logical problem of evil is found (among other places) in Steven B. Cowan and James S. Spiegel, *The Love of Wisdom: A Christian Introduction to Philosophy* (Nashville: B&H Academic, 2009), 296.

follow from premises 2–4, and premise 6 seems to be clearly true. Premise 7 follows of necessity from the combination of premises 5 and 6. Thus, the anti-Christian objection seems to be quite strong: given the presence of evil in the world and the traditional Christian understanding of God, there is a logical inconsistency.

How can Christians respond to this logical problem of evil? I suggest that there are two missteps in the argument as presented.

First, I think premise 4 is imprecise. The claim stands as an absolute stance that permits no exceptions. "If God is omnibenevolent (all-good or all-loving), then God would desire to prevent or eliminate any and all evil in the world." Although the claim is generally accurate, it is relatively easy to identify exceptions to the rule.

Consider a human analogy. As parents, my wife and I have always applied the general rule, do not permit strangers to stab our children with sharp objects. Whenever we walk down the street and encounter a wild-haired rowdy with crazy eyes carrying a sword, we shield our children and would fight to the death to protect our kids from being stabbed by that stranger wielding a sharp object. Nonetheless, several times during their childhood, we visited the local medical clinic for our kids to receive their vaccinations. On those occasions, we not only permitted, but *encouraged and facilitated*, the evil and suffering of having strangers stab our children with sharp objects. Why? The apparent evil of the experience was the necessary means to accomplishing an otherwise-unattainable good: inoculation against potentially deadly diseases. That is, the evil was both permitted and permissible in pursuit of a "greater good."

If we can understand parents permitting apparent evil to accomplish a greater good, then we should be able to expect the same of God—whose knowledge far exceeds our own. The "greater good" response suggests that while God *in general* desires to prevent or eliminate evil and suffering, nonetheless there is a morally sufficient reason for which God permits the evil and suffering that occurs. In some cases (e.g., Good Friday), we can identify in retrospect God's morally sufficient reasons for permitting the evil; in other situations, God's reasoning might be beyond our (current) comprehension.[2] Nonetheless, the greater good response claims that it is reasonable to believe that God always and only permits evil when it is accomplishing some higher-order value. A more precise articulation of premise 4, then, would be "If God is omnibenevolent, then God has the general desire to prevent (or eliminate) evil; but God can have a morally sufficient reason for permitting some evil to exist in pursuit of an otherwise-unattainable greater good."

Second, a similar imprecision exists in premise 2: "If God is omnipotent, then he has the power (ability) to prevent (or eliminate) evil." The critic of Christianity suggests that an omnipotent God can do all things; therefore, God could eliminate all evil in the world. Indeed, the critic might even suggest that God could achieve the "greater good" without needing to use evil or suffering in the process. After all, if God can do all things, then God could accomplish good ends by any means; he would not need to use evil or suffering.

According to many (most) Christian theologians and philosophers, however, God's omnipotence ought not to be understood as the ability to do absolutely anything, but rather as the ability to do all things that are logically possible. On this understanding, God's very nature is rational, such that what we understand as the laws of logic

---

[2]  The Christian might cite Isa 55:8–9 in support of this contention. "'For my thoughts are not your thoughts, neither are your ways my ways,' declares the Lord. 'As the heavens are higher than the earth, so are my ways higher than your ways and my thoughts than your thoughts.'" In traditional Christian conception, God's vision, wisdom, and knowledge can encompass all of time and space, including eternity; it therefore takes into account far more possibilities and outcomes than our finite brains are capable of calculating. Hence, God can be legitimately pursuing a greater good of which we are entirely ignorant.

are simply reflections of the character and essence of God. God is naturally bound to operate in accordance with his own divine nature; thus, God will act in accordance with the laws of logic. This is not a limitation upon the power of God, such that God is no longer seen as omnipotent; rather, it is a clarification of the nature of omnipotence. God possesses all power, or maximal power, and can do all things that are logically possible.

But God cannot, for example, create a square circle—a two-dimensional figure that simultaneously (1) has four equal sides with four right-angled corners and (2) has no sides and no corners. Such a figure (which I fondly call a squircle) is a logical impossibility and therefore cannot be created by anybody, not even God.

How does this apply to the problem of evil? The skeptic suggests that God could accomplish his purposes without using evil and suffering. A fairly typical Christian response is known as the free will defense and suggests that the source of evil and suffering in the world is the exercise of human free will. On this understanding, God has endowed human beings with the ability to choose good or to choose evil; when we use our will wrongly, we cause others to suffer and bring evil into the world.[3]

Why couldn't God create us with free will, but in such a way that we always and only use our free will to choose good rather than evil? The free will defense suggests that such an option is logically impossible. God cannot create free-willed creatures who always freely choose the good—such creatures would not be free at all. Moral freedom will involve not the possibility but the actuality of freely chosen evil. To be more precise, perhaps premise 2 should read, "If God is omnipotent, he possesses maximal power; but even an omnipotent God cannot create truly free creatures who never

---

[3]  The classic expression of the free will defense is found in Alvin Plantinga, *God, Freedom, and Evil* (Grand Rapids: Eerdmans, 1989).

freely do wrong." God can indeed prevent or eliminate all evil, but only by not creating free-willed creatures in the first place (or by exterminating them all when they use their free will to cause evil and suffering).

Given the greater good and the free will responses to the problem of evil, there is no contradiction between the traditional understanding of God (as omnipotent, omniscient, and omnibenevolent) and the existence of evil and suffering in the world. Here is the revised argument with its outcome:

1. If God exists, then God is omnipotent (all-powerful), omniscient (all-knowing), and omnibenevolent (all-loving/all-good).
2. [Revised] If God is omnipotent, then God has all power, but even an omnipotent God cannot create truly free creatures who never freely do wrong.
3. If God is omniscient, then God knows how to prevent (or eliminate) evil.
4. [Revised] If God is omnibenevolent, then God has the general desire to prevent (or eliminate) evil; but God can have a morally sufficient reason for permitting some evil to exist in pursuit of an otherwise-unattainable greater good.
5. Therefore (from 1–4), if God exists, then evil and suffering in the world is (a) accomplishing a greater good and/or (b) the result of human misuse of free will.
6. There is evil in the world (i.e., it is false that there is no evil in the world).
7. Thus, there is no contradiction between the existence of an omnipotent, omniscient, omnibenevolent God and the existence of evil and suffering in the world.

The logical problem of evil, then, although it makes the strongest claim, fails to achieve its goal. There is no reason to think that God is incompatible with evil, and there is good reason to think that God permits evil in pursuit of the general greater good of free-willed creatures.

### *The Evidential Problem of Evil*

Philosophers and theologians are generally agreed that the logical problem of evil fails to show that God cannot (or does not) exist. Nonetheless, non-Christians suggest that evil in the world still poses an insurmountable challenge to Christian belief. The *evidential* version of the problem of evil claims that the existence of God is unlikely given the *amount* and *type* of evil we see in the world.

*Amount*—on the one hand, we see a *lot* of evil on planet Earth. The daily newspaper recounts the exploits of free-willed creatures causing immense amounts of suffering for other free-willed creatures. We do not have to go far or think hard to see significant suffering and extreme evil.

1. The greater the amount of evil and suffering in the world, the less likely it is that God exists.
2. There is an overwhelming amount of evil and suffering in the world.
3. Therefore, it is unlikely that God exists.

*Type*—on the other hand, we see much evil that does not seem to be accomplishing any "greater good." From animals slowly dying in a forest fire, to the brutal rape and dismemberment of toddlers, there are instances of evil that defy all reasonable attempts to find a correlative greater good. Such evil seems gratuitous or unnecessary.

It does not bring about some better state of affairs; it is just plain evil.

1. If God exists and permits evil to occur only when it is accomplishing some greater good, then there would be no pointless (or gratuitous) evil in the world.
2. There is (probably) pointless evil in the world (i.e., it is false that there is no pointless evil).
3. Therefore, God (probably) does not exist.

The evidential problem of evil makes a modest claim, suggesting that it is unlikely or improbable that God exists given the amount and type of evil and suffering that we encounter. It is worth noting three brief responses to the evidential version of the problem of evil.

First, many philosophers note that human beings are not well situated to know whether an individual instance of evil or suffering is truly pointless.[4] The traditional Christian conception of God holds that God is omniscient (all-knowing) and atemporal (outside of time) and therefore is able to see and know far more than is accessible to our finite time-bound minds. So if we encounter evil and cannot see purpose in it, we should hesitate to conclude that therefore the evil is pointless. There may in fact be some good that God is working in the midst of the evil, and we are just incapable of seeing it.

Second, it is interesting that humanity's sensitivity to the amount and type of evil in the world has grown in apparently inverse proportion to the scale of evil and suffering across the world. This is a very delicate subject and a difficult point to establish without

---

[4]   The type of response is known as skeptical theism and is articulated by Stephen Wykstra, Alvin Plantinga, William Alston, and Peter van Inwagen (among others). See, e.g., Trent Dougherty, "Skeptical Theism," *The Stanford Encyclopedia of Philosophy*, January 25, 2014, https://plato.stanford.edu/entries/skeptical-theism/.

appearing insensitive. So let me emphasize at the outset that this is a purely intellectual response to a purely intellectual question, and I do not think this is ever a helpful thing to say to a friend who is in the midst of suffering. But if someone is raising the amount and type of evil in the world as a rational reason to doubt or disbelieve in God, then that rational objection requires a rational response.

It seems to me that the overall scale of suffering and evil in the world has been declining for the past several hundred years. This is particularly true in "Western" or "first-world" nations, which are (somewhat ironically) home to a higher proportion of people who are liable to raise the problem of evil as a reason to reject faith in God. It is, in general, mostly comfortable middle-class Westerners who raise the amount and type of suffering in the world as a club against Christian faith. We are rightly repelled by the ravages of disease, natural disasters, institutional oppression, personal violence, and other causes of evil and suffering in the world.

Third, it is helpful to remember the insights of the greater good and the free-will responses to the logical problem of evil. If it is true that evil and suffering in the world are (primarily) the result of our misuse of free will, then in one sense we (corporately, as a human race) have no one to blame but ourselves for the prevalence of evil and suffering in the world. But, you might suggest, couldn't God prevent some people from expressing the evil in their hearts? Certainly this would be possible—it seems to me that God has the ability and the authority to overrule our creaturely freedom whenever and wherever he sees fit. But if it is also true that the very possession and expression of human free will is itself one of the "greater goods" that God is pursuing in the created universe, then it would follow that God would be rightly hesitant and sparing in overruling our freely chosen evil acts.[5] So it may be that there is no truly pointless evil, simply because all of the evil that occurs is the outcome of freely chosen human acts, which are a part of God's good creation. Again, someone might disagree with God regarding the relative goodness of human free will, but that's a different kind of problem.

## *The Existential Problem of Evil*

Bart Ehrman writes,

> I don't know if you've read any of the writings of the modern theodicists, but they are something to behold: precise, philosophically nuanced, deeply thought out, filled with esoteric terminology and finely reasoned explanations for why suffering does not preclude the existence of a divine being of power and love. Frankly, to most of us these writings are not just obtuse, they are disconnected from real life, life as lived in the trenches. . . . Many of the attempts to explain evil can, in the end, be morally repugnant. . . . Suffering, at the end of the day, should not

---

[5] As a purely abstract thought experiment, it is also interesting to note that if God does regularly intervene to thwart people from acting upon their freely chosen evil intentions, then God would never get credit for preventing those evils. After all, given that God (in this thought experiment) thwarts the evil, the evil never actually occurs, so nobody would be aware that God had done anything at all and prevented a tremendous evil from happening. Following this thought experiment through, it is possible that God is actively stopping huge amounts of pointless evil from occurring, and the evil that actually happens and which we encounter is far less than it would be were it not for God's interventions. I do not think this is the case, but it is interesting to note that if it were the case, none of us could ever know of it, and we would never give God thanks for stopping the evils that we never knew would otherwise have occurred.

lead merely to an intellectual explanation. It should also
lead to a personal response.[6]

My articulation of and response to the logical and evidential
versions of the problem of evil have been exclusively rational in
nature. As I noted, rational objections require rational responses.
In light of Christian philosophers and theologians defending God
against the problem of evil, Bart Ehrman voices the concern of
many non-Christians: those defenses (known as theodicies) are cold,
impersonal, and insensitive. The philosophical responses miss the
personal nature of suffering and come across as "disconnected from
real life" or, worse, as "morally repugnant."

I firmly believe that the philosophical responses to the logical
and evidential problem of evil are necessary. But I am also convinced that for the average person today, the question or problem or
objection we have with respect to God and evil is not the abstract
philosophical problem. Rather, the problem is much more personal
and existential: If God is loving and powerful, then why would he
allow *this* to happen to *me* or to my loved ones? Where is God when
I am hurting? Where is God in the midst of the evil that I see around
me? Where is God when I observe such intense suffering in the
world?

The real problem of evil, then, is a deeply personal and emotional problem: I feel abandoned by God and therefore question his
love, presence, and very existence. I see God fail to address the suffering around me and wonder if God cares at all. If the sufferings of
the world do not seem to matter to God, I wonder why God ought
to matter to me.

---

6   Ehrman, *God's Problem*, 121–22 (see pt. 4, n. 2).

In traditional Christianity, though, our suffering most definitely matters to God. He is never indifferent to or callous toward the evil and suffering that occur in the world. Through the incarnate Son of God, we are invited to a relationship with the transcendent God who brings us comfort in the midst of the trials of this life.

> [Jesus said,] "Come to me, all you who are weary and burdened, and I will give you rest. Take my yoke upon you and learn from me, for I am gentle and humble in heart, and you will find rest for your souls. For my yoke is easy and my burden is light." (Matt 11:28–30)

> [Jesus said,] "I have told you these things, so that in me you may have peace. In this world you will have trouble. But take heart! I have overcome the world." (John 16:33)

Christianity does not pretend that evil and suffering do not exist or that they do not matter. Rather, the Christian faith proclaims that evil and suffering are not the last word. We know that, whatever our sufferings may be, "this too shall pass." There will be an end to pain, an end to suffering, and an entrance into eternal life where a new order, free from evil, will be initiated.

> I saw a new heaven and a new earth, for the first heaven and the first earth had passed away, and there was no longer any sea. I saw the Holy City, the new Jerusalem, coming down out of heaven from God, prepared as a bride beautifully dressed for her husband. And I heard a loud voice from the throne saying, "Now the dwelling of God is with men, and he will live with them. They will be his people, and God himself will be with them and be their

> God. He will wipe every tear from their eyes. There will
> be no more death or mourning or crying or pain, for the
> old order of things has passed away."

> He who was seated on the throne said, "I am making
> everything new!" (Rev 21:1–5)

The Christian thus looks forward to life after death, where the wrongs of this life will be set right, our sufferings will be redeemed, and we will experience the glory of eternal life with God the Father, Son, and Holy Spirit. Thus, the apostle Paul, despite the myriad of sufferings he experiences (see 2 Cor 11:16–29, where he recounts his beatings, imprisonments, etc.), is able to proclaim with confidence and hope:

> Therefore, we do not lose heart. Though outwardly we are
> wasting away, yet inwardly we are being renewed day by
> day. For our light and momentary troubles are achieving
> for us an eternal glory that far outweighs them all. So we
> fix our eyes not on what is seen, but on what is unseen.
> For what is seen is temporary, but what is unseen is eter-
> nal. (2 Cor 4:16–18)

The Christian faith gives the believer tremendous assurance of an eternity that will more than sufficiently make up for all the evil and suffering we might experience in this life. That divine and eternal comfort allows Christians first to endure their own suffering and, second, to turn to others who are suffering to provide that same comfort.

Praise be to the God and Father of our Lord Jesus Christ, the Father of compassion and the God of all comfort, who comforts us in all our troubles, so that we can comfort those in any trouble with the comfort we ourselves have received from God. For just as the sufferings of Christ flow over into our lives, so also through Christ our comfort overflows. (2 Cor 1:3–5)

Furthermore, Christianity teaches that God is not distant or detached from our suffering. Indeed, God becomes human through the incarnation of Jesus of Nazareth and experiences the most intense suffering imaginable during Easter week. As he anticipates his soon-impending death, Jesus tells his followers, "My soul is overwhelmed with sorrow to the point of death." He then prays that he might not have to go through the suffering to come: "My Father, if it is possible, may this cup be taken from me" (Matt 26:38–39).

What follows, instead, is a litany of excruciating pain and suffering on every level—physical, emotional, and spiritual. Jesus, though innocent of wrongdoing, is betrayed by his close friend Judas (Matt 26:14–16, 47–49), arrested and hauled before an illegal midnight court (vv. 57–62), convicted of blasphemy and beaten by the Jewish leaders (vv. 63–68), disavowed three times by his closest follower, Peter (vv. 69–74), sentenced to death by the reluctant Roman governor Pilate (Matt 27:11–25), beaten and mocked again (vv. 26–31), nailed to a cross (vv. 32–37), mocked by the gathered crowd and abandoned by his friends and followers (vv. 39–44), before dying alone on the cross (27:50).

Christians do not worship a God who is above suffering and indifferent to the pain we experience. Rather, we worship a God who *entered into* our suffering, took our pain and sin and punishment upon himself, and died so that we might have the hope of redemption and eternal life.

> Therefore, if anyone is in Christ, he is a new creation; the old has gone, the new has come! All this is from God, who reconciled us to himself through Christ. . . . God was reconciling the world to himself in Christ, not counting men's sins against them. . . . We implore you on Christ's behalf: Be reconciled to God. God made him who had no sin to be sin for us, so that in him we might become the righteousness of God. (2 Cor 5:17–21)

> You see, at just the right time, when we were still powerless, Christ died for the ungodly. . . . God demonstrates his own love for us in this: While we were still sinners, Christ died for us. (Rom 5:6, 8)

Though evil and suffering are caused by our misuse of creaturely freedom, God condescends to take our suffering and pain upon himself, dying in our place to provide eternal salvation.

At this point, it might be tempting to conclude that Christianity encourages people to minimize earthly suffering in the light of eternal life. But this would also be a mistake. Yes, Christianity puts suffering in eternal perspective, reminding us that evil is temporary and will be outweighed by the glory to come. But Christianity also provides a robust call to oppose injustice and evil, to mitigate and alleviate suffering, and to comfort those who are hurting.

When Old Testament Israel neglected to practice the social compassion and concern God had mandated, God sent prophets to correct, rebuke, and warn the nation. One brief example will have to suffice, from the prophet Amos:

[The LORD says,] "I hate, I despise your religious feasts; I cannot stand your assemblies. Even though you bring me burnt offerings and grain offerings, I will not accept them. Though you bring choice fellowship offerings, I will have no regard for them. Away with the noise of your songs! I will not listen to the music of your harps. But let justice roll on like a river, righteousness like a never-failing stream!" (Amos 5:21–24)

When people who profess to belong to God live in a way that causes suffering and perpetrates evil, God declares that he is utterly opposed to them and their actions. God will not look favorably upon their worship or their religious professions so long as they live in a way that violates the goodness and compassion he commands. Hence, "away with the noise of your songs"; they need to be replaced with "justice" and "righteousness" toward others. Similarly, the prophet Micah tells the people that offerings are useless compared to the most important thing: what God requires of his people is "to act justly and to love mercy and to walk humbly with your God" (Mic 6:8).

As human beings, we experience evil and suffering in the world existentially, emotionally. We encounter hurt, and we naturally question the love and presence of God. But it seems to me that it is only by embracing the love and grace of God as demonstrated in the death and resurrection of Jesus Christ that we can both see evil and suffering in its proper perspective and have a confident hope that evil does not have the last word.

Bart Ehrman concludes his book-length objection against God based on evil with this dual thought:

In my opinion, this life is all there is . . . .

[Thus, we should be] working to alleviate suffering and bringing hope to a world devoid of hope.[7]

The sad irony, however, is that Ehrman's worldview precludes the existence of a real hope, particularly for people suffering the ravages of disease, oppression, persecution, slavery, or impending death. Hope, it seems to me, can be found in the presence of a transcendent God who hates evil, desires to alleviate suffering, and offers the free gift of eternal life to all who would come. For the abandoned widow, the abused child, the enslaved migrant, the impoverished day laborer, the subsistence farmer, it is the good news of Christianity that provides true hope in the midst of evil and suffering.

What does Christianity have to offer those who experience evil and suffering and question God? I conclude by repeating the invitation of Jesus and the profession of Paul.

Come to me, all you who are weary and burdened, and I will give you rest. Take my yoke upon you and learn from me, for I am gentle and humble in heart, and you will find rest for your souls. (Matt 11:28–29)

Therefore we do not lose heart. Though outwardly we are wasting away, yet inwardly we are being renewed day by day. For our light and momentary troubles are achieving for us an eternal glory that far outweighs them all. (2 Cor 4:16–17)

---

[7] Ehrman, *God's Problem*, 276 (see pt. 4, n. 2).

## The Hypocrisy of Many Christians

If belief in God is true and life-changing, then why are so many Christians hypocrites? When non-Christians are asked why they reject belief in God, one of the most frequently cited reasons is the hypocrisy of churchgoers: Christians frequently do not live as if what they believe is true. Christianity preaches compassion for the poor and the outcast; Christians are often close-fisted and hard-hearted toward the vulnerable in society. Christianity teaches us to love all people, even the most flamboyant of sinners; Christians are often judgmental toward sinners. Christianity preaches forgiveness and turning the other cheek; Christians often carry grudges for years. Should the hypocrisy of many Christians be a reason to doubt or reject Christianity? Let me suggest three considerations against that conclusion.

First, citing the hypocrisy of *Christians* to reject *Christianity* is a type of category mistake.[8] Christianity stands or falls on the foundation of its core proclamations—particularly the deity, atoning death, and resurrection of Jesus of Nazareth (see chaps. 7–9). A worldview, including a religious worldview, should be judged on the merits of the *worldview*, not its *practitioners*. A religion should be judged on the truthfulness of its *beliefs*, not on the faithfulness of its *believers*.

Perhaps a couple of analogies would help. Consider an imaginary leader of MADD (Mothers Against Drunk Driving) who has advocated for stringent laws against and severe penalties for drunk driving. Imagine that this leader is then caught driving with a blood

---

[8]    Chandler Warren puts it this way: "Can a person make a good/true argument against smoking with a cigarette in their mouth? If the answer is yes (and it is), then Christianity can be true, and its advocates can live in opposition to the truth." Personal correspondence, February 2020.

alcohol level of 0.24, three times the legal limit. Would her hypocrisy be sufficient cause to reject the tenets and merits of MADD? Clearly not. MADD should be judged on its own merits, not the failures of its leaders.

Or consider an imaginary president of the American Secular Humanist Society who has long argued for the establishment of a purely secular social morality built on the insights of the social and physical sciences. Among his stances is the immorality of sexual abuse. Imagine this president is credibly accused of molesting multiple teenage girls over a decades-long span, abusing his position of trust and authority to secure unwanted sexual relationships with students. Would his hypocrisy be sufficient cause to reject secular humanism (atheism)? Clearly not. Secular humanism should be judged on its own merits, not on the failures of its believers.

Why then should the hypocrisy of Christian believers be used as a reason to reject Christianity?

Second, if Christianity is in fact true, we should (lamentably) *expect* there to be a strong element of hypocrisy among professing Christians. On the one hand, Christianity tells us to expect there to be numerous people who claim to be Christian but do not in fact belong to Christ.[9] The hypocritical actions of many so-called Christians may well be on account of the fact that they are not in reality Christians at all!

On the other hand, Christianity also teaches that we are all fallen and prone to evil thoughts and deeds, even when we belong

---

[9]   See, e.g., Matt 7:21–23, where Jesus says, "Not everyone who says to me, 'Lord, Lord,' will enter the kingdom of heaven, but only he who does the will of my Father who is in heaven. Many will say to me on that day, 'Lord, Lord, did we not prophesy in your name, and in your name drive out demons and perform many miracles?' Then I will tell them plainly, 'I never knew you. Away from me, you evildoers!'"

to God and have the best of intentions.[10] We need to be consistently reminded that "sin is crouching at your door; it desires to have you, but you must master it" (Gen 4:7). So yes, even authentic Christians will often act in a way that is inconsistent with Christian belief and teaching; we will (intentionally or unintentionally) cause hurt and pain to others. This does not *excuse* the hypocrisy of Christians (including myself), but it does help to *explain* it. As Christians, we must be constantly reminded that there is no excuse for sin. We must be faithful about confronting sinful and hurtful behavior when we observe it. And we must be humble and self-convicting in confessing and repenting of our wrongdoing when it occurs.

Third, although there is a distressing amount of hypocrisy among Christians, there is exponentially more common decency and faithfulness among believers than is often acknowledged. What often makes media headlines and sticks in personal memories are the times when Christians do not live up to their beliefs. But when Christians live in accordance with the general teachings of Christianity—love, compassion, forgiveness, gentleness—it frequently goes unnoticed. Again, I think that ultimately a worldview stands or falls on the truthfulness of its claims, not on the faithfulness of its followers, but we should in fairness recognize the general goodness of the average Christian in society.

So, although the hypocrisy of Christians, including myself, sickens me, it is not ultimately a very good rational reason to reject the Christian faith.

---

[10]  See e.g., Rom 7:15–18, where Paul writes, "I do not understand what I do. For what I want to do I do not do, but what I hate I do. And if I do what I do not want to do, I agree that the law is good. As it is, it is no longer I myself who do it, but it is sin living in me. I know that nothing good lives in me, that is, in my sinful nature. For I have the desire to do what is good, but I cannot carry it out."

## The Injustices of the Christian Church

If Christianity is life-giving, then why have Christian churches sponsored so much violence and oppression? The litany of injustices perpetrated by Christian churches and leaders is long and illustrious: the Crusades, witch hunts, subjugation of women, the transatlantic slave trade, imperialism and colonization, attempted extermination of indigenous culture and language, oppression of sexual and gender minorities, sexual abuse scandals. It seems that not only are everyday Christians frequently hypocritical, but that the church and its leaders have institutionalized injustice. Surely *that* should count against the truthfulness of the Christian faith, shouldn't it? After all, if even the leaders are evil, then the religion as a whole must be bankrupt.

Although church-sponsored injustices may prompt an *emotional* aversion to Christianity, they do not provide *rational* reasons to reject the Christian faith. The considerations from the previous section on individual hypocrisy all apply here as well. A worldview must be adjudicated on the merits of the worldview itself, not on the faithfulness of its practitioners or even of its leaders! If the core claims of Christianity are true, then the religion is true regardless of how unfaithful the church may be.

Thus, although the injustices of the historical and contemporary church sicken me (and, I trust, you as well), they do not pose a good rational reason to reject Christian faith.[11]

---

[11]  For more on the charges of Christian hypocrisy and church-sponsored injustice, see Paul Chamberlain's excellent work, *Why People Don't Believe* (see pt. 4, n. 3).

## The Conflict between Science and Faith

If Christian beliefs are true, then why does science prove Christianity to be false? In the eyes of many contemporary Westerners, both Christians and everyday people, there is a deep and unresolvable conflict between the claims of religious faith and the discoveries of modern science. On this understanding, science uncovers deep truths about the structure and workings of the universe that contradict the orthodox affirmations of the Christian faith.[12]

Although the science-faith conflict thesis is widely held, it needs to be identified for what it is: a myth! There is, to put it bluntly, no contradiction between the deliverances of science and the core tenets of Christianity.

One can certainly point to potential areas of tension, where some people think that modern scientific discoveries pose challenges for specific beliefs held by some religious people—for example, the scientific claims for an ancient earth, a heliocentric (rather than geocentric) solar system, global climate change caused (at least in part) by human activity, biological evolution and common ancestry of all living creatures, and the vastness of the physical universe. But with some of those areas of tension, there are many (though a minority of) scientists who dispute the claim, while the majority of Western Christians accept the scientific claim but do not consider it to be in conflict with their religious beliefs. Furthermore, the specifically *scientific* claims in these areas of possible tension do not affect any core doctrine of the Christian faith: the potential difficulties surround either tertiary matters or expressions of doctrines.

---

[12]  For two contemporary examples of this position, see Victor Stenger, *God: The Failed Hypothesis—How Science Shows That God Does Not Exist* (Amherst, NY: Prometheus, 2007); and Richard Dawkins, *Outgrowing God: A Beginner's Guide* (New York: Random House, 2019).

For example, consider the scientific claim that the earth is ancient—billions of years old, rather than thousands of years old. Some in the ranks of science (Dawkins, Stenger, etc.) *and* faith (Answers in Genesis, Creation Research Institute, etc.) argue that the scientific claim directly contradicts the Christian doctrine of creation, which requires a recent (6,000–10,000 years) creation. But an ancient earth would not debunk the belief that God created the universe *ex nihilo* (out of nothing)—at most, an ancient universe would mean that God created the universe longer ago than some Christians believe he did. The age of the earth is a *working out* of the doctrine of creation; it is *not* the doctrine of creation itself! So, whether young-earth proponents are correct in claiming that contemporary scientific dating of the universe is grossly mistaken, or old-earth proponents are correct in claiming that the universe is tremendously old, all that is affected is the timing and means of creation and the interpretation of the poetic description of God's creative activity contained in Genesis 1.[13]

Two more brief considerations.

First, the myth that science and religion are locked in mortal combat was created intentionally by John William Draper and Andrew Dickson White in the 1800s. Their books *The History of the Conflict between Religion and Science* (Draper, 1874) and *A History of the Warfare of Science with Theology in Christendom* (White, 1896) effectively spread the myth, which relied upon exaggeration, misinterpretation, and even deliberate misinformation.[14] In the study

---

[13]   For a helpful and (mostly) charitable discussion on the timing and means of creation, see J. B. Stump, ed., *Four Views on Creation, Evolution, and Intelligent Design* (Grand Rapids: Zondervan Academic, 2017).

[14]   Critiques of the Draper-White thesis came immediately, as contemporary scholars pointed out historical errors, flaws in references, and outright lies. See James Joseph Walsh, *The Popes and Science: The History of the Papal Relations to Science during the Middle Ages and Down to Our Own Time (1908)*. In the contemporary

of the historical relationship between science and Christianity, virtually all scholars agree that the Draper-White conflict model is an intentional myth that bears no resemblance to the historical reality.

Indeed, in the medieval and modern period, the church was the largest, most generous, and most faithful patron of science and scientists: church leaders sponsored and funded the studies undertaken by Kepler, Copernicus, Galileo, Newton, etc. The majority of those scientists were themselves devout believers striving to understand God's creation more thoroughly.[15]

Not only is modern science rooted *historically* in Christendom, but it is also rooted *philosophically* in the Christian faith. Philosophers of science note that the practice of modern science requires the embrace of numerous philosophical presuppositions: the general reliability of sensory perception, the regularity of nature, the rational order and discoverability of natural law, the goodness of creation, the worthwhileness of studying the natural order, the laws of thought (logic), moral values (honesty in reporting data), and the law of causality.[16] Some of these philosophical presuppositions can be supported by other worldviews, but the combination of presuppositions provided by the Christian faith allowed for modern science to get started in the first place.

Second, the Draper-White conflict myth actually gets the historical claim backward. There is not an irresolvable conflict between modern science and Christian faith. Instead, there is deep concord

---

study of the history of science, the Draper-White thesis is thoroughly discredited and rejected. See, e.g., David Lindberg and Ronald Numbers, eds., *God and Nature: Historical Essays on the Encounter between Christianity and Science* (Berkeley: University of California Press, 1986); Gary Ferngren, ed., *Science & Religion: A Historical Introduction* (Baltimore: Johns Hopkins University Press, 2002).

15   See, e.g., chap. 2 in Stark, *For the Glory of God* (see chap. 1, n. 6).

16   See, e.g., J. P. Moreland, *Christianity and the Nature of Science* (Grand Rapids: Baker, 1989).

(and only surface tension) between Christianity and science. Christianity provides the rich philosophical, theological, and practical environment in which modern science is birthed and nurtured. As discussed in Chapter 4, scientific discoveries also provide considerable evidence supporting Christian belief.

Finally, as argued by Alvin Plantinga (among others), any science-religion conflict is not at the level of the deliverances of physical science, but rather at the level of the *naturalistic worldview* held by *individual scientists*. Individuals are certainly free to interpret scientific evidence in such a way that it contradicts tenets of Christian faith, but in such cases it is a clash of worldviews, not a conflict between science and religion. Indeed, Plantinga concludes, if there is a conflict between the deliverances of modern science and a particular worldview, then it seems that the conflict is between science and naturalism, not science and Christianity.[17]

## The Exclusivity of Christian Beliefs

If God is loving and desires all to be saved, then why does Christianity insist that one can be saved only through faith in Jesus Christ? Christians profess that "God so loved the world that . . ." (John 3:16), but the majority of the earth's population throughout history, and even today, will never come into contact with the teachings of Jesus Christ. Why would God require that Jesus is "the way and the truth and the life" and that "no one comes to the Father" except through Jesus (John 14:6) if most would never even hear of him? Doesn't it seem unfair and unjust that Jesus is the only "name under heaven given to men by which we must be saved" (Acts 4:12)? What about the billions of people who faithfully follow other religions or no

---

[17]  Plantinga, *Where the Conflict Really Lies* (see chap. 6, n. 11).

religion at all? Why would God condemn them to hell for the simple mistake of embracing the wrong religious beliefs or being born into the wrong religious tradition?

I may be unusual in this regard, but of the five issues or objections raised in this chapter, it is *this* one, the exclusivity of Christian belief, that causes me the most discomfort. On one hand, I wish that everyone in the world could know God personally and experience the peace and joy of redemption in Christ that I have experienced. If that were to happen, then all would be saved and enjoy an eternity with God in heaven—and that would make me very happy indeed. On the other hand, I also wish that kind, peace-loving, and devout followers of other religions would be found faithful by God and granted salvation. In general, I would very much like for heaven to be heavily populated, and for the population of hell to be as sparse as (or sparser than) Alaska or Canada's three northern territories. It bothers me to think of people being separated from God for all eternity, regardless of the reasons for that separation.

But my discomfort has no bearing on the truths of the matter. As conservative commentator Ben Shapiro is fond of saying, "Facts don't care about your [my] feelings." As I tell my students every semester, truth is true for all people in all places at all times, whether they know it or not, believe it or not, and like it or not.

Let me propose three quick lines of thought that help me in wrestling with the question of Christian exclusivism and the fate of those who never hear of Jesus.

First, although it is popular to believe that all religions are fundamentally the same (and are just superficially different), in reality religions are fundamentally different (and only superficially the same) Even if we look only at the rituals and practices of different religions, it is quite clear that Hinduism, Buddhism, Islam, and Christianity are radically diverse. But if we look even more closely, into the essential truth claims of various religions, we see that they embrace contradictory positions on fundamental worldview questions about life, the universe, and everything.[18]

Consider two such questions: (1) the nature of divine reality and (2) humanity's postmortem fate (what happens when we die). Buddhism says (in textbook versions) there is no god; popular Hinduism embraces the existence of a plethora of minor deities and several major deities; textbook Hinduism is pantheistic, embracing the permeating of all reality with deity; Islam proclaims a unitary monotheistic deity; Christianity proclaims a triune all-powerful Godhead.

Buddhism claims that our postmortem goal is cessation of personal existence in nirvana, and until then we will be continually reincarnated; Hinduism states the goal of being united with Brahman but the continuation of reincarnation in samsara as we pursue greater holiness; Islam asserts that we have one physical life to live, and we will be judged to an eternity in heaven or hell based on our faithfulness to Allah's revealed will in the Qur'an; Christianity agrees with Islam that we will be judged after this life but argues that our judgment is based on our acceptance (or lack thereof) of the atoning death of Jesus of Nazareth.

On these questions, religions are *not* the same; they cannot all be true. The central truth claims of the world's major religions are irreconcilable and mutually exclusive. So, although we might wish it were otherwise, religions are fundamentally different, not the same.

Second, I do not know precisely how God will judge those who have never heard the good news about Jesus Christ. I have no doubt

---

[18] For a helpful treatment of diverse and contradictory beliefs in different religions, see James W. Sire, *The Universe Next Door: A Basic Worldview Catalog*, 6th ed. (Downers Grove, IL: IVP Academic, 2020).

that I personally will be judged based on my response to God's invitation through the life, ministry, death, and resurrection of Jesus. But what about those who have never heard? I do not know how God will deal with them. Perhaps there are no such people—perhaps God has revealed enough of himself to all people that they can respond to the gospel if they are willing to. Perhaps God will judge them based on "the light they have received," that is, what they *can* be expected to know and believe given their circumstances. Perhaps when Jesus says, "I have other sheep that are not of this sheep pen" (John 10:16), he is referring to people whom he will redeem out of other religious traditions. Perhaps God will provide opportunities for others to respond to his offer of salvation after they die if they have not heard before then. Perhaps C. S. Lewis is right, that those who are in hell have deliberately chosen hell over heaven.[19]

But based on my experience of God's redeeming grace and my understanding of his self-revelation in both nature and Scripture, I do know that I can trust "the Judge of all the earth [to] do right" (Gen 18:25). I understand (rightly, I think) that God is "not wanting anyone to perish, but everyone to come to repentance" (2 Pet 3:9). Given God's expansive love and my experience of his redeeming (and undeserved) grace, I can and do trust God for what I do not know—namely, how he will judge rightly those who have never heard of Jesus of Nazareth, even those who have devoutly followed other religions. I do not know precisely what that will look like, but I do trust his judgment. I certainly trust his judgment over my own in the matter!

Third, regardless of how God might deal with those who follow other religions and have never heard God's offer of salvation through faith in Christ, I am not one of those people, and neither

---

[19]   See C. S. Lewis, *The Great Divorce* (1946; repr., San Francisco: HarperSanFrancisco, 2000).

are you. For anyone reading this book—indeed, anyone living in a culture where books like this are available—we have had ample opportunity to hear about, learn about, and respond to God's invitation. We might choose, like Bertrand Russell, to protest that we have not received enough evidence, but we cannot pretend that we did not have the opportunity to investigate the truth claims of Christianity for ourselves.

## Conclusion

I do not pretend to have dealt in full measure with any of these five objections, let alone with all of them! There is, as always, much more to say, both in support of the objections and in response to them. My goal has been to give a simple presentation of the typical problems and indicate some straightforward ways of responding. I hope to have shown, at least, that there is no reason to think that any of the five objections provide a falsification of Christian belief: at most, they provide a critique of much Christian practice and/or tension within a Christian worldview.

### Recommended Resources for Further Exploration

Chamberlain, Paul. *Why People Don't Believe: Confronting Seven Challenges to Christian Faith.* Grand Rapids: Baker, 2011.
———. *Why People Stop Believing.* Eugene, OR: Cascade, 2018.
Lewis, C. S. *The Great Divorce.* 1946. Reprint, San Francisco: HarperSanFrancisco, 2000.
Plantinga, Alvin. *God, Freedom and Evil.* Grand Rapids: Eerdmans, 1989.
———. *Where the Conflict Really Lies: Science, Religion, and Naturalism.* New York: Oxford University Press, 2011.

Sire, James W. *The Universe Next Door: A Basic Worldview Catalog*. 6th ed. Downers Grove, IL: IVP Academic, 2020.

Stark, Rodney. *For the Glory of God: How Monotheism Led to Reformations, Science, Witch-Hunts, and the End of Slavery.* Princeton, NJ: Princeton University Press, 2003.

# CONCLUSION

# *Why Believe?*

## Why We Should Want and Believe Christianity to Be True

T he primary question of this book is, *Why believe*? In Chapter 1, I responded to contemporary apatheism (disinterest in the big questions of life) and argued that we should all care to know whether Christianity is true. I also suggested that regardless of what we currently believe, we should also *want* Christianity *to be* true. I want to revisit that discussion briefly and conclude this book with an appeal to both *heart* and *head*.

### The Heart: Why We Should *Want* Christianity to Be True

Christianity provides a satisfying and desirable worldview, such that we should *desire* that the Christian faith be true.

First, Christianity provides objective and knowable moral values and duties. Second, Christianity provides the platform for an objective and knowable physical reality. Third, Christianity provides for an objective and transcendent value to human life. Fourth, Christianity provides for an objective and transcendent purpose and meaning in human life. Fifth, Christianity provides a basis for the possibility of temporal and eternal forgiveness for wrongdoing.

Sixth, Christianity guarantees the reality of life after death. Seventh, Christianity offers the fulfillment of a core human desire: to know and to be known by God in an ultimate divine-human relationship.

Sigmund Freud rightly recognized that Christianity answers some of the deepest longings of the human heart. In fact, Freud was so convinced that the Christian faith satisfies our strongest longings that he concluded Christianity was made up as a type of wish fulfillment—we so desperately *want* there to be life after death (and transcendent meaning and knowable morals, etc.) that we (or at least someone, somewhere) *invented* Christianity as a way of achieving those objectively unattainable longings.

Freud was at least half right: Christianity, if true, *does* answer the deepest cries of the human heart. Indeed, it seems to me that we should all deeply desire for Christianity to be true.

## The Head: Why We Should *Believe* Christianity to Be True

But, as I mentioned briefly in Chapter 10's discussion of the problem of evil, desires do not create reality. Perhaps you agree that we should (and perhaps do) *want* Christianity to be true: but our desire for Christianity to be true does not *make* Christianity to *be* true.

Is there reason for the head to follow the heart and *believe* Christianity to be true? In a nutshell, yes: Logic, evidence, and rational arguments point to the truth of the Christian worldview. That is why Freud was only *half* right. He was also half wrong. Christianity is not "too good to be true": it is infinitely good *and* it also happens to be true. Or at least so I have argued.

The burden of chapters 4–9 was to provide reasons to believe Christianity to be true. To wrap up this literary journey together, then, let me recap why I think we should believe Christianity to be true.

First (chap. 4), scientific evidence points strongly toward the existence of a powerful, creative divine designer who brings this universe into existence (cosmological arguments) and designs the macro- and microlevels of the universe to be suitable for the development and sustenance of human life (design arguments).

Second (chap. 5), logical arguments establish the existence of a perfect divine being (ontological arguments) who is both a moral agent and the standard for objective moral values and duties (moral arguments).

Third (chap. 6), clues from human nature and experience suggest the reality of a transcendent personal being who can be experienced (arguments from religious experience) and desired (arguments from religious desire), and who has endowed humans with otherwise inexplicable libertarian freedom (arguments from free will) and trustworthy rational capacities (arguments from reason).

Thus, there is good reason to believe that God exists—and not just some random or undefined deity, but an all-powerful, creative, moral, all-good, personal, and loving Creator who remains in intimate relationship with what he has created. Then there are further reasons to believe that Christianity specifically is true, with its embrace of the deity, atoning death, and bodily resurrection of Jesus of Nazareth as narrated in the New Testament.

Fourth (chap. 7), we have good reasons to trust the text containing (the quantity and quality of the New Testament manuscript tradition) and story contained in the New Testament Gospels.

Fifth (chap. 8), the evidence of Jesus's life and ministry establishes that he believed himself to be divine (the titles used by and of Jesus in the Gospels) and both claimed and demonstrated divine authority (Jesus's actions). It is reasonable to believe, then, that Jesus of Nazareth was (and is) who Christians traditionally proclaim him to be: the incarnate Son of God.

Sixth (chap. 9), the historical evidence that is broadly accepted by virtually all scholars can only be sufficiently explained by the conclusion that Jesus was raised from the dead. It is reasonable to believe, then, that the Christian doctrine of the resurrection is true.

Again, the governing question of this book is, why believe? I have suggested that (1) we should care to know if Christianity is true; (2) we should want Christianity to be true; and, at most length, (3) we should believe Christianity to be true based on the cumulative strength of the arguments and evidence presented in chapters 4–9.

Perhaps you read this book as a hardened skeptic. I hope that some of the considerations have given you reason to reconsider your opposition to the Christian faith. At the very least, perhaps you can now accept that someone could be both reasonable and truth-seeking *and* believe Christianity to be true.

Perhaps you read this book as a former believer. I hope you have been introduced to logical and evidential supports for Christianity that were unknown to you when you were a believer. Maybe you will even reconsider your rejection of the faith you once held.

Perhaps you read this book as a questioning seeker. I hope you have found at least plausible answers to some of the questions you have been asking, and perhaps you have been given reason to seriously consider accepting the truth claims of Christianity.

Perhaps you read this book (or at least part of it) as a disinterested secularist. I hope you have found some reason to care about the big questions of life, the universe, and everything, and that you are now expending more intellectual and emotional energy pursuing truth.

Perhaps you read this book as a struggling follower. I hope the questions and doubts you've had have been addressed to some degree in this book, and that you have found a new confidence in the reasons for the hope that you have.

Perhaps you read this book as a tentative apologist. I hope you have found some solid reasons and evidence to add to your repertoire, to be able to share with others the good news that you have found in Christ.

In the end, every reader is left with an existential question. What are you going to do with the reasons and evidence presented? What are you going to do with the professed truth of Christianity? Ignore it and lapse (back) into an apathetic unconcern with fundamental worldview questions? Deny it and embrace your current worldview as your truth? Or embrace it and seek to know Jesus as the Messiah and Lord of your life?

My sincere prayer is that you will have come closer to a personal knowledge that Christianity is both true and beautiful—and that you will give (or will have already given) your life to Jesus as "the way and the truth and the life" (John 14:6). Whoever you are, whatever your situation in life and faith is, I hope you have at the very least enjoyed this dialogical journey together.

# Name and Subject Index

# *Scripture Index*